The Classic Collection

Heritage Hotels & Luxury Lodgings from East and West

The Classic Collection

Heritage Hotels & Luxury Lodgings from East and West

by **Kim Inglis**
photography by **Jacob Termansen**

TALISMAN

Contents

First published in 2016

Published by:
Talisman Publishing Pte Ltd
52 Genting Lane #06-05
Ruby Land Complex 1
Singapore 349560

Text © Kim Inglis
Photography © Jacob Termansen
Art Direction and Design Norreha Sayuti
Designers Foo Chee Ying, Stephy Chee
Publisher Ian Pringle

Printed in Singapore
ISBN 978–981–07–8441–6

Page 1 *A coloured elevation of The Majestic Malacca.*
Page 2 *The spa pool at The Majestic Hotel Kuala Lumpur overlooks the Railway Station Administration Building.*
Previous page *The figure of Justice surmounts the Guildhall (1775–78) in the UNESCO World Heritage Site of Bath Spa.*
This page *An overview of the centre of town in Bath Spa.*
Overleaf *View of the River Thames and riverside homes in the pretty Royal Berkshire village of Bray-on-Thames.*

HERITAGE AND TOURISM
Introducing the Classic Collection

You don't have to be a student of architecture to appreciate the beauty of a Palladian-style villa, an old Chinese courtyard house or an archetypical English country cottage. Nor do you need to be a heritage specialist to enjoy wandering through the cobbled streets of a medieval town, perhaps stopping for a break in an outdoor café situated in a finely proportioned square. Similarly, the delights of shopping for handmade crafts or local goods shouldn't be the preserve of the curator or museum manager.

Finding interest and enjoyment in the past is nothing new. Taking a vacation in a historic town or hotel, learning about a new culture, sampling local foods and interacting with different people has been a form of recreation for millenia. And today, it is also a means of preserving built and natural environments, all the while providing employment and a sense of pride for the local populace.

In the past, such journeys have taken many forms: there's the medieval pilgrimage; the 18th-century Grand Tour when aristocrats searched for the picturesque in classical antiquity; the factory workers' trip to the seaside town during the Industrial Revolution; the 20th-century package holiday. All have allowed certain segments of different populations to interact with history, make sense of the past and enjoy some well-deserved rest and relaxation away from the confines of home.

Recently, with increased mobility and prosperity, the net has been cast wider as so many more people are now included in this modern tourism industry. The democratisation of travel has allowed

Opposite and below *History, culture, architecture, retail and food and beverage are all draws for tourism, as illustrated clockwise from opposite top: A bridge in strict Palladian style in Prior Park, Bath; Moorish design in Masjid Jamek, Kuala Lumpur; Sir Victor Sassoon's Art Deco Grosvenor Mansions apartment block in Shanghai; Windsor Castle; rickshaws in Malacca; Guildhall, Bath; night market, Malacca; retail therapy in Bath.*

the industry to diversify like never before. Examples include holidays for environmentalists, sports vacations, culture-vulture tours, mini-breaks in country houses, or a week or two in an exotic country soaking up sun, sand and sea. In this book, we are concerned with one specific segment of the industry — that of heritage tourism.

WHAT IS HERITAGE?

Heritage is a broad concept and includes the natural as well as the cultural environment. It can encompass landscapes, historic sites, as well as bio-diversity, sociological practices, knowledge and living experiences. In this book we are mainly focusing on architectural heritage in the form of six specific historic hotel sites, but naturally these hotels bring with them different agendas: the culture of the areas in which they are situated; the local identities specific to each of their individual locales; distinctive histories; customs and peoples. Each has a fascinating story, highlighting a variety of traditions that developed in the past as well as ones that will continue to grow and change in the future.

The heritage encountered in this book is extremely varied, spanning as it does both East and West. We cover three distinct geographical areas — the UK, Malaysia and China (and within those three countries, there is further diversification) — and six very unusual architectural styles. We take readers on a tour of each location's history and culture, and place our hotels and lodgings within their own discrete cultural and architectural milieux. If it is diversity you are after, you won't be disappointed.

Naturally, one of the key factors behind the heritage industry is conservation — how best to preserve heritage and keep it intact for future generations. Understanding the significance of places

Above A modern gym and swimming pool have been incorporated into The Majestic Malacca, a mansion turned boutique hotel in Malacca.

is vital, and including people in sustaining historic environments needs to be at the forefront of any agenda. Today, buildings, whole towns, even certain regions have become designated historical sites. Sometimes they've been given UNESCO World Heritage Site status — indeed we feature two such areas in this book — and often there is dissent as to how and even why heritage needs to be preserved.

A UNESCO World Heritage Site is a place designated by the United Nations Educational, Scientific and Cultural Organisation as having special cultural or physical significance. Administered by a UNESCO World Heritage committee that pledges to conserve the site, it sometimes administers funds to help with preservation as well. As of 2013, there are 981 sites, the overwhelming majority of which are considered of cultural importance to humanity.

In this book, we feature two such sites: the historic Straits of Malacca city of Melaka (Malacca) and the English country town of Bath (increasingly known as Bath Spa). The former showcases influences of Asia and Europe in a specific multicultural environment that dates from the early stages of the 15th-century Malay Sultanate, through 300 years of Portuguese, Dutch and British rule. The latter is well known for its Roman baths and its classical Georgian architecture, as well as its Gothic-style cathedral. Our two hotels are situated at the heart of these well-preserved, culturally rich towns.

This is not to say that the other places we feature are any less interesting: there's the fascinating port city of Shanghai with its rich collection of early 20th-century architecture along the Bund and in the former foreign concessions; the quintessential English country village of Bray in Royal Berkshire (think Tudor-beamed cottages clustered in an idyllic spot on the River Thames); the Malaysian capital city of Kuala Lumpur, where we focus on the older colonial section with its Moorish-inspired

Above *Increasingly, English country cottages are no longer charmingly ramshackle, but attract visitors with both character and modern amenities. These two examples are in Bray-on-Thames, now reinventing itself as a foodie destination.*

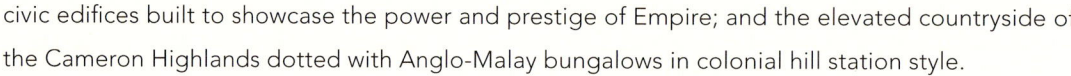

Above The imposing Georgian facade of The Gainsborough Bath Spa (1826) features a four–column portico and pediment.
Below The Swatch Art Peace Hotel on Shanghai's Bund is in elegant Victorian Renaissance style and dates from 1909.

civic edifices built to showcase the power and prestige of Empire; and the elevated countryside of the Cameron Highlands dotted with Anglo-Malay bungalows in colonial hill station style.

In each locale we place heritage in its context — architectural, cultural, and environmental. Whether it's a neo-Classical building, an Art Deco gem on a grand scale or something more intimate like a Chinese shophouse or an English country cottage is irrelevant. What's important is that it has a story to tell that is worth recording. And of course there are the visuals: all are brought to life in beautiful full colour photographs.

THE CLASSIC COLLECTION

All of our luxury lodgings are located in these colourful, historic locations and all have been restored and/or renovated so that they reflect their past glories. Some were hotels in the past, others private homes or simpler hostelries. Many have had to comply with stringent conservation policies during renovation, retaining original facades and sometimes interiors. Naturally, interior decoration has been sensitive to time and place, with no expense spared to produce high-quality, authentic décor that is responsive to the history of the accommodations. The hotels are also equipped with everything the modern-day guest requires — and some have new additions behind the original structures to maximize amenities and space.

In Kuala Lumpur, for example, when it opened in the 1930s the Hotel Majestic was the first high-end hotel in the then colonial administrative headquarters of Malaya. Its spacious public rooms, high ceilings, sumptuous accommodations, fabulous fixtures and fittings, not to mention excellent

standards of service, ensured its success with both the colonial élite and wealthy locals. It became the venue of choice for celebrations locally and the only place to stay for visitors — and remained so for around 50 years.

After its closure, the hotel became the subject of great debate. To renovate and resurrect it would be extremely expensive, but, according to some, to pull it down would be tantamount to treason. Local architect Hajeedar bin Haji Abdul Majid declared: "An old man without memories is not an old man, is he? A city like ours needs buildings like the Majestic. They are a measure, a physical form, by which we measure time and the progress we have made." To people like him, the building was much more than a building; it was part of the country's fabric. Therefore, there was much relief when it was gazetted in 1984 under the Malaysian Antiquities Act of 1976.

This meant that the building had to be saved, but the form it would take had to be very carefully planned and executed. In essence, it took a very specific vision to regenerate this past icon of hospitality into something that honoured its history, but looked firmly to the future. It also took some time — more than a decade, in fact — to work through red tape and comply with preservation regulations. It is unsurprising that many developers prefer to work with new-builds only.

The result, however, has been nothing short of phenomenal. When the hotel reopened its doors under the Malaysian brand of YTL Hotels, it had undergone an extensive rehabilitation under the careful eye of Zaidan Tahir, an architect with extensive heritage experience. The original 1930s building was maintained relatively intact and rebranded as the Majestic Wing, while a new tower emulating the Art Deco style of old added further accommodations, food and

Above left *Glamour and glitz have been resurrected at The Majestic Hotel Kuala Lumpur, through high-quality interior décor and excellent service, entertainment and amenities.*
Above right *A reproduction of a Roman mosaic at Spa Village Bath found beneath the building and now sealed below for eternity.*

beverage outlets, and a fabulous ballroom. Now, once again, the hotel wines and dines élites, from within the country and without.

The same can be said for The Gainsborough Bath Spa consisting of three listed buildings — the 1800s Gainsborough and Bellott's buildings with Georgian facades and Hetling House, the one remaining Elizabethan building in the heart of Bath, UK. Renovated, redesigned and regenerated to offer superlative accommodations and amenities firmly rooted in its classical heritage, the hotel also has the only natural thermal spa situated within a luxury hotel in the UK. Advantageously situated in the heart of this UNESCO World Heritage Site, the hotel has been furnished to the highest standard with design cues referencing period detail combined with contemporary forms.

Visitors can enjoy all that Bath offers — its Roman ruins, its Georgian architecture in soft ochre-toned local stone, its thriving antiques markets, its waters, its museums and other cultural attractions — from *within* a heritage building rather than without. This enables guests to fully immerse themselves in the city's culture. One of the key activities at The Gainsborough is a therapeutic bathing treatment in the hotel's spa: harnessing the area's subterranean natural thermal waters via a borehole that leads directly up into the basement, there are a variety of pools, suites with pools, cast iron roll-top tubs and more, all delivering a dedicated thermal water service directly to hotel guests.

"Taking the waters" was one of the main reasons people visited Bath in the past: Harnessed through three hot springs in the centre of the city, the 45°C water contains over 42 different minerals, the most concentrated being sulphate, calcium and chloride. Believed to benefit body, mind and spirit, this "health through water" or *Salus Per Aquam* (the forerunner of today's acronym of SPA) has

Above and opposite *Food and beverage, often served in the privacy of one's own suite or surrounds, is a major tourism draw. From left to right: A quintessential English afternoon tea in a cottage garden in Bray-on-Thames; the pizza oven in the garden of Lavender Cottage, Bray-on-Thames; afternoon tea and snacks in Peranakan style at The Majestic Malacca.*

a long and illustrious wellbeing history. Today, as in the past, guests at The Gainsborough can take advantage of Bath's mineral-rich waters, but now it is pumped directly into their residence.

Other hotels in this book are no less enticing: there are some sweet "home from home" cottages also in the UK; a mock-Tudor hotel in the Cameron Highlands; an old Chinese mansion in the heart of the UNESCO Heritage Site of Malacca; as well as a superbly renovated neo-Classical hotel on Shanghai's Bund. All offer superb accommodations, excellent standards of food and beverage, and some contain capacious conference facilities. All are united in their commitment to service.

PERSONALISED HERITAGE EXPERIENCES

In an era of heightened experiences, where the world literally can be one's oyster, hoteliers are increasingly trying to offer something a bit more than superior accommodations, food and beverage, spa treatments and general pampering. All our lodgings are deservedly celebrated for their high standards of service and amenities, but they also offer something more.

This comes in the form of highly personalised local excursions, often conducted by hotel guides and tailormade to guests' individual desires. Bespoke concierge experiences, where guests really do make the most out of their time at their destinations, is where the future of hospitality lies. The jewel in the crown of YTL Hotels' commitment to service, they are a major attraction for repeat guests.

Take the Cameron Highlands, for example. Surrounded by some of Malaysia's most beautiful scenery — jungle-clad mountains and expansive tea plantations set amongst colonial hill station architecture and rugged hiking trails — the area lures visitors seeking both tranquility and a

cooler climate. The Cameron Highlands Resort offers a number of trips that celebrate the region's environmental heritage: there's an idyllic tour through a nearby tea plantation that culminates in a sumptuous picnic laid out al fresco on a ridge overlooking velvety hillsides planted with *Camelia sinensis*. Others may prefer a trip to what locals call the Mossy Forest, an amazing botanical phenomenon coating slopes close to Gunung Brinchang, or a hike with the resort guide who regales guests with stories of the fabled Jim Thompson. Combining a love of nature with history, local lore and a penchant for the outdoors, these off-the-beaten-track excursions make a stay at the Cameron Highlands Resort that little bit extra special.

Elsewhere, architectural heritage is honoured with guided walking tours through historical areas: whether it is Chinese shophouse architecture you're interested in or stories of opium dens, intrigue and secret deals, hotel history tours are a must at The Majestic Malacca and The Swatch Peace Art Hotel in Shanghai. All the exotica of the Orient is neatly packaged into a number of two- or three-hour walking tours through ancient streets, parks and alleyways, home to traders and triad members in the past. For something a little more sedate there is the outstanding architectural legacy of Georgian Bath: imagine how author Jane Austen lived her genteel life amongst the town's 18th- and 19th-century élites — and how the town, its buildings and occupants influenced her acerbic tongue in the novelist's justly famous books.

This multiplicity of experiences is something that YTL Hotels prides itself on: not only are guests feted and indulged within the hotels and lodgings, they are also able to experience history when without. As far as heritage goes, what could be more authentic than that?

Above *Locally-grown fresh strawberries and champagne cocktails are served in front of a roaring log fire at Cameron Highlands Resort, Malaysia.* **Opposite** *Night falls outside The Gainsborough Bath Spa where vintage street lamps illuminate the way home along old cobbled streets lined with honey-toned Georgian buildings.* **Overleaf** *The tranquil bathing pool at Spa Village Bath was specifically designed with the Roman history of Bath in mind.*

The Gainsborough Bath Spa

THE GAINSBOROUGH BATH SPA

 oused in three interlinking Classical-style buildings in honey-toned Bath stone, The Gainsborough Bath Spa is an exciting addition to this UNESCO World Heritage site. With a direct link to mineral-rich thermal waters below and two distinguished Grade II-listed Georgian facades looking out to the Roman Baths area, its interiors have been designed to be grandiose, yet intimate.

A member of the prestigious Leading Hotels of the World, the hotel is a magnet for both the local populace and visitors from afar. Its five-star status fills a void in the city, while its world-famous spa via the Hetling Spring features a bespoke menu of aquatic therapies along with other healing modalities. Added to these impressive credentials is a relaxed, yet rigorous,

restaurant under the Teutonic eye of Michelin-starred chef Johann Lafer and a plethora of conference facilities.

Ninety-nine guest rooms and suites in a variety of styles now grace the corridors of buildings that served a variety of functions in the past. At one time a hospital, an almshouse and an educational facility, The Gainsborough Bath Spa is now an international hotel of the highest calibre. A creative example of architectural adaptive re-use, it has been receiving many an accolade since its grand opening in September 2015.

Previous page *The facade of the Albert Wing, a Victorian addition to the original hospital building.* **Opposite, above and right** *The Georgian facade of the original hospital building now receives hotel guests through its grand entrance. The modern glass building on the opposite side of the road is the Thermae Bath Spa, also owned and operated by YTL.*

ARCHITECTURAL HERITAGE IN BATH

Roman — Elizabethan — Georgian

The World Heritage city of Bath (also known as Bath Spa) is best known for its pristine Georgian architecture and its Roman remains. Each year four and a half million tourists visit this attractive city to view its ancient heritage, partake in the many cultural events it hosts, "take the waters" and enjoy its thriving community life. As such, its function is not so different as during its heyday in the 19th century.

Bath owes its existence to its thermal waters. "Discovered" by the Romans some time after they invaded Britain in 43 AD (although the waters were revered by the Celts much earlier), they consist of springs that release water that fell as rain up to 8,000 years ago and has been heated between hot plates of rock two miles below the earth's surface. Between 60 and 70 AD these waters were harnessed in a bathing and temple complex that, according to archaeologist Barry Cunliffe, was "one of the wonders of Roman Britain". Dedicated to Sulis Minerva (Sulis was a Celtic goddess, Minerva a Roman one), the sacred springs attracted visitors from all across the Roman Empire: some came to enjoy the social and curative aspect of the baths, others came to make sacrifices and worship, yet more did both.

Today's The Gainsborough Bath Spa hotel is situated in this thermal spring area — thereby explaining how engineers were able to install a borehole in Hot Bath Street in front of the hotel to guarantee a supply of thermal water to its basement spa. But, because the Roman complex fell into ruin after the Romans retreated and various other structures were built on top of these ruins, their remains are now 12 feet below ground level. Various parts have been restructured and re-imagined and it is well worth visiting what was once one of the tallest buildings in Roman Britain.

Opposite and left *A variety of structures, below ground dating from Roman times and above from Georgian, comprise the wonderful Roman Bath complex.*

Sadly, very little is known about Bath between the departure of the Romans and the Norman Conquest, but it was noted that William the Conqueror's son, William Rufus, entrusted his physician John of Tours to instigate a huge building programme in the Bath spring area and later, by the end of the 15th century, the Anglo-Saxon Abbey was rebuilt by one Oliver King, Bishop of Bath and Wells. Even though there was damage to it during the Reformation, Bath Abbey stands today as one of the finest examples of late medieval Gothic architecture.

Then as now, royal patronage had a great deal of influence on the rise and fall of cities — and Bath was lucky to find favour with Queen Elizabeth I. She visited the city in 1574 and granted it a charter in 1590. This effectively gave it a local governing body that undertook to modernise both the baths and the amenities around them. Unfortunately, there is only one extant residential edifice from this time: the Abbey Church House, now called Hetling House, one of the grandest of the houses around the baths, which at the time had its own private bath drawn from the Hot Bath (see pages 50–51).

As the royals and their entourages came to Bath, so did a number of less desirable members of society — pickpockets, gamblers and a plethora of quack doctors pandering to the whims of the unhealthy rich. It took one man to turn the city's fortunes around: John "Beau" Nash, a Welshman who came to Bath in the mid 18th century. He became the unofficial Master of Ceremonies of the city and ultimately established it as a centre for fashion, decorum, taste and elegance.

Above *The soaring sight of Bath Abbey built in Gothic style in creamy Bath stone.*
Opposite *Bath's elegant and symmetrical Georgian architecture often featured Roman statuary and motifs. Clockwise from top left: The world-famous Crescent; the Abbey; the Circus; the Guildhall.*

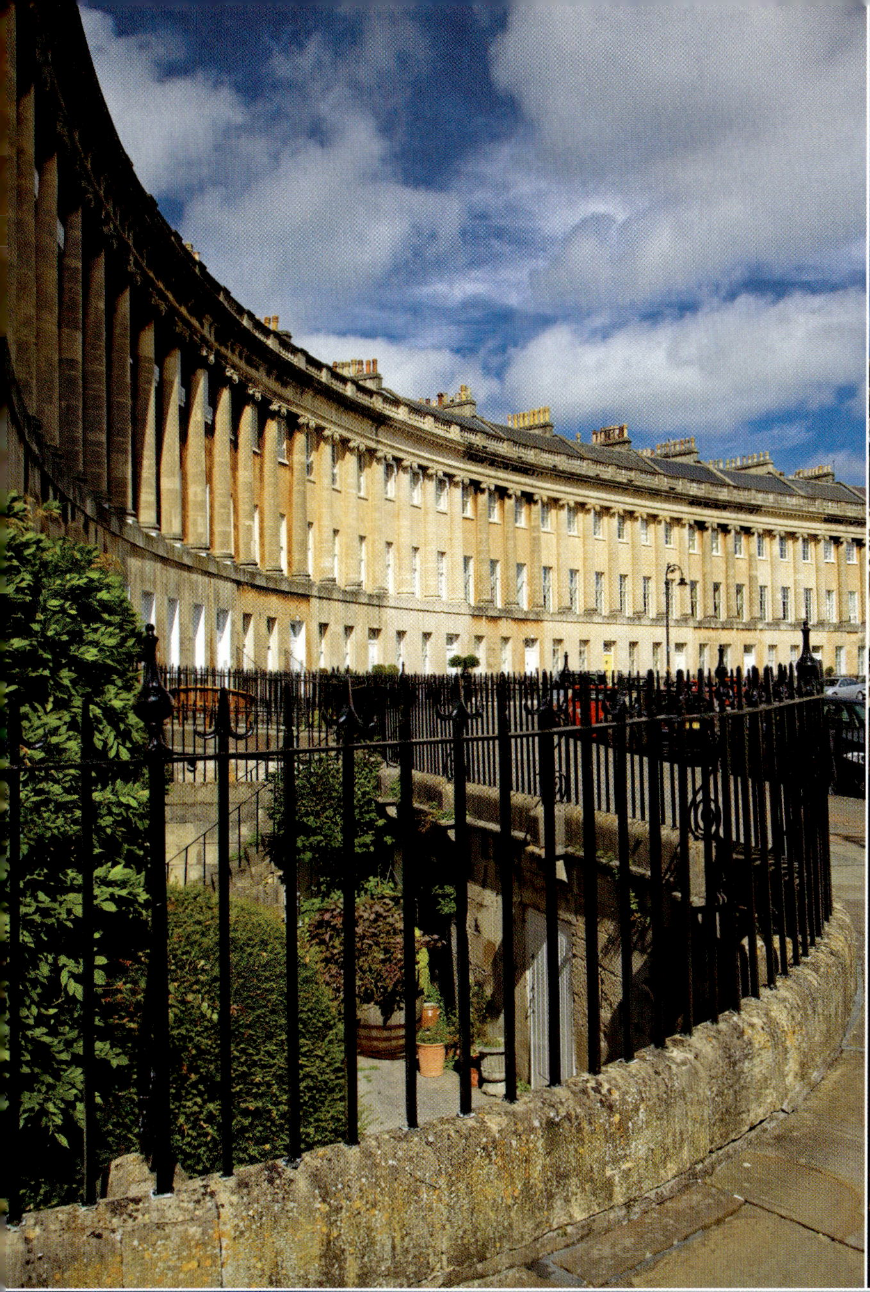
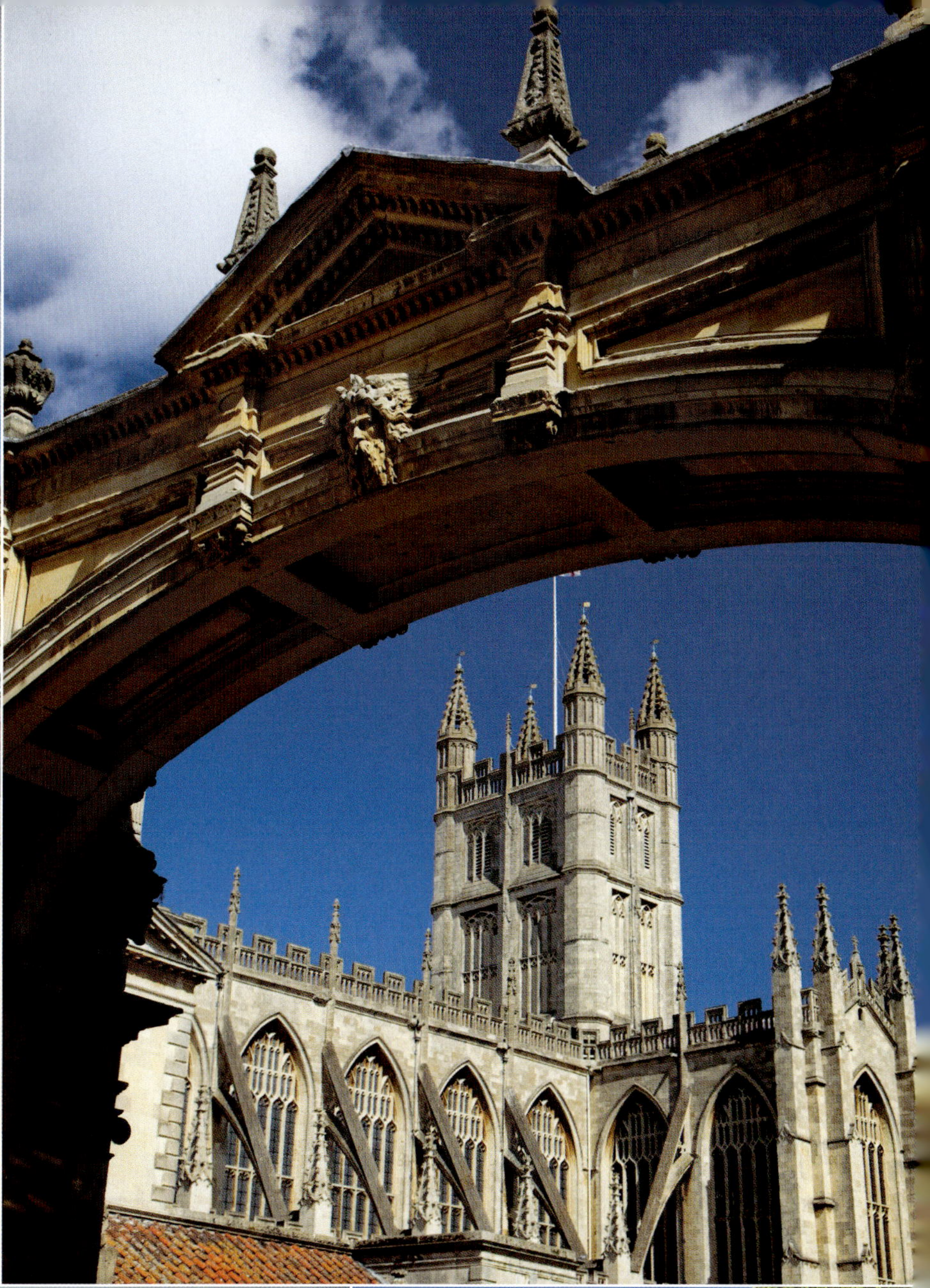
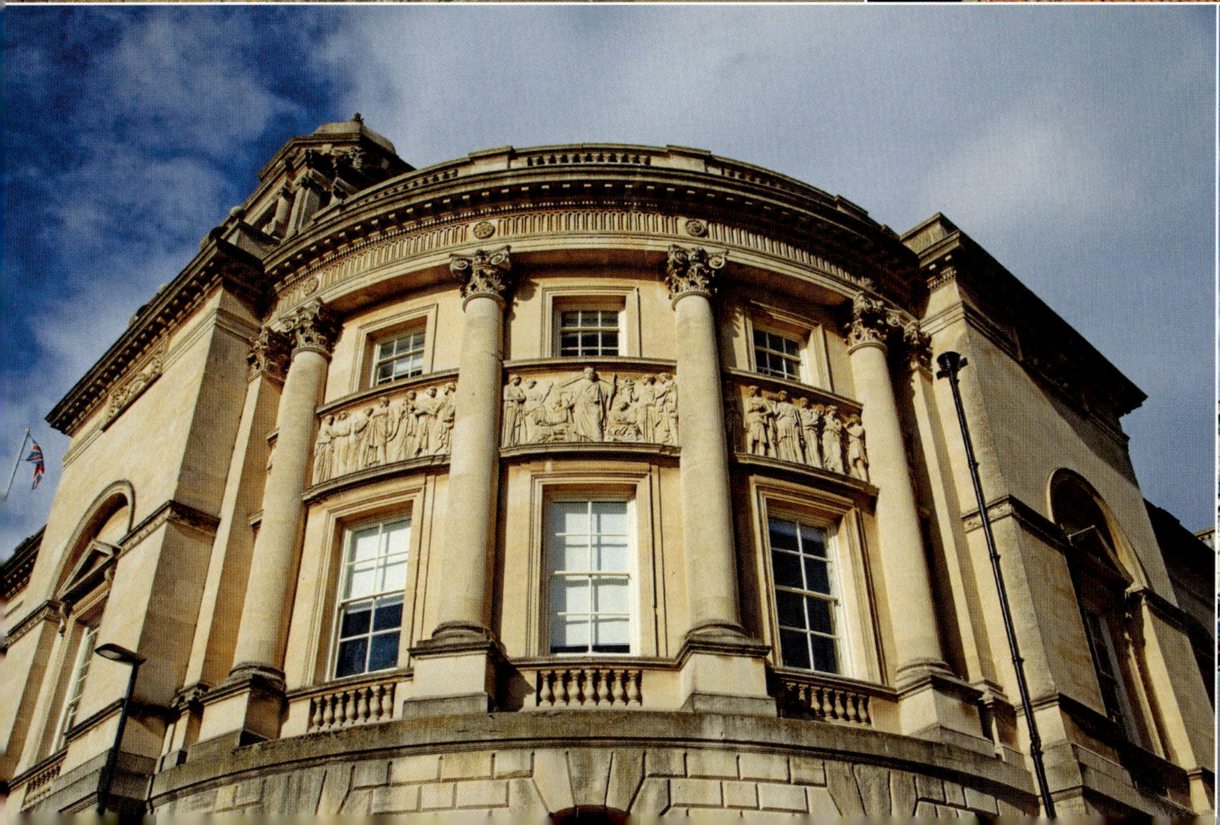
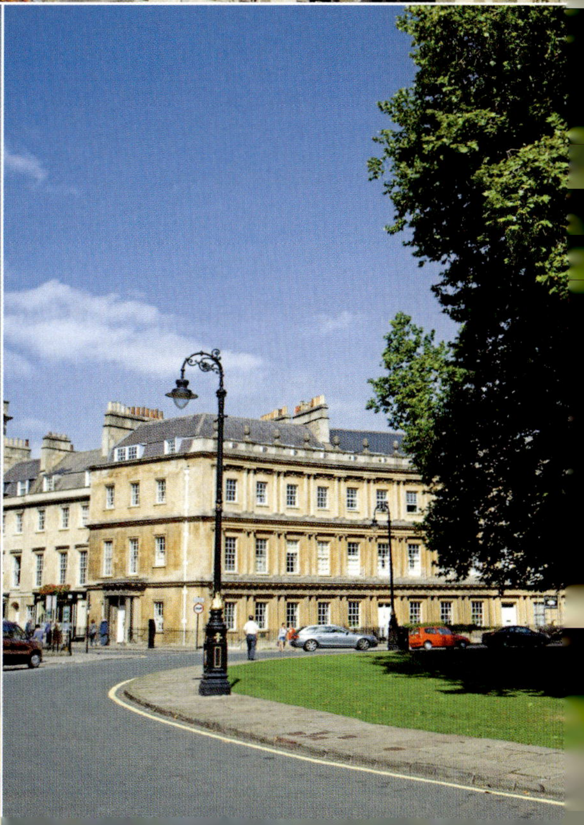

Bath's most famous architect, John Wood (1704–54) claimed that 12,000 people visited Bath in 1749; at its height, 8,000 came in a week during the Season. Naturally, they had to be housed, fed and watered — so, during the Georgian period, Bath expanded outside its medieval walls with the construction of a number of elegant terraces hugging the contours of the surrounding hills interspersed with parks and gardens. Two men can mainly be credited for creating these gently curving Palladian terraces from warm-toned local stone: the father and son duo, John Wood the Elder and John Wood the Younger.

Between them, they fashioned the spacious streets of the Georgian Upper town — Queen Square, the Parades, the Circus and, finally, the Crescent. In 1789, the City Council turned its attention to Bath's centre and organised the demolition and rebuilding of the baths, the Pump Room and the surrounding area. New buildings, still in the Classical style but softened by delicate decoration in the style of Robert Adam, replaced the older bathing facilities. Fortuitously, all these parts of town have been magnificently preserved to the present day.

However, as with many other culturally and architecturally significant sites, Bath is also a living, breathing modern city. Its present-day needs have to be met while its heritage is preserved for future generations. This delicate balancing act is exemplified at the newly restored and re-opened The Gainsborough Bath Spa: marrying the need for conservation with the demands of contemporary convenience, amenities and innovation, the five-star hotel is helping to regenerate the Roman Bath area. Turn overleaf to see more.

Above, left to right *Pulteney Bridge, spanning the River Avon (1774); columns from the Palladian-style bridge in Prior Park; Roman Bath arcade.*
Opposite *The honey hues of Bath stone are found everywhere in the city. On far right is St Michael's church, designed by G P Manners in 1835-7.*

CLASSICAL HERITAGE RESTORED

The Gainsborough Bath Spa heralds a new Era

In the same way that the painter Sir Thomas Gainsborough is inextricably linked to the city of Bath, this hotel is part and parcel of the city's architectural and social fabric. While Gainsborough spent time painting portraits of the city's fashionable residents and visitors in the 1760s, the various hotel buildings housed many of them in different guises over the centuries. It is fitting that today it once again welcomes visitors from all over the world.

Consisting of three distinguished historic structures (and one new one), The Gainsborough Bath Spa is a fine example of how old buildings can be renovated and refashioned into something new and lasting. Setting a benchmark for architectural adaptive re-use, YTL Hotels has saved three near derelict heritage edifices and returned them to relevance in the 21st century.

The main building originally housed the Bath United Hospital and was built in 1826 to a design by John Pinch the Elder. Bold, yet austere, it featured 11 bays with a four-column attached portico and pediment and was considered a handsome addition to the town at the time. It was awarded the title 'Royal' by Queen Victoria in 1864, when a new wing, named the Albert Wing after the recently deceased Prince Consort, was added. This was designed by local Bath architect, John Elkington Gill, and included the addition of a chapel. In 1935 the hospital moved to Combe Park, and the buildings were turned into premises for the Bath Technical College (which then merged with the Bath College of Art & Design). Prior to its conversion, they had been vacant for a decade.

These two buildings are linked by an underground walkway to the Bellott's annex, the oldest of the three edifices. First

Opposite *A pretty courtyard in the Bellott's building affords a private outdoor space for hotel guests.*
Above *The Burghley coat of arms and inscription above the entrance to the Bellott's building. This building houses 14 guest rooms and may be rented out as a totality if a smallish group so requires.*

This page *Exterior and interior of The Chapel, a Victorian addition. Today, this is used for conferences.* **Opposite** *Adjacent to The Chapel are two stained glass windows, believed to have been installed when the building housed the Bath College of Art & Design.*

mentioned in 1608, it was originally built as a "hospital" or almshouse by one Thomas Bellott for poor visitors seeking treatment at the spa in Bath. Bellott had served as Steward of the Household to William Cecil, Lord Burghley (1521–98), so he placed the Burghley coat of arms above the door to commemorate his late master. Beneath was an inscription in Latin that read: "Do not leave dormant in your store that which would relieve the poor. If the poor sleep soundly, so will you." During Victorian times the building was remodelled but still bears the coat of arms above its main entrance.

It is a testament to the architects, London-based EPR Architects in collaboration with DA Architecture, that such a disparate collection has been harnessed into a cohesive and attractive whole. It could be argued that the central court housing 1,300 square metres of thermal pools within an airy atrium is the architectural "glue". Flooded with natural light, it was designed with the Roman history of Bath in mind. It is fitting that during excavation, Roman mosaics and a significant collection of Roman coins were found where these pools now stand. A selection of the coins are on display in the hotel's lobby.

CONTEMPORARY INTERIORS, CLASSIC STYLE

 ll the public areas of the hotel are housed in the original building that is accessed off Beau street through an imposing arched entranceway. New York-based Champalimaud Design is responsible for the contemporary interiors that are luxurious, social and welcoming yet retain respect for the strong Georgian and Victorian characteristics of the buildings. On the one hand the hotel is clearly steeped in history; on the other, it is undeniably modern. Such a balancing act is difficult to achieve, but the design team has risen to the challenge with panache.

An airy lobby surmounted by an elegant and historic central stair greets visitors on arrival. At the top of the staircase is a glass occulus that brings light into the building; it is accompanied by a cascading lamp sculpture that descends from the uppermost level to the spa reception at lower ground. Elegant and imposing in cool tones of grey and taupe, the lobby is nonetheless warm and inviting as well.

The same can be said for the other public areas at ground-floor level. First up is the lobby lounge, an attractive sitting room that hosts afternoon teas and drinks and cheeseboard in the early evenings. Paying homage to Gainsborough, it is quintessentially British in style and has been aptly named The Canvas Room. A

Above, right and opposite top *The hotel lobby is thoroughly contemporary with Deco-style furniture, lamps and marble floors. Nonetheless , the original columns remain intact.*
Opposite bottom *Two views of the original stair with cascading lamp sculpture flank the ground-floor corridor that connects the public rooms.*

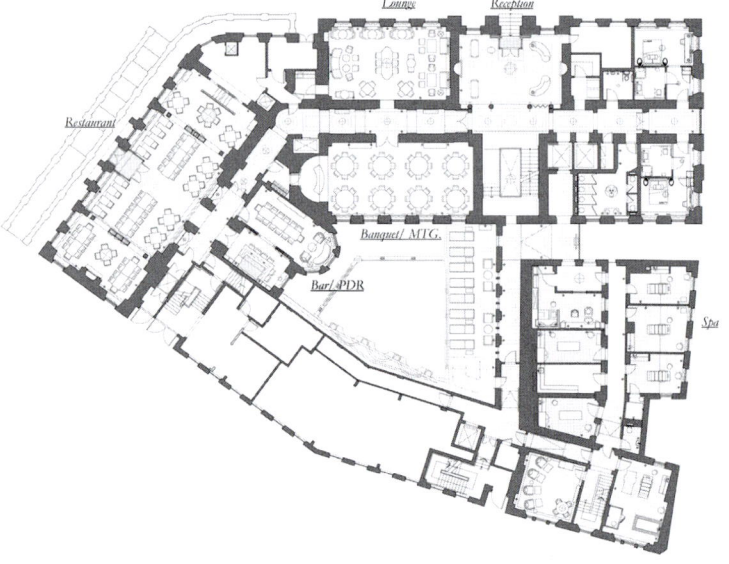

little past this room one comes to the hotel's bar on the left and a striking dining room on the right. Both rooms feature artworks from students at the Bath School of Art & Design.

The dining room is a collaboration between YTL Hotels and the Michelin-starred chef, Johann Lafer, well known in Germany not only as a cook, but also as a television personality. For many years he has collaborated with YTL Hotels' Group Corporate Chef Wai (the duo even authored a book together called *Two Chefs, One Cuisine*) and the restaurant serves the type of food that the two have championed for years. Fresh local produce cooked in innovative and unusual ways is the order of the day and night at Johann Lafer at The Gainsborough.

Above *The Gainsborough Bar and adjoining lounge.*
Left *Drawing of the ground floor, showing how the various buildings surround the central spa atrium, the pool of which is in the basement.*
Opposite *The comfortable Canvas Room hosts afternoon tea and drinks. The Deco-style tea set was specially commissioned from Villeroy & Boch.*

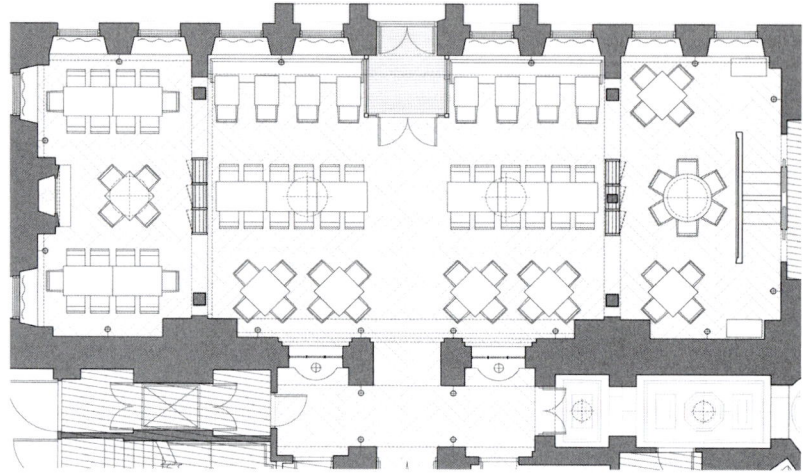

Left, above and opposite *Various views of the restaurant with its different areas clearly marked in the plan. A number of different seating options are available in this welcoming room.*

Thankfully, the design of the 94-seat restaurant acts as the perfect backdrop for the food. Convivial yet elegant, it is warmly appointed with butterscotch-coloured leather seating, herringbone floors and high ceilings. A semi-transparent wine cellar wall provides a dramatic focus off-centre, while a large mural by one of the college students dominates the other end of the room. For more intimate dining there is a smaller area arranged around an open fireplace, while taller, communal-style tables take centre stage for livelier gatherings.

The hotel is not short of conference and banqueting facilities, so it is suitable for large groups as well. The Somerset Room sits on the ground floor of the hotel and accommodates up to 70 people for luncheons, dinners and meetings. It is supplemented by a beautiful hall housed in what used to be the original chapel.

Left and right *A variety of guest rooms and one bathroom are showcased here: luxurious and restful in tones of grey and white, there are nine different permutations to choose from.*

Elegant Georgian windows flood this room with light from two sides and an exquisite silk awning beneath the ceiling gives the room undisputed drama. On one side there are views of the thermal pools, while on the other there's an open-air terrace for additional events. The hotel further benefits from conference facilities in a nearby YTL-owned building (see pages 50–51).

Because of the nature of the original buildings, no two guest rooms are alike at The Gainsborough Bath Spa. Ranging in size and style according to the layout of the various floors, many feature incredibly high ceilings and huge Georgian windows. A couple take the form of duplexes, while another two have an adjoining balcony that overlooks the thermal pools. Where they are united, however, is in the interior design that can best

be described as classic with a modern twist. Local reference is noted in the black and white toile antimacassars depicting playful bathing scenes draped over headboards, while burlwood inlaid wardrobes match black-and-gold consoles. Bathrooms are a sumptuous mix of marble and glass — and feature underfloor heating for that added touch of luxury.

One further attraction for smallish groups is that the 14 guest rooms located in the Bellott's Building may be rented out as a totality if required. The building benefits from its own private access and has a picturesque courtyard garden, yet is still fully integrated with the hotel. For special events such as wedding parties and the like, it affords extra privacy but still benefits from all the hotel's amenities.

SPA VILLAGE BATH

aving the exclusive privilege of being the only hotel in the UK to have direct access to natural thermal waters, The Gainsborough Bath Spa is setting a precedent that will be hard to follow. Measuring a massive 1,300 square metres, Spa Village Bath features three therapeutic pools set within an atrium flooded with natural light. In addition, there are treatment rooms, an ice room, infra-red sauna, traditional sauna, steam room, luxurious men's and ladies' changing rooms — and three exclusive Spa Suites. These are the only guest rooms in the UK to offer in-bathroom access to the thermal waters via a third tap, giving guests the luxurious choice of bathing in thermal or non-thermal water.

Designed with the Roman history of Bath in mind, the complex is a stunning sight. Romanesque columns, arched niches clad in custom-crafted blue and grey glass mosaics, sparkling aqua-blue tiles and Georgian-style lanterns surround the main pool that stretches out beneath an expansive glass ceiling. There is something infinitely luxurious about floating in thermal waters looking up to the Bath sky or soothing tired muscles against powerful water jets in such a setting.

A special pre-treatment thermal water journey that respects the Roman tradition of sequential temperature bathing has been devised for guests. Alternating hot steams, saunas and waters with chilly showers and the ice room, it allows guests to fully immerse themselves in the mineral-rich waters. A touch of "naughty but nice" comes in the form of a specially concocted chocolate and chilli drink.

Elsewhere, a Roman mosaic floor, uncovered during 19th-century archaeological works and sealed beneath the surface,

Left *Various views of the thermal baths: harking back to the days of Roman bathing, the pools offer salubrious surroundings for mineral-rich immersion.*
Above *Personalised aromatheraphy treats are one of the specialities of Spa Village Bath.*

has been replicated above (see opposite). The beautiful pattern has been transformed into a special logo for the spa.

The second level of the spa is dedicated to Spa Village treatments, some honouring Asian hydrotherapy traditions, others using the powers of organic and restorative fruits and flowers. There's the UK's first Ofuru-style wooden tub accented with river rocks, as well as a tatami room and a cloistered space called the Fountain Room where guests are invited to contemplate on the thermal waters before treatments.

Above and left *One of the specialist Spa Suites.*
Far left *Spa Village Bath reception.*
Opposite *Reproduction Roman mosaic floor in the tranquil relaxation chamber.*

Far left *A cast iron roll top tub in one of the Spa Suites; Ofuro-style tub in hinoki wood is used in a Japanese aromatic bathing ritual.* **Left and opposite** *Cross Bath, once considered a sacred site, houses a beautiful pool and one of three springs connected to Bath's thermal waters. It is the only source that visitors are allowed to touch.*

An extra-special experience around the corner in the Cross Bath, one of the town's original bathing pavilions, can be organised on request. Part of the YTL-operated Thermae Bath Spa directly opposite the hotel, it houses a beautiful spring next to an open-air immersive pool in a Classical-style pavilion built in Georgian times from beautiful Bath stone. Centuries earlier, different baths were believed to have different healing properties. The Cross Bath was recommended for "young, tender bodies" while the adjacent Hot Bath was believed efficacious for "colds and moist diseases".

Today, groups of up to 12 people may hire the Cross Bath premises on an exclusive basis, and the team is happy to provide light bites with champagne, wine or fruit juice. What could be more indulgent? Bathing in a real Roman bath in the open air, surrounded by warm-toned Bath stone, occasionally dipping one's fingers into spring waters that rise to the earth's surface from their ancient repository, all the while sipping on the nectar of the gods. For many, it's a unique experience that lasts a long time in the memory.

HETLING HOUSE

The Last Remaining Elizabethan Mansion in Bath

t is widely believed that Bath only became a fashionable resort under the guidance of Beau Nash, but it was actually an extremely popular destination during Elizabethan times. Many members of the Elizabethan court frequented Bath, taking the waters and approving of its convivial atmosphere. The Queen's favourite, Robert Dudley, Earl of Leicester, came four times and Sir Walter Raleigh was particularly enamoured of the city.

With such an élite flocking to Bath, houses were very much in demand among Elizabethan physicians competing for wealthy patients; if the location was in the vicinity of the baths, so much the better. Today, there is only one surviving lodging house dating from that time — the Abbey Church House (also called Hetling House) in Westgate Buildings. A fine gabled mansion, it was built by Dr Robert Baker around 1590 and benefited from a private bath drawn from the Hot Bath. It is a stone's throw from The Gainsborough Bath Spa.

Even though the mansion was badly hit in the Bath Blitz and the west front is a post-war restoration, it still retains much of its original form. The lower-storey windows have been altered, but the upper-storey ones are authentic and the gables have been scarcely altered. The corner gable, angling towards Hetling Court, still bears its projecting window. Furthermore, the house's fine wainscotted Great Room with Elizabethan panelling and elaborate chimney-piece survived the bombings. The only room of importance remaining, it has been transformed into conference chambers to service guests at The Gainsborough Bath Spa. Naturally, the chimney-piece, over nine feet wide and fourteen feet high, with its elaborate carving and heraldic details takes pride of place in this 86-square-metre hall.

As is to be expected, the restoration has been overseen very much in keeping with period detailing, yet all modern amenities are included. Incidentally, the name 'Hetling House' likely dates from the end of the 19th century when a wine merchant of that name used the building as premises for his business.

Opposite *Two views of the facade of Hetling House — in the present day and from an 1886 etching by Fred E Ellison. Printed at the Chiswick Press by Charles Whittingham & Co, Bristol.*
Above and opposite bottom right *The fireplace in the Great Room (detail of coat of arms from today and etching from 1886).*

THE TOWNHOUSE AT HETLING COURT BATH

ituated just round the corner from The Gainsborough Bath Spa is a beautifully renovated townhouse at 3 Hetling Court which offers additional accommodation for those who want privacy and seclusion, yet are still invited to use the hotel facilities. Set on a pretty paved passageway that runs between Westgate Street and Hot Bath Street, the four-storey townhouse is adjoined on its western side by the Abbey Church House (see previous page) and appears to have been built around the same time. A Tudor building, it is one of the few pre-Georgian buildings surviving in Bath.

Believed to date from around 1590, the townhouse oozes period character and charm, but is also thoroughly modern with amenities suitable for a contemporary luxury retreat. Each floor is different; each room reveals a different character behind original wooden doors. It is the perfect bijou bolthole for a family or group of up to five people.

A discreet doorway leads into an entrance hall that has been designed as an indoor representation of a Georgian garden. It leads on to a staircase and a rear kitchen with tiny outdoor court. The main living room, decked out in scarlet and grey hues, is on the first floor and boasts floor-to-ceiling panelling. The impressive fireplace and grate are mid- to late-18th century with contemporary panelling above the fireplace. Above on levels two, three and four are three bedrooms — a superb master bedroom with a silver-and-grey colour scheme, canopied bed and a copper bathtub thoughtfully placed before the fireplace and two further guest bedrooms — as well as two luxurious and sybaritic bathrooms.

During the renovation, all care and consideration was given to the protection and retention wherever possible of the existing historic structure and detail. As such, the townhouse offers authentic accommodations a stone's throw from Bath's historic centre. What's not to like about that?

Opposite top *A view of Hetling Court's paved passageway, with number 3 roughly at centre right.*
Opposite below *A variety of interior views of the townhouse which has been decorated in luxe finishes.*
Above *A watercolour of the Abbey Church House.*

CONCIERGE

Take a Tour of the Assembly Rooms

During Bath's heyday in the 18th century, visitors to Bath would surely have visited the Ball Room, Octagon, Tea Room or Card Room here to participate in some light socialising, flirting and one-upmanship! Dances, tea parties, conversation and card playing were the order of the day and evening in these magnificent rooms designed by John Wood the Younger in 1769. Today, the Assembly Rooms are open to the public, giving visitors a chance to re-imagine those days of yore. Other attractions include a world-famous Fashion Museum, a quality café and an extensive fashion bookshop.

Take in a Theatre Show

One of the oldest and most beautiful theatres in Britain, the Theatre Royal Bath has an illustrious history that dates back to 1705. The present building was designed by George Dance, a professor of architecture at the Royal Academy, and opened on 12 October 1805 with a performance of Richard III. Today, it has three auditoria, and offers a varied and exciting calendar of productions.

Enjoy the Great Outdoors in Prior Park

Created in the 18th century by a local entrepreneur called Ralph Allen, with advice from landscape architect "Capability" Brown and the poet Alexander Pope, Prior Park is set in a sweeping valley where visitors can enjoy magnificent views of Bath. The park's most famous sight is its Palladian bridge, one of only four of this design in the world. Other must-sees include an area at the top of the valley called the Wilderness with a lake and water cascade and the reconstructed Summerhouse. A five-minute walk leads to the Bath Skyline, a six-mile circular route encompassing beautiful woodlands and meadows, Roman settlements and 18th-century follies.

Concierge

Visit the Roman Baths

The magnificent temple and bathing complex built by the Romans in 60–70 AD still flows with natural thermal water, and is now open to the public for a fee. Located below street level, there are four main features: the sacred spring, the Roman temple, the bath house and a museum displaying finds from Roman Bath. Beautifully preserved and presented, with ancient statues, columns and stone pavements set around a steaming pool, the Roman Baths are situated at the heart of this World Heritage Site. Above street level are a number of 18th-century structures including the magnificent Pump Room that offers morning coffee, lunch and afternoon tea.

Indulge in a Thermal Water Spa Treatment

The Gainsborough Bath Spa is the only hotel in the UK that houses a natural thermal spa, so a sampling of its dedicated thermal water service is an absolute must for hotel guests. With three mineral-rich thermal water pools, three exclusive Spa Suites, various relaxation areas and a plethora of therapies that honour the wellness traditions of thermal bathing, there is no lack of choice here. In addition, there is an ice chamber, steam room and a choice of saunas to complement the hydrotherapies. Located over two levels, Spa Village Bath also offers a number of treatments drawn from the surrounding locale but interwoven with Malaysian interpretations linking back to the spa brand's roots.

Visit the Jane Austen Centre

Situated at 40 Gay Street in a beautiful Georgian building, this beguiling museum is a must visit for Jane Austen fans. Telling the story of the author's Bath experience — the effect the city had on her and her writing — it has a lovely period atmosphere. Featuring film costumes, contemporary exhibits, maps and books, it is the perfect starting point to an exploration of Jane Austen's Bath. An added bonus is the Champagne Afternoon Tea or Morning Coffee at the elegant Regency Tea Room.

The Majestic Hotel
Kuala Lumpur

THE MAJESTIC HOTEL KUALA LUMPUR

ust over 80 years since its first opening, The Majestic Hotel Kuala Lumpur, flung open its doors in grand style to paying guests once again. Hosting a party on 8th December 2012 that vied with the celebrations of old, it heralded a new era in hospitality. For, even though the hotel had been closed for nearly 30 years, it had not been forgotten.

In its post-World War I heyday, Hotel Majestic was *the* place to see and be seen. Writers, singers, dignitaries, politicians and, later, film stars stayed or came to dine, drink and party. Author Graham Greene partook of afternoon tea and, in the 1970s, actor David Niven drank at the rooftop bar. It was one of actress Maria Menado's favourite haunts; she brought film-maker Tan Sri Datuk Amar Dr P Ramlee to the hotel in the 1950s. On a more serious note, the hotel served as a venue for *eminences grises* like Abdul Rahman and Tun Razak planning for an Independent Malaysia.

Clearly, history played out within its walls. But, by the end of the 1970s, the hotel was struggling to compete with Kuala Lumpur's newer, flashier outposts and it closed in 1983. After a 14-year stint housing the National Art Gallery, the building lay empty for many years. Fortuitously, YTL Hotels spearheaded plans for its restoration as the jewel in the crown of its Classic Hotels' collection, spending vast sums on saving its heritage structures and building a large, modern Tower Wing behind.

Now, once again, the hotel is meeting the challenges of hospitality head on. Combining Art Deco glamour and an atmosphere of old with futuristic amenities and technology, the hotel has truly risen from the ashes. Located along the "historical mile" of colonial Kuala Lumpur (see overleaf), it seeks to regenerate a culture of old-fashioned hospitality and an entire area of the city. For a taste of tradition, but one that is firmly fashion-forward, there is no other place to stay in the city.

Previous page and opposite *The hotel's imposing facade, although cement rendered, has been fully restored to its former glory with the use of a traditional lime-wash finish.*

COLONIAL KUALA LUMPUR

Neo-Classical Heritage in the Tropics

y the time the Hotel Majestic opened in 1932, Kuala Lumpur was a forward-looking, thriving city. The new construction — the grandest hotel and most modern building in town — was built on a rise and overlooked the cluster of neo-Classical civic buildings that made up Kuala Lumpur's colonial core. Situated a stone's throw from the impressive railway station, the hotel quickly established itself as the premier destination for both the colonial and local élites.

Only decades earlier, it had been a very different story. In the mid 19th century, Kuala Lumpur was a rough-and-ready Chinese tin-mining settlement, an insanitary frontier town of timber and *attap* that was subject to frequent fires and floods. But, with the introduction of commercial rubber planting, increasing British influence, and the eventual formation of the Federated Malay States (FMS) with Kuala Lumpur as capital, the town transformed itself into a busy administration centre for the colonial authorities.

Much of this transformation can be attributed to Sir Frank Swettenham, a British civil servant who began his career in 1871 in Singapore and was appointed the FMS Resident-General in 1881. Upon taking office, he immediately set about conferring

some order to the haphazard streets of downtown Kuala Lumpur. Even though there wasn't any centralised planning, as had been the case with Singapore under Raffles, for example, the last two decades of the 19th century saw a plethora of brick-and-tile constructions — commercial, civic and residential — replacing the makeshift wooden buildings in the downtown area. A hybrid of European and Chinese forms, they were characteristic of the architecture of the day. The original Chinese town stayed, for the most part, east of the Klang river, while colonial Kuala Lumpur stretched along its west bank.

Comprising an area of swampy, uneven land (that became the *padang* or parade ground), a line of government offices snaking from the original High Court building to the railway station, and a number of bungalows on higher ground, the new town gradually took shape. Civic buildings followed the typography of typical British public buildings in the Tropics: built by military and public works' engineers, they were designed as an expression of dominance and power. Many — just down the road from the present-day hotel — are still extant today. Other less elevated buildings were much like the Chinese buildings in Singapore, Malacca and Penang: Taking the form of the row- or

Early Kuala Lumpur

Literally translating as "Muddy Confluence", Kuala Lumpur was sited at the spot where the Klang river joined the Gombak river, adjacent areas originally opened up for tin-mining in the Klang Valley. Predominantly Chinese, the settlement attracted prospectors, traders, merchants and the like — but its early days were marred by feuds between triads, Selangor princes and other interested parties. It was only in 1857 when Kapitan Yap Ah Loy was appointed leader of the Chinese community and introduced a system of frontier justice that peace and order were conferred upon the unruly settlement. Thereafter, Kuala Lumpur — a higgledy-piggledy mass of wooden and *attap* buildings, with some later shophouse rows — flourished, especially after the first railway connecting the town to Port Klang opened in 1886.

Previous page and left *A short stroll down Jalan Sultan Hishamuddin leads to these colonial civic buildings — literally a stone's throw from the entrance to The Majestic Hotel Kuala Lumpur.*

terrace-house, with a five-foot way in the front, shop premises on the ground floor and living quarters above, they were found on both sides of the river.

Because fire was a major problem, Swettenham issued a decree in 1884 requiring new buildings to be built of brick or wattle and to have tiled roofs. The Royal Selangor Club, formerly constructed from timber, was replaced in 1890 by its present Tudor-styled form, while other infrastructure projects continued to sprout up: the British Residency building, the police headquarters, the barracks and more. The river was straightened and embanked by degrees to prevent flooding.

From the turn of the century through the boom times of the 1920s, Kuala Lumpur flourished economically. As a result, the town continued to grow. The colonial core saw the addition of the Anglican St Mary's church, the Sultan Abdul Samad building, the General Post Office, and other buildings — the Public Works Department building and the Sanitary Board building, amongst others. For the most part, these were Palladian in style, sporting a profusion of stucco decoration, pillars and porticoes, statues and steps. However, it is interesting to note that many of these buildings included Moorish design motifs such as Moghul arches, cupolas, colonnades and onion domes (see opposite).

By the 1930s, despite the global economic downturn, the bustling town was ready for a world-class hotel which came in the form of the Hotel Majestic. Turn overleaf to see more of this magnificent edifice, now lovingly renovated for the 21st century.

Moorish Design Elements

It is fitting in a predominantly Muslim country that so many civic buildings in the capital sport Moorish design elements — yet it should be noted that this "Mahometan style" was not integrated into Kuala Lumpur's skyline as an homage to the Malay population. Rather, it may well have been borrowed from similar architectural trends in British India, the result of the various manuals and plans that were available to colonial engineers in the early 20th century.

There, the most spectacular early 20th-century public buildings were found in New Delhi. In 1912, when the British decided to move their Indian capital from Calcutta to Delhi, English architect Edwin Lutyens was chosen to lay out the new city. Famous for his English country house designs, Lutyens disliked Indian architecture, but was persuaded by the then British viceroy, Lord Charles Hardinge, to incorporate some accents into his overall plan. Borrowing from India's Mughal, Hindu and Buddhist past, they took the form of *chattris* (pavilions), stone lattice screens, carved images of elephants and a colossal Buddhist dome, all of which were combined with traditional neo-Classical forms. The resulting new style of architecture was lauded all over Empire.

As the British expanded eastwards, they would have distributed these building plans to other Public Works Departments in Malaya, Singapore, Hong Kong and even China. Hence, many of Kuala Lumpur's civic buildings (seen on previous page, opposite and above), with their emphasis on authority and grandeur, also included a plethora of Moorish design details.

A Malaysian Icon
The Majestic Hotel Rises Again

When the Hotel Majestic burst on to the architectural scene in 1932, it was a success in more ways than one. Kuala Lumpur's equivalent of the Raffles in Singapore, the Eastern & Oriental in Penang, the Strand in Rangoon (Yangon) or the Oriental in Bangkok, it became a magnet for lavish receptions, New Year's Eve parties and society weddings. Within its walls, there was no shortage of glitz and glamour, no lack of elegance and élan.

Stories abound about its impeccable service, its fabulous cocktails and food, the new standards it set in hoteliering. The hotel quickly gained status as the *grande dame* of Kuala Lumpur hospitality — beloved and loved by many a customer. Servicing all types of traveller in the era of leisurely voyages, it provided the necessary levels of comfort and service along with a hefty dose of the exotic. Uniformed representatives met guests at the railway station, transported them across Victory Avenue (as

Jalan Sultan Hishamuddin was then known) and escorted them into the confines of the vast lobby. There they may well have come across an acquaintance or two, taken tea in the lounge, then transferred over to the bar.

A cocktail or two later, it would have been dinner in the formal dining room. Fans whirled lazily overhead, while bone china and silver service glittered on starched linen, and food (some familiar dishes, some unknown ones) appeared in the hands of deft, besuited waiters. Apparently, some guests never left: Mrs Buxton, High Commissioner Sir Gerald Templer's secretary, and theatre buff and author Donald Davies made the hotel their home for over 20 years. For those on more of a timetable, it would have been a stiff stengah at the bar, a pot of afternoon tea, or a rendezvous on the rooftop.

Dato' Maria Menado, the Sulawesi-born star who was later signed up as a Cathay Cinema Production actress, remembers

Left *A grand piano sits beneath the gold-leaf dome at The Bar in the Majestic Wing. Evening entertainment takes the form of jazz, courtesy of the Solianos, one of Malaysia's leading musical families and descendents of the original hotel's musicians.*

Left and right *The open-plan ground floor of the Majestic Wing comprises a full-width tea lounge, a dining area split into two, and a cosy, clubby bar.* **Above** *An old advertisement illustrates how the hotel was a veritable institution in the past.*

her stay at the Hotel Majestic in 1959. She had travelled to Kuala Lumpur for a film festival and says: "It was like a fairytale. I had never stayed in a hotel like the Majestic. It was, indeed, a majestic hotel and there was nothing else like it anywhere."

What was also marvelled at was the design. Built by Dutch architect Van Leangeanderg of the firm Messrs Keys & Dowdeswell, the hotel was lauded by all and sundry for its forward-looking aesthetic. By the late 1920s, new technologies in the form of reinforced concrete, modern sanitation, electricity, lifts and even early air-conditioning had arrived in Malaya. These, along with the new Modernist sensibility that had become popular in Europe and America, resulted in a new direction in architecture in Kuala Lumpur. Classical motifs were eschewed for pared-down Art Deco ornamentation, a cleaner, more geometric look, and a

preference for function over adornment. The Hotel Majestic was a marvellous example of this shift in emphasis.

Originally destined to be a block of luxury apartments, the property was listed under the Trustees of the Estate of Loke Wan Tho, the youngest son of Kuala Lumpur's famous philanthropist and businessman, *Towkay* Loke Yew. Because of the recession that occurred in the years between the wars, the developers decided to reconfigure the building into a hotel. This can be verified by what is almost certainly a later addition in the form of the cubist geometry of the Modernist entranceway that leads up to the entrance proper. Whilst the building itself has a neo-Palladian facade with a porch sporting doors and windows with fanlights, the protruding black-and-white entranceway is Art Deco through and through. Strong horizontal lines, lines of small square windows and a central flagstaff are all hallmarks of the utilitarian approach of what later came to be termed "tropical Deco". In addition, there is a pair of swagged garlands in stucco on the facade, no doubt added after such motifs came into vogue.

Left and opposite *Original features, such as airwells, light fixtures, floor tiles, windows and the staircase, have been meticulously restored.*
Below right *An architect's drawing depicting the elevation of the Majestic Wing.*

This Modernist sensibility with Art Deco flourishes was followed through into the interior, in a style that was new and exciting to the general public at the time. Zaidan Tahir, the architect in charge of the hotel restoration, says materials used were functional and there wasn't much in the way of luxury finishes. "The overall look, both inside and out, was clean-lined and cement rendered. There was no marble, no decorative excess, no mosaics, as would have been found in earlier neo-Classical buildings." Rather, luxury is noted in the spatial quality and functionality of the architecture, the modern lighting and light fixtures, and the Art Deco details such as staircase woodcarving and a sunburst within a central decorative dome in the bar.

Boasting 51 rooms, all with hot and cold running water, and 18 with a long bath, the hotel was considered the height of luxury in the 1930s. As its reputation grew, so did its clientele. However, after Independence, the days of leisurely travel came to an end and this lack of customers along with the prohibitive costs of running and maintaining a hotel of its size and stature resulted in the hotel closing in 1983. Its glory days appeared to be over.

THE MAJESTIC WING

ecause the building had been gazetted as a heritage structure and YTL Hotels was keen to retain as much as possible of the architecture and design of the old hotel, restoration of the various edifices proved a long, arduous task. It was decided that the original hotel building would be resurrected as a suite-only, luxurious lodging with a colonial atmosphere. In the meantime, further facilities and rooms would be housed in an adjoining tower.

Thus, the Majestic Wing was born. Wishing to maintain the building's practical nature, architect Tahir chose to stick to the hotel's original *partie* as much as was possible. For example, the ground floor is not too different in layout in its new incarnation and suites are adaptations of the earlier rooms. A pair of airwells has been retained (though they are now roofed over to maintain the air-conditioned interior) and the staircase has been renovated, but sadly the old elevator was deemed too unsafe for retention by the authorities. Nonetheless, the walls have been repainted with a plaster and lime mix used in colonial times giving a smooth elegant finish.

As far as the interiors are concerned, very little documentation about the building was found, but a number of black-and-white photographs gave hints as to the general scheme. What is known is that fixtures and fittings were extremely modern for the time, and no expense was spared on details. All the furniture was supplied to the hotel by the firm of Messrs Storch Brothers, merchants of fine goods based in Kuala Lumpur. The lighting was entrusted in its entirety to General Electric Co of England and was extremely up-to-date: Of particular note was the ground-floor dome lit by 65 Osram lamps fitted in specially designed trough reflectors, thereby hiding the bulbs from sight and cutting out glare — the height of sophistication at the time. Tahir has retained the dome, but painted it in gold leaf, thereby keeping the visual aesthetic of the '30s.

Furniture is similarly authentic with The Tea Lounge featuring comfy sofas and leather armchairs beneath old-fashioned grid ceilings. Cut-glass lights with antique brass fittings were custom crafted after some of the original light fittings that were sold at auction in the '80s; these cast a soft glow over floral decorations on low tables. The Bar and The Reading Room are clubby colonial in atmosphere with dark wood panels, glittering mirrors and brass. Perfect for a cocktail, the bar also evokes a nostalgic atmosphere when musicians descended from the original pianist

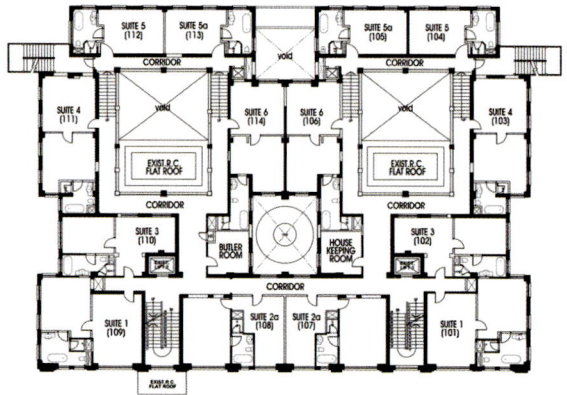

Previous page *The luxurious lounge laid for tea.*
Left and opposite top *One of 47 suites with bathroom, living room and bedroom.*
Above *Layout of a typical floor showing rooms.*
Opposite below *Colonial-inspired Drawing Room and clubby Bar.*

that played in the old hotel take to the floor. Adjacent is the Colonial Cafe: jutting into the original lightwells on either side of the bar, its tones of taupe and gold, reminiscent of the original colour code, are especially resplendent in the evenings.

There's no doubt that Tahir has successfully recreated the type of atmosphere that would have permeated the 1930s, yet has endowed the public spaces with a fresh modernity. "I tried to be very sensitive to the original design," explains the architect, "After all, the Majestic was the grandest hotel in its day; I wanted to recreate its old-world charm." Mission accomplished, I would say.

Upstairs, 47 suites are accommodated over five floors. Fitted out with a lounge, a bedroom and elegant colonial-style bathroom with claw-foot tub and a separate shower stall, they are elegant and comfortable, but fully up-to-date now. Butler service is supplied to all guests, and — alleviating bureaucratic formalities — check-in takes place within the privacy of the suite. Other hotels should take note of this sensible practice: no waiting in a busy lobby, no looking desperately for rest rooms on arrival!

Also sensible is the lack of numerous light switches and various contraptions allegedly turning on TVs or Internet access. Everything is easily navigable and easily sorted — and, if there are any glitches, the butler sorts them out instantly. In a similar way, the rooms are tastefully fitted out and equipped, but are not fussy or over-designed. Easeful living is achieved through the restful colour scheme, comfortable furniture, and all the amenities a guest would require.

It's this attention to detail that really shines in the Majestic Wing: service was always a high priority in the hotel of old, with many repeat guests returning because they knew that standards were always maintained. Former Chief Psychiatrist to the government and founder of the Malaysian Psychiatric Association, Tan Sri Dato' Seri Dr M Mahadevan reminisced about visits to the hotel in his youth: "It was upmarket and exclusive," he remembers. "It was a classy place and people who dined, partied or stayed at the hotel expected the best." He felt he was never let down by the service and continued to patronise the hotel with friends for many years.

Today is no different. High levels of personalised service, from the personal butler to waiters, bar staff and other members of staff, make a stay at the Majestic Wing memorable. These well-trained, friendly folk open a window to the past, but also provide everything the modern traveller requires in the 21st century.

Situated between the Majestic and Tower Wings is a unique Orchid Conservatory that houses a fantastic array of Phalaenopsis orchids, many of which are large-petalled varieties. Probably named after the scientific genus Phalaena, the name given to a large moth, they are sometimes called Moth Orchids. This room is not only a delight to look at, however. If guests fancy a meal within its colourful, airy surrounds, staff can set up a table for lunch, afternoon tea or dinner here.

THE TOWER WING

I f the Majestic Wing harks back to an era where life was lived in a leisurely manner, the Tower Wing acts as its counterpart in style, tempo and sheer size. Nonetheless, there is no jarring when one walks from one wing to the other: the rhythm and proportions of the original architecture are carefully maintained in the Tower Wing, though the scale is considerably magnified.

Art Deco is the name of the game here: there's a vast lobby (below) with geometrics in the floor, wrought ironwork, polished chrome, sparkling mirrors, pendant glass-and-metal lanterns and

a giant chandelier hanging from a ceiling specked with gold leaf. "The Art Deco period represents luxury, glamour, exuberance and technological progress," notes Tahir, "and I wanted to inject those elements from the past into the new tower block."

This is amply illustrated at Contango, the full-service restaurant that seats 250 people (opposite). Deco lighting and ironwork illustrate service counters and pillars, while the cuisine is freshly prepared to order in front of guests' eyes. The ornate, pillar-free ballroom is another case in point: with chandeliers casting a magical glow on a cavernous room that has the capacity to seat 1,200 guests, it has fast become a popular venue for weddings and special events. The Roof Garden of the Hotel Majestic of old had a dance floor and an area that could seat 350 people; today's Tower Wing follows in its footsteps — albeit on a far more capacious scale.

Opposite *The central serving station in Contango.*
Left *The vast lobby is a vision in marble and metal.*
Above *The Hotel Majestic's rooftop was a popular venue for all manner of parties, gatherings and dances. Here, we see a joyful family celebration from the heady days of the 1950s.*

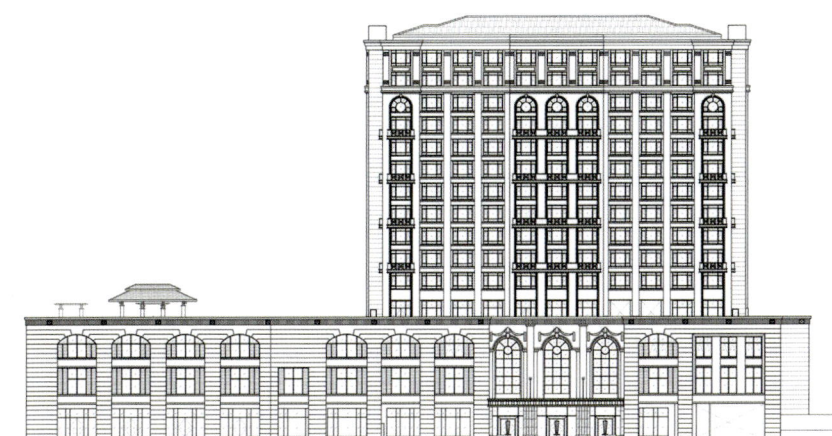

The Deco theme is followed through to the 300 bedrooms and suites, although many are given a contemporary twist with floor-to-ceiling glass walls separating bathrooms from bedrooms (opposite). Each room has butterscotch interiors with Art Deco-style geometric wallpaper and wooden floors in the bedrooms and black-and-white tiles in the luxurious bathrooms. Decadent touches include TV screens in the bathrooms, so guests can catch up with their favourite soaps while soaping.

Also in the Tower Wing is a large fourth-floor roof terrace that features a geometric-styled swimming pool and a huge al-fresco space that is used for parties, product launches and the like. Loungers surround the pool that looks on one side to the gym, on the other to the neo-Classical Kuala Lumpur of old. What could be more fitting? Old melds perfectly with new; the past merges with the present.

Above & bottom right *Architectural drawings show the Tower Wing front elevation and a typical floor of guestrooms. Suites are located in the central section near the lifts, while the slightly smaller rooms radiate out on the two side wings.*
Top right *This view of the hotel clearly shows the relationship between the Majestic and Tower Wings. The swimming pool in foreground is adjacent the spa; there is a second tranquil pool and deck on the fourth floor of the Tower Wing.*
Opposite *A variety of guest rooms and bathrooms in the Tower Wing.*

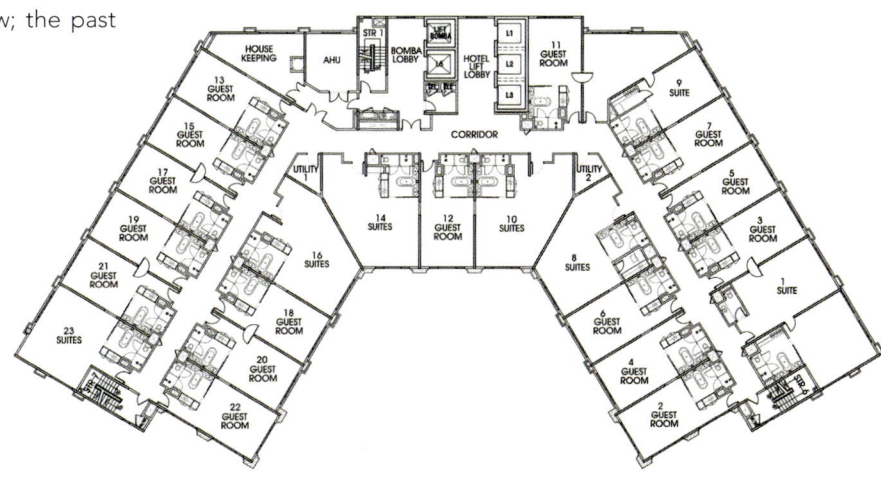

Heritage Dining

lthough the sun has set on the British Empire, some of its culinary vestiges — classic prawn cocktail, custard, faggots, to name a few — continue to make their last gastronomic stand at the Colonial Cafe (see opposite, far left). A meal here represents a nostalgic culinary journey that began some 150 years earlier.

The British first arrived in Malaya in the latter part of the 18th century when the East India Company set up a trading post in Penang. Over the next couple of decades, as a result of increased trade and the growth of the tin-mining and rubber industries, they extended their stretch inland. Many of the initial arrivals came from India where they had previously worked and acquired a taste for spices and curry. They brought with them their love of "home food" (albeit adapted somewhat because of climactic differences) and Indian curries, as well as a need to eat in a manner they were accustomed to.

At the same time, many Chinese were migrating to Nanyang (as they called South East Asia), fleeing economic hardship in their homeland. Thus, it came to pass that many British planters, bureaucrats and families employed Hainanese cooks in their households. Luckily these intrepid chefs did not baulk when they were given the task of recreating British recipes in the tropics with a set of ingredients that were totally different from the originals — and the rest, as they say, is history.

The result of this harmonious situation was the birth of a type of colonial cuisine that took traditional British staples and turned them on their head, utilising Asian cooking styles and exotic local ingredients. Curry Kapitan, for instance, is a mild curry that takes its name from when servants would announce dinner with the words: "Curry, Captain". The Sunday tiffin is an adaptation of the Indian curry lunch, while Roti John, thick slices of bread spread with minced meat dipped in egg and fried was so called because all English men were referred to as John! Chicken Chop is another favourite: pieces of chicken tenderized by pounding, then dipped in a batter and deep fried, and invariably served with a brown gravy of cloudy origins, peas and fries.

The menu at the Colonial Cafe includes many of these much-loved dishes along with some ingenious desserts: swiss roll using local *kaya* instead of fruit jams, spicy spotted dick, and bread and butter pudding with Madagascar vanilla. When served on starched white tablecloths with super attentive service, one can easily imagine dinner at the Hotel Majestic in earlier times.

THE MAJESTIC SPA

 oused in a stand-alone two-storey annex that nestles between the grand Indo-Saracenic Railway Administration Building and the Majestic Wing is The Majestic Spa. With a sweet swimming pool out front and an airy double-height reception lobby, it is both a design statement and a tranquil retreat.

Taking its inspiration from Arts and Crafts proponent Charles Rennie Mackintosh and his Willow Tearooms in Scotland as well as the hotel's heritage, the lobby is enlivened with Art Nouveau motifs, leaded glass panels, geometric timber panelling and a fresh aquamarine-and-white palette. A pair of high-backed chairs (right), of which Mackintosh designed many variations, creates an elegant enclave by the door, while comfy sofas and low chairs allow guests to sip tea or water pre- or post-treatment. Therapy rooms are on either side of the atrium lobby.

Nostalgia is carried through to the therapies themselves with genteel-themed rituals such as the English Afternoon Tea experience that starts with a scrumptious berry scrub, segues into a massage and ends with a fragrant English rose facial. Other treatments pluck herbs from the English garden and utilise the power of lavender, for example, while the pre-treatment ritual, a

hallmark of YTL Hotels' spas, is named Gift from the Garden. This starts with a soothing lavender foot soak and is followed by a stimulating rosemary scalp massage, before guests are escorted to their treatment room for the therapy proper to begin.

As befits the colonial Malaya ambience, chamomile tea is the beverage of choice here, although Pimms could be an option post-treatment. Another alternative is a stint in the steam room: with its glistening mosaic tiles and mood lighting, it provides just the atmosphere for a post-massage pamper.

THE SMOKE HOUSE

lamour has been well and truly revived at The Majestic Hotel's Smoke House, a convivial smoking zone styled on the gentlemen's clubs that proliferated in London's West End in the 19th century. Frequented by the upper echelons of society, they provided a home away from home — with bars, restaurants and overnight rooms. They were also patronised by expatriates visiting London: many had membership at the East India Club in St James or the Oriental Club, just off Oxford Street.

Situated in a heritage building that may have served as the General Manager's home or the Caretaker's house, today's Smoke House is accessed via a covered walkway attached to the hotel. Inside it's all dark wood panelling and shiny wood surfaces — clubby colonial in feel, companionable in atmosphere. This hits just the right spot, as The Smoke House contains a billiard table, two card rooms and a luxe private dining room (opposite), as well as a dedicated lounge and bar (right), all geared up towards social interaction. It's the place to go for a girly chat, a boys' night out, or some pre-dinner drinks and cigars.

However, that isn't all. Downstairs, there's a 12-seater dedicated screening room that shows wonderful old films and a gentleman's barber in the form of London's Truefitt & Hill. Operating as a Royal Warrant holder to the Duke of Edinburgh, it can provide a trim and wet shave before a night out. There's also an excellent tailor for custom-designed suits and dresses.

Above *The Smoke House comprises a substantial colonial building in its own right. Beautifully proportioned, its symmetrical facade looks out over Jalan Sultan Hashamuddin.*

CONCIERGE

Visit the Lake Gardens

The brainchild of Alfred Venning, the State Treasurer in Sir Frank Swettenham's time, the Lake Gardens are not only a pleasant place to stroll around, they are close to the Majestic. Spanning 100 hectares, this late 19th-century botanical garden contains a variety of attractions such as a Deer Park and a Bird Park. It also houses the Islamic Arts Museum with more than 7,000 artefacts, many from China and South East Asia, as well as an exceptional library of Islamic Art books.

Go for Grooming at Truefitt & Hill

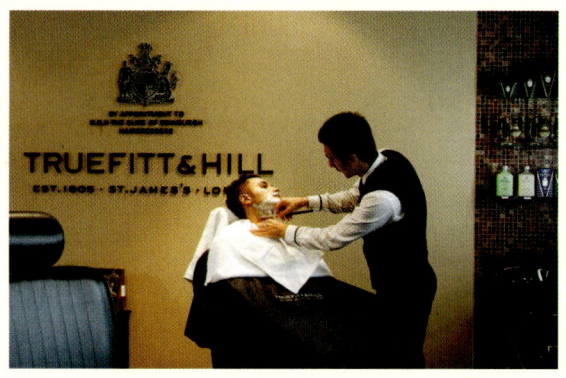

Gents cannot go wrong at The Smoke House's bespoke grooming outfit, Truefitt & Hill. This isn't the world's oldest and most respected barber for nothing: a hot towel shave and haircut here needs to be experienced to be believed. With a history on London's Old Bond Street dating back to 1805 and a client list that reads like a Who's Who of the British aristocracy, the KL outpost has much to live up to. Never fear, the traditions continue with aplomb here at The Majestic Hotel's Smoke House.

Take a Treatment at The Majestic Spa

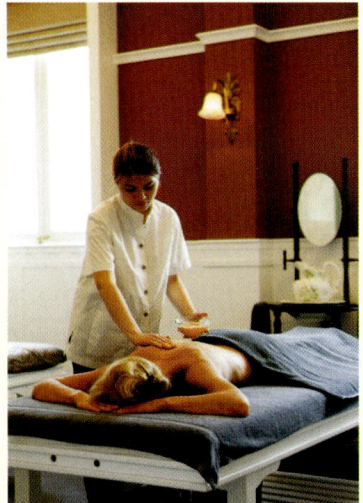

With an airy, Art Nouveau-inspired interior and innovative therapies, an afternoon ritual at the spa is a must-do for anybody requiring a pick-me-up. The menu isn't extensive, but as with all Spa Village outfits, the products are derived straight from nature and the therapists are supremely considerate and skilled. As befits the heritage property, rituals take their inspiration from either Colonial Malaya or Olde-Worlde England, with evocative names such as Queen Victoria's Lavender or English Afternoon Tea. The pre-ritual "Gift from the Garden" lavender and rosemary foot soak and scalp massage is a real treat too.

CONCIERGE

Visit the National Museum

Located along Jalan Damansara, a 20-minute walk from the hotel, the National Museum provides an overview of the history and culture of Malaysia. Housed in a striking building that takes inspiration from traditional Malay and Minangkabau architectural features, the museum was upgraded in 2008. With artefacts covering early Malay pre-history, the Malay Kingdoms, colonial times, the Japanese occupation and Post-Independence Malaysia, the museum is quite comprehensive. The one-hour guided tour comes highly recommended.

Take in some Shopping at Starhill Gallery

Hop on to the free shuttle bus that plies the route between the Bukit Bintang shopping district and The Majestic Hotel and indulge in some retail therapy. Starhill Gallery offers a smorgasbord of all the top brands, as well as some wonderful eateries, either in the basement Feast Village, or in some of the different outlets dotted on different floors. And if you literally shop until you drop, rest tired toes at the up-market Newens Tea House (left): intricate gold themed décor and wonderful service beckon for an afternoon cuppa.

Visit the Petronas Twin Towers

Designed by Argentine architect, César Pelli, these post-modern twin towers were the tallest buildings in the world from 1998 to 2004 until they were surpassed by Taipei 101. However, they remain the tallest twin building in the world — and are well worth a look. Featuring a double decker Skybridge connecting the two towers on the 41st and 42nd floors and an Observation Deck on the 86th floor, the views of the city are breathtaking. There are also the usual gift shop and various changing exhibits.

The Swatch Art
Peace Hotel

THE SWATCH ART PEACE HOTEL

hortly after the establishment of Shanghai's British Settlement in 1842 until the present day, a hotel has stood on the site of today's Swatch Art Peace Hotel. The first to grace this prime site on the Bund was the aptly-named Central Hotel built in the early 1850s. Renamed the Palace Hotel in 1903, it was then housed in a new, fashion-forward building that was completed in 1909, a building that remains to this day. Designed by the British firm, Scott & Carter, the hotel's design, facilities and construction scale were top class even then.

Consistently sought after as a venue for high-level events, the Palace Hotel saw history unfold around it. Many important meetings with the Concession administrations were held in the hotel, as was the first International Opium Conference in 1909. Widely regarded as the event that started the global anti-drugs campaign, it is commemorated by a copper plaque that still hangs on the wall of the hotel. On 29th December 1911, Dr Sun Yat-Sen arrived in Shanghai and gave a speech at his welcome party in the Main Hall. The well–known slogan "The revolution has not yet prevailed, and comrades still need to struggle on" was taken from his speech that night.

Later, in the 1920s, Chiang Kai-Shek announced his engagement to his future wife, Soong May Ling, at the hotel — and the room on the fifth floor where the engagement party took place has been named after this happy occasion. The 1920s and '30s were boom years for the hotel, but, as with all the Bund buildings, post World War II the hotel fell into decline. In 1956, when the Cathay Hotel across the road was seized by the government and opened as the Peace Hotel, the Palace was also requisitioned to serve as the South Building of the Peace Hotel, until Switzerland's Swatch Group conceived and completed an extraordinary restoration of the landmark building.

Its present incarnation has seen the hotel's 120 rooms reduced to just seven suites and guest rooms on the fourth floor, with the second and third floors hosting an artists' residency programme in 18 workshops and apartments. The ground floor is given over to a number of watch boutiques, while further private dining, exhibition and conference rooms, the world-class Shook! restaurant and a rooftop terrace complete the hotel's facilities. Still at the centre of the Bund and still at the centre of Shanghai life, The Swatch Art Peace Hotel is justly celebrated as an international art centre and unique boutique hotel.

OLD SHANGHAI

Heritage Architecture in the International Style

xtensive books by any number of experts have been written on the subject of Shanghai's extraordinary array of 19th- and 20th-century architecture, so this author isn't going to try to compete with an in-depth analysis. Suffice it to say that the city is well worth a visit — for both architecture aficionados and those who enjoy a heritage experience.

Two hundred years ago, Shanghai was already a trading port lying at the mouth of the Yangtze River. But, when the British were allocated land there under the terms of the 1942 Treaty of Nanking at the end of the First Opium War, the city entered a new phase in its life — one of Western commercial activity. Stretching from Soochow Creek in the north, down along the Bund in the east, and extending westward and inland a few miles, the area

Left and top *The Western appearance of the Bund buildings feature palatial Italianate interiors and imposing facades in a variety of architectural styles.* **Overleaf** *Soaring Deco towers, exposed brickwork, classical columns and cupolas, and an all-pervading aura of history pervade the multiple apartment and office blocks, as well as ecclesiastical buildings, in both the French Concession and the Bund.*

eventually became home to two enclaves of foreigners, namely the International Settlement (ruled by the British and occupied by both British and Americans) and the French Concession.

Initially, both areas were envisaged as purely for foreign occupation, but they soon became home to tens of thousands of Chinese as well. Attracted by the security guaranteed by the foreign governments, Chinese residents comprised by far the majority of their inhabitants. In addition to the British, French, Americans and Chinese were numbers of Jews from both Russia and the Middle East as well as a significant population of White Russians: the former contributed greatly to Shanghai's wealth and built heritage, while the latter, mainly from the upper classes and minor nobility, were often impoverished and ill-used to earning a living. Their role was often in the service and nightlife sectors.

Within a couple of decades, both concessions were awash with offices, residences, clubs, restaurants, brothels and more. Boom time had come to Shanghai — and the city was pleased to accommodate it.

Today, the first thing one notices about these enclaves is how European most of the architecture is. Remarkably, much of it is extremely well preserved — and restorations continue to this

day. From the beginning, the Bund (taken from a Hindustani word meaning "embankment") was dominated by offices and banks built on a grand scale along the bustling waterfront, while private residences and apartments tended to be located further west along the tree-lined avenues of the French Concession.

Architecturally speaking, the 1920s was the decade that shone the brightest in bricks and mortar. New construction techniques in the form of reinforced concrete, improved engineering, the advent of electrical lifts and modern heating and cooling, resulted in the advent of the high-rise. In Shanghai, most specifically, this was the era of Art Deco apartment building. These stunning edifices, complemented by the grandiose Romanesque Revival, Gothic Revival, Renaissance Revival, Baroque Revival, Neo-Classical and Beaux-Arts styles that already lined the Bund, came to embody the dizzying heights (literally and figuratively) of prosperity that Shanghai had attained.

Naturally, pride comes before a fall, and Shanghai's residents — accustomed to its free-wheeling mercantile environment and high living standards — somehow felt themselves immune to events in the rest of the world. Even a massive influx of European Jews, fleeing the Nazis in the 1930s, didn't seem to impact the locals' imperviousness to encroaching disaster. However, the advent of World War II and Japanese occupation, followed by postwar fighting between Nationalist and Communist forces, finally took their toll on Western business. By the time of the 1949 "liberation" of the city by Communist forces and the establishment of the People's Republic of China, the time for Westerners in Shanghai was over.

Even though the Westerners left, their buildings remained. Sadly, the ensuing period of enforced isolation, exacerbated by the activities of proponents of the Cultural Revolution, resulted in the dilapidation and destruction of much of Shanghai's built heritage. Also, with Shanghai's more recent resurgence from the 1990s onwards, many more buildings have fallen prey to the wrecker's ball. Nonetheless, there is still a sizeable body of sophisticated work that has survived the vagaries of time, and, as Shanghai once again rises on the international stage, they are being sensitively renovated and revitalized. The Swatch Art Peace Hotel, occupying a central Bund location, is one of many such historic edifices (see overleaf).

ENGLISH STYLE ON THE BUND

A Revolutionary Hotel — Past and Present

espite construction problems, the six-storey structure that houses today's Swatch Art Peace Hotel was lauded as revolutionary when all its floors became fully operational in 1909. Boasting 120 guest rooms all with baths, it was the most capacious and comfortable hotel in Shanghai at the time. Its two lifts were the first to be installed in Shanghai, even in China, and were viewed with awe. Then as now, the ground floor was taken up with shops, while the whole of the top floor accommodated a dining room that could seat 300 people and a 200-seat banqueting hall with access to the roof garden.

Built in a locally interpreted Victorian Renaissance style, with red brick and cream-white tile veneer, when viewed from Nanjing Road East the building appears grand; when viewed from the Bund it seems altogether more slender. The architects favoured an English style for the facade and interiors, while the two pavilions on the roof were Baroque with an Oriental flavour. Unfortunately, in the early 20th century the roof garden suffered from a fire that destroyed the pavilions, but they were rebuilt only slightly amended from their original style. Today, along with the rooftop terrace, they are top venues for drinks, dinner and views.

Even though the interiors are markedly modernised now, the Nanjing Road entrance with its revolving door remains the same (despite the contemporary addition of a canopy) and the lobby retains its marble and dark wood panelling. Opening onto a broad wooden staircase that sports exquisite enchasing on the railings and stained glass windows, it is an imposing sight. This respect for the hotel's heritage is maintained in the fifth-floor Chiang-Soong room, where dark wood panelling complemented by gold inscription is maintained in pristine condition (see these pages).

Above *One of the rooftop pavilions, now called the Corner Tower, illuminated by candlelight and chandelier.* **Opposite** *A private dining room named after Chiang Kai-Shek and his fiancée Soong May Ling.*

Elevated Dining in Salubrious Surrounds

he floors housing the artists' workshops and apartments and the seven guest accommodations are markedly different from the exterior style of architecture, as is the top-floor Shook! Shanghai restaurant. However, while the former make reference to both Chinese and British history in an abstract manner, the design of the award-winning restaurant is a modern, modish interpretation of Chinese high style.

Guests walk through a stunning floor-to-ceiling wine cellar corridor to access the bar and restaurant, both of which sport textural finishes in the form of lacquer, metallics, silk and glass. With the convivial Time Bar on the left and an open-plan kitchen on the right, dining options are divided into sections, ensuring that Shook! is both airy and intimate. It's undeniably sexy too, with Chinoiserie touches, *Shoji*-style screens and more than a nod to the decadent Deco style of Old Shanghai. Gold and red predominate along with the shiny waxy sheen of dark wood.

Entirely in keeping with the international flavour of the Bund, food is a mix of Malaysian, Thai, Chinese, Japanese and modern Western. Choose from a table *à deux* or for four with fabulous river views or more enclosed seating clusters behind dark wood and lacquered screens. Either way, the lunch or dinner delights with an opulent Oriental ambience and flavourful cuisine.

Further personalised experiences are to be had in the roof's two pavilions: with views over the Bund and river to the modern high-rises of Pudong, there's exclusive private dining in the Corner Tower or a cigar and cognac experience in the clubby Blancpain Room. For most people, a visit to the expansive roof terrace for pre-dinner cocktails, post-prandial coffees and cigars and panoramic views is a highlight.

Previous page *A semi-enclosed dining space (left) and the restaurant's floor-to-ceiling wine cellar that doubles as an entrance corridor (right).*
Above *The Corner Tower (top left), the clubby Blancpain Room (right) and a sexy table setting with beautifully rendered screen (above left).*

Opposite left *The Time Bar with its high-backed stools and comfortable U-shape is just visible behind an intimate seating booth.*
Opposite right *Textural touches — shiny wood, heavy lacquer, metallic beading — form the backdrop to this restaurant, as do views all around.*

Concierge

Take A Walking Tour in the French Concession

A number of heritage guides offer walking tours in different parts of the French Concession — meandering slowly by foot is the best way to take in some of the extraordinary architecture still extant. Furthermore, many of the streets are lined with plane trees, the branches of which bend inwards and join in the middle, making for a shaded path beneath which to walk. There's the Little Russia area with its former Russian Orthodox Mission church, rows of English-style villas in Tudorbethan style, narrow streets lined with lane houses, as well as the former French Club set within verdant gardens. A highlight is the beautifully renovated Art Deco apartment building, Grosvenor House: owned by Victor Sassoon (of the Cathay Hotel fame), and known to locals as "Eighteen Floors", it was (and still is) one of the city's premier addresses.

Have a Private Dinner in the Corner Tower on the Roof Terrace

With panoramic views over the Huangpu River to the sparkling sight of Pudong on the other side, the roof terrace at the Swatch Art Peace Hotel is worth a visit for the vista alone. However, if you fancy something a bit more special, you can hire the octagonal pavilion on the roof for a private dinner for two or four. With beautiful deep green walls and a candlelit interior, the setting is both cosy and impressive. Personalised dining in your own private cupola … what could be more romantic?

Shop for Antiques in one of Shanghai's Markets

No trip to Shanghai is complete without a foray into its world of antiques and curios. Selling everything from Mao memorabilia, Deco artefacts, to porcelain, calligraphy, jade and embroideries, as well as a range of increasingly hard-to-find early 20th-century furniture, there is no end to the collectibles on offer. Most popular is the Dongtai Lu antiques market with an assorted mishmash of vintage items, traditional crafts, various knick-knacks, as well as some high-end pieces. Despite the blatant copies, experienced collectors may pick up some excellent buys. There are also the weekend Fuyou Road Crafts Market and the Jing'an Temple Jewellery and Curio Market in the Jing'an District.

CONCIERGE

Delve into Shanghai's Street Food

Shanghai is well known for its dedication to street food, with the Shanghainese even having a name for late night snacking: *ye xiao* refers to any meal taken after midnight. Nonetheless, you'll easily find an assortment of home-cooked, super fresh snacks or *xiao chi* on any street corner at any time of day. Thin skinned dumplings filled with piping hot pork soup or *xiao long bao* are served with straws to drink up the broth; the so-called stinky tofu is usually fried and served with a chilli sauce (don't be put off by the smell!); and those hankering after a breakfast snack would do worse than try one of the fresh, floppy scallion pancakes, brushed with fermented bean paste. The best bet is to wander, buy and try.

Cross the Huangpu River to Pudong

Literally translating as "Huangpu East Bank", this area with its modern skyscrapers opposite the Bund symbolises the brave new face of China. In addition to being Shanghai's financial centre, it also has fantastic views over to the Bund from both the riverside and from some of its tall buildings. Radiating out from the central Century Square are the Oriental Art Centre and the Shanghai Science & Technology Museum — both illustrating how far China has advanced in recent years. It's a sobering thought to realize that the whole of Pudong simply didn't exist 25 years ago!

Enjoy a Cuppa in an old Teahouse

Ever since the Emperor Chen Nung "discovered" tea in 2,737 BC when a leaf from a wild tea plant reputedly fell into his bowl of hot water, the Chinese have been drinking tea as a social habit. By 500 BC, *yum cha*, as it is known, had become a mark of friendship and hospitality with hosts offering tea to guests as a sign of welcome, but — contrary to general perception — tea is not often drunk with meals. Generally it is consumed between meals, or alone, in teahouses. Shanghai is known for its plethora of teahouses; check one out and savour a cup of green tea, the leaves steeped in a teapot and the liquid drunk from a porcelain cup usually with a lid.

CAMERON HIGHLANDS RESORT

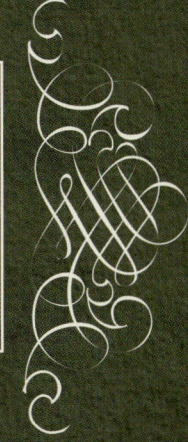

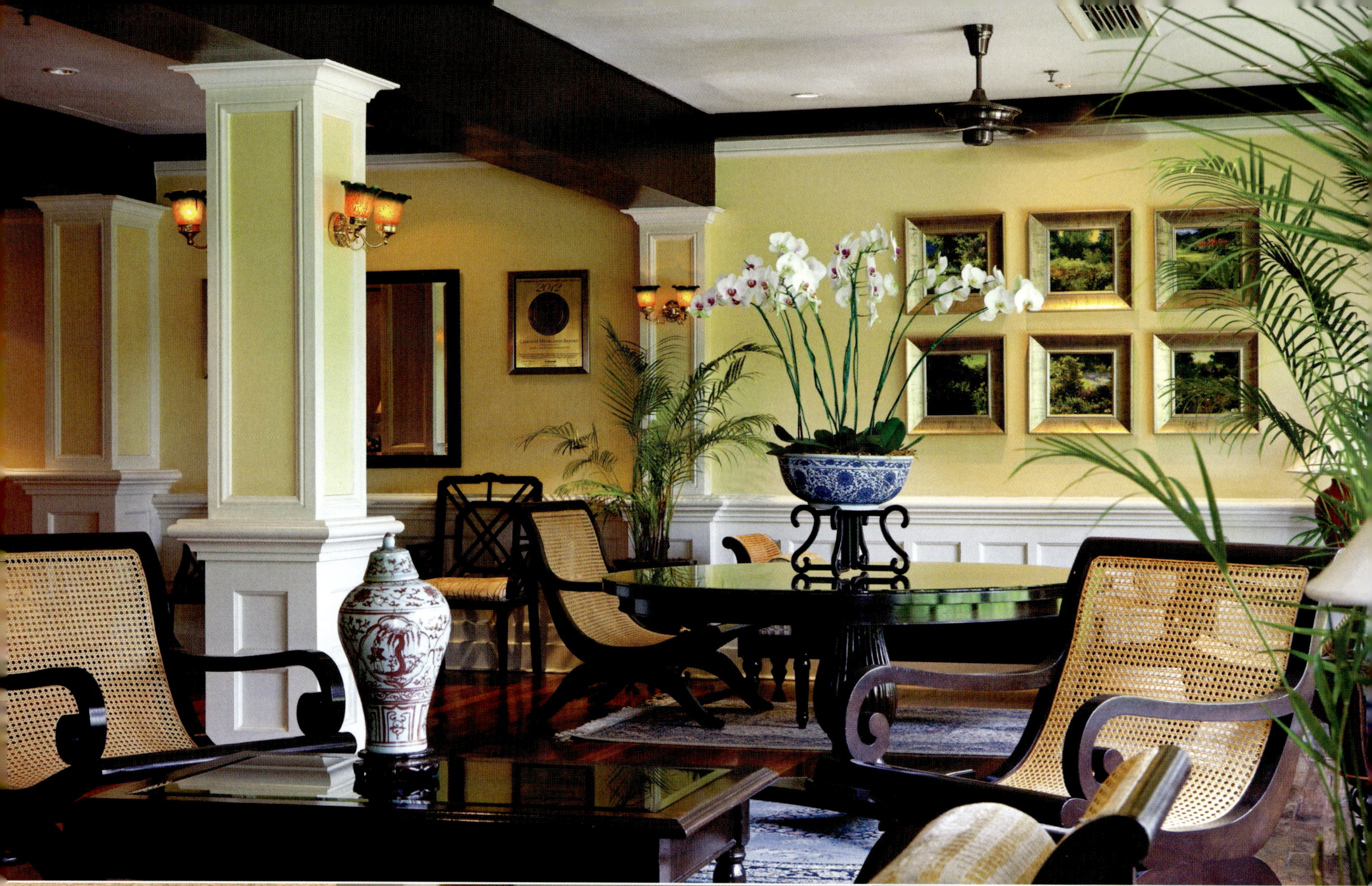

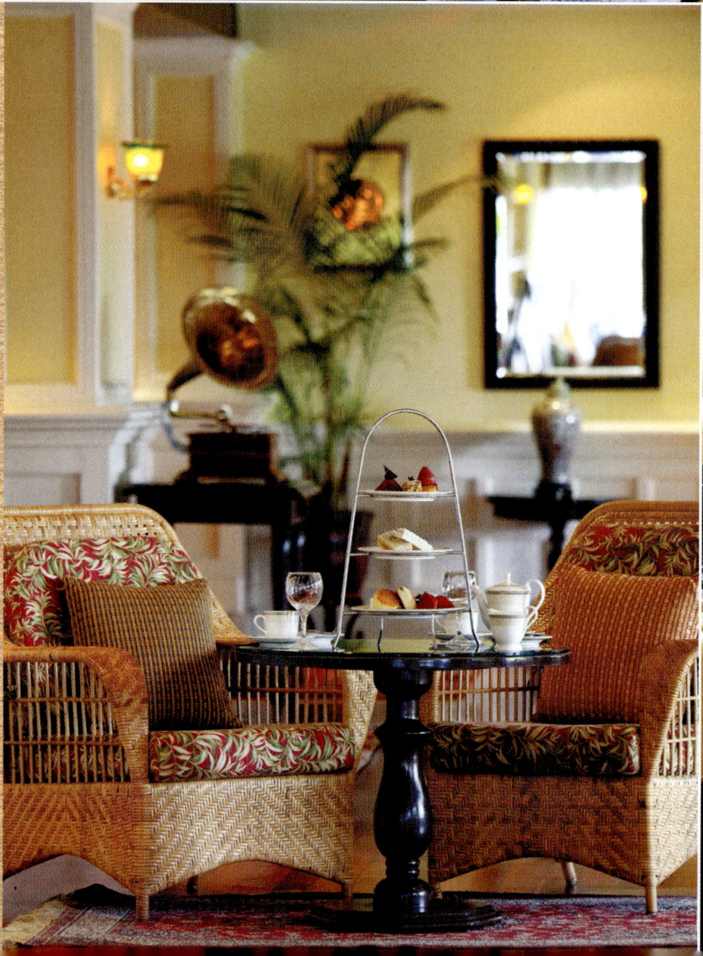

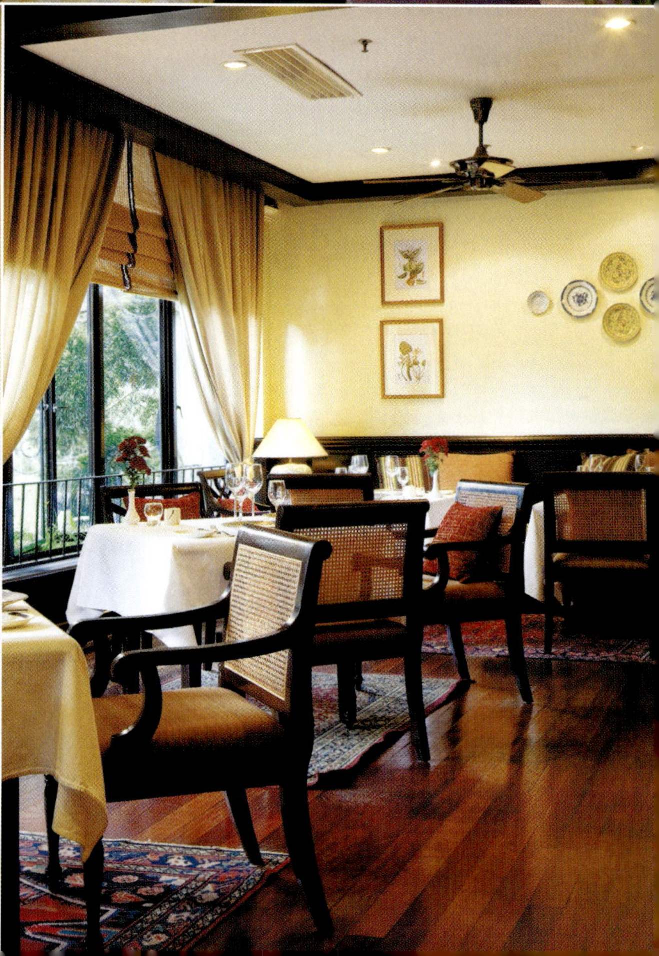

CAMERON HIGHLANDS RESORT

 boutique hideaway with a nostalgic air, Cameron Highlands Resort has an atmosphere reminiscent of colonial times, even if most of the actual building dates from the 1970s. Styled to mimic the ambience of a plantation house, the hotel has always been a stalwart of the hospitality scene in the peaceful surrounds of the Cameron Highlands.

Set 1,500 metres above sea level just outside the small settlement of Tanah Rata in a forested mountainscape, the hotel is built around a two-storey cottage that was probably a British home in the 1930s or '40s. The rest of the hotel is also set over two storeys — but was designed in the mock Tudor architectural style that was so popular in British hill stations in the colonies.

Featuring a handsome facade in black and white, with French doors sporting fanlights, plantation-style shutters, wrought ironwork balconies on the first storey (above) and attic windows peeping through a tiled roof, the hotel boasts fantastic views over the local 18-hole golf course. It is the perfect retreat for those wishing to get away from the heat, humidity and hectic activity of towns down at sea level.

This, of course, was why the area was settled in the first place. As with other hill stations in India, Sri Lanka, Burma (now Myanmar) and elsewhere, the Cameron Highlands served the purpose of being "a little piece of England in Asia". It gave the planters and bureaucrats that made the area their home stability and reassurance; in the same way, it was a tranquil escape for the British and well-to-do Asians who frequented it at weekends.

To this end, the Cameron Highlands Resort perpetuates the atmosphere of those long-gone days: through its heritage-style architecture and ambiance, its personalised service and its slightly wistful air (it's as if everybody is harking back to the past), the hotel evokes an era when elegance, luxury and bespoke facilities were a given. After all, who isn't guilty of wanting to turn the clock back once in a while?

Opposite *The hotel interiors are colonial chic in style — think planters' chairs, potted palms, lazy fans whirling overhead, and plenty of warm wood.*

THE ANGLO-MALAY HILL STATION

Mock Tudor in the Cameron Highlands

The "hill station" was a term coined in India by British civil servants during the era of the Raj: with the approach of summer, first the *memsahibs* and children, and later the menfolk, flocked to higher elevations in order to escape the intense heat on the plains. There, they set up shop in outposts that came to resemble mini recreations of Surrey or Sussex villages. Chocolate-box cottages with English country gardens, look-out posts, a recreational club, and cool fresh air all contributed to the charm of such settlements. It also helped that they were situated in areas of beautiful natural scenery.

As the British extended their sphere of influence eastwards, they brought the concept to Malaya. "Discovered" in 1885 by William Cameron, a British colonial government surveyor, the Cameron Highlands ticked all the boxes for a hill station: it comprised a series of green plateaus in the Titiwangsa mountains, its temperature seldom rose above 25°C by day and could drop to as low as 9°C at night, it had gorgeous views, and it was sparsely inhabited by local *orang asli* populations.

It, along with other hill stations such as Fraser's Hill in Perak and the Genting Highlands bordering the states of Pahang and Selangor, was mainly developed in the 1920s and 1930s. A 1927 article in *The Singapore Free Press and Mercantile Advertiser* noted that the main object of the Cameron Highlands was "the creation of a healthy Hill Station, similar to Nuwara Eliya, rather than the extension of agriculture, but as it should be possible to supply foodstuffs that will be of benefit to people who cannot use the Station itself, the reservation of areas suitable for agricultural development will be considered at a later stage." The article then went on to outline the plans to construct a road, the setting up of an experimental plantation to grow cinchona, tea and coffee as well as other vegetables and fruits, and the stationing of 36 Tamil coolies to clear land.

As is now known, the terrain lent itself beautifully to the cultivation of tea, vegetables and fruits — and, after the access road was completed, development of the area was fairly swift. Attempting to recreate a "little bit of home", architects and engineers followed the precedent laid out in India and Sri Lanka: small settlements sprang up incorporating all the features of the sub-continental hill station. Residences were rustic in style, often sporting Tudor-style beams, stone and tile floors, fireplaces and chimneys, as well as shuttered windows. They were surrounded

by perennial English gardens with cool-climate flowers and plants that reminded the inhabitants of "home" — roses, phlox, chrysanthemums and the like.

Infrastructure came in the form of the newly completed road in 1931, a six-hole golf course, three inns, a police post, two boarding schools and a couple of churches, as well as a variety of Chinese-run vegetable gardens and nurseries. Naturally, tea plantations led the way commercially and aesthetically with the surrounding hillsides becoming tamed by acres of velvety *Camellia sinensis*. The area became popular with the European community and wealthy Asians, many of whom visited for holidays or extended weekends.

Their choice of lodgings was in a "Tudorbethan" cottage, a style that became popular from the 1900s to the 1930s, both in Britain and its overseas outposts. In fact, it became almost *de*

rigueur in the Cameron Highlands, as it had in Simla in the Indian Himalayas some decades earlier. Generally, such houses harked back to a style of "Old English" architecture, where timber details were painted black and the rendered surfaces white. This style grew out of the anti-industrial Arts and Crafts Movement, popular in Britain from the 1860s to 1910. Celebrating old forms of construction, traditional craftsmanship, romantic styles of decoration and the like, it emerged as an antidote to the mechanisation of the day.

YTL Hotels' Cameron Highlands Resort, with its black and white facade, is a wonderful example of this Tudor revival style. Turn to the following pages to see inside its doors.

A COUNTRY RETREAT

Pastoral Pursuits in an Elegant Setting

ameron Highlands Resort is a handsome building facing the golf course a few miles out of the settlement of Tanah Rata. With its mock Tudor facade and plantation-style interiors, the guest experience is one of nostalgia and heritage. Built as a long extension from an existing 1930s cottage (see opposite), the architecture dates from the 1970s, but the interiors successfully hark back to an earlier era.

The resort combines friendly service with comfortable accommodation in an area that is renowned for its natural beauty. As such, most guests take advantage of the various outings that are organised at the hotel — visiting a tea plantation for a tour and a high-class picnic tea, viewing the spectacular cloud forest, playing golf and trekking with the resident trek leader in the surrounding hills are enticing examples.

When guests are at the hotel, the emphasis is very much on relaxation and recuperation. The public rooms, furnished with cane loungers and comfy sofas beneath lazily circling fans, encourage curling up with a good book. Whether it is in the clubby-style library or the large open-plan lounge, local juices and teas are on offer all day — and the atmosphere is quiet, but welcoming. A large jardinière with sprays of orchids sits before a grand piano, which comes alive during the evenings for convivial cocktails around a freshly-laid wood fire.

The dining room, with vistas overlooking the golf course, serves a selection of fresh food sourced from the surrounding hills — traditional English cuisine, Asian dishes, and grilled items with a local twist are part and parcel of the culinary agenda. Guests are also advised to sample a whisky or cocktail, perhaps with a game of snooker, in the Highlands Bar.

Opposite *The original section of the resort houses the suites. There is a Deco element in the rounded balconies and square fanlights, and the rooms are slightly larger than elsewhere at the resort.*

In addition to lazing and dining, guests would be well disposed to sample a treatment at the resort's first-class spa. Utilising local ingredients, such as tea leaves, strawberries and other plants, its menu tantalises with fresh natural therapies. Another alternative is one of any number of local walks in the hotel vicinity: ranging in difficulty from simple strolls to more challenging hikes and climbs, you'll be rewarded by the variety of exotic flora and fauna on display in the stunning jungle environment.

Many guests, however, find the highlight of a trip to the Cameron Highlands Resort to be the traditional afternoon tea. Comprising freshly-made scones, locally-made jam, just ripe strawberries, cucumber sandwiches and other delights artfully set out in front of a roaring log fire, it is an all-English affair. What could be more appetising than that?

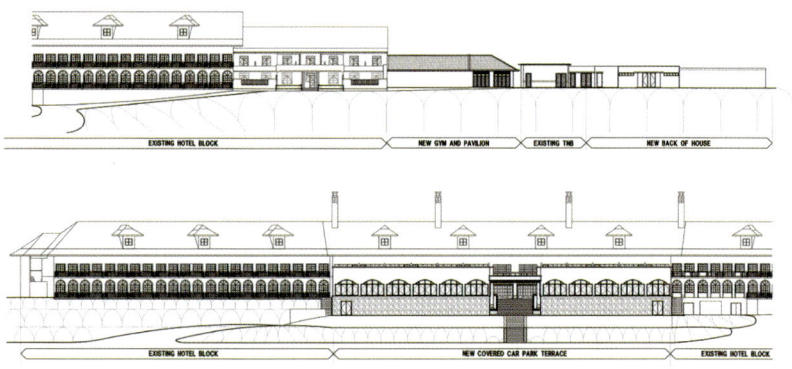

Top and opposite *An all-pervasive genteel air, reminiscent of colonial times and lifestyles, permeates the resort. Old-fashioned, honest service is another plus.*
Above *Architect's drawings of the front elevation: note how small the original cottage is compared to the '70s structure.*

CONCIERGE

Visit the Mossy Forest

One of the Cameron Highlands' unique attractions is its patches of "mossy forest" that grow at the highest elevations. Low-level clouds driven by winds blanket these forests with constant mist and moisture, creating an ideal habitat for moss, ferns and lichen. Furthermore, there are plenty of other exotics like pitcher plants, orchids, bromeliads and the like. One such area is found close to Gunung Brinchang, some half hour's drive from the resort. It's well worth the trip to walk through this magical environment — many locals compare it to some of the scenes in the Harry Potter movies!

Visit the Night Market at Brinchang

A popular shopping attraction amongst visitors and locals alike, the night market occurs every Friday and Saturday starting from 4pm and ending late at night. Occupying two clearings opposite each other across the main road, it consists of a variety of stalls retailing the best products from the Cameron Highlands — strawberries, vegetables, flowers, plants and kitsch souvenirs. It's also an excellent place to go food hunting, with many hawker stalls serving up local favourites and continental snacks.

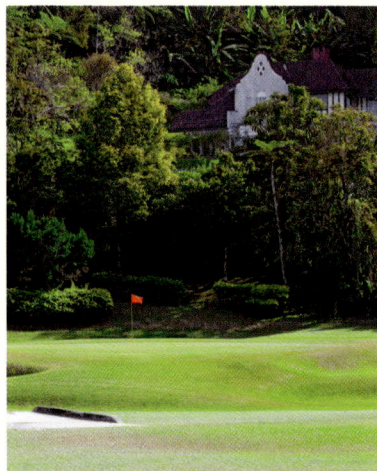

Play a Round of Golf

Situated directly in front of the resort, the par-71, 6,101 metre, 18-hole golf course provides a wonderful opportunity for a full day's golf in fresh mountain air. The well-manicured course comprises luxuriant green fairways with mature trees, fine sand bunkers, tricky greens and thick rough, providing what is probably the coolest and most pleasant golfing environment in Malaysia.

CONCIERGE

Tour a Tea Plantation

No trip to the Cameron Highlands would be complete without a visit to a local tea plantation. One of the resort's fabulous excursions involves a visit to the famous BOH Plantations, followed by a gorgeous, bespoke picnic tea amongst the velvety tea gardens. See the tea pickers at work, take a tour round the factory to learn about the different processes for tea preparation, then enjoy a cuppa at the tea shop. Afterwards, a private butler serves a sumptuous picnic set beneath an umbrella high above the plantation — what could be more decadent?

Take a Treatment at Spa Village Cameron Highlands

Set in a sweet wooden building that used to comprise the old servants' quarters, the resort's Spa Village offers a number of tea-inspired therapies designed to nurture body and soul. Before each healing therapy, there is a signature tea-leaf bath, then guests can choose from any number of treats that celebrate the local area. There are some *orang asli* adaptations "borrowed" from the indigenous residents' extensive knowledge of local plant life, as well as plenty of pampering treatments involving regional produce such as strawberries, avocado, mint and rose petals. Whatever you choose, you'll be sure to emerge glowing and relaxed.

Go on a Trek with the Resident Naturalist

Tailored to every level of fitness, the resort offers a number of guided walks in the surrounding jungle. Most guests will know this as the place where Jim Thompson took his last fatal walk: follow along part of his path, check out a couple of the local waterfalls, or go for something a little more challenging in the form of a peak hike. All afford sensational views over the surrounding mountains and the resort's knowledgeable naturalist provides information about local history, flora and fauna.

The Majestic Malacca

THE MAJESTIC MALACCA

 bijou boutique gem in a unique port town steeped in history, The Majestic Malacca receives travellers with warmth, wit and gracious hospitality. Housed in a 1920s' former mansion with a new building mirroring the original architecture behind, the hotel possesses a rare combination of qualities — it's refined and sophisticated, yet homely and welcoming as well.

A wonderful example of adaptive re-use of architectural heritage, the original building retains many authentic features, yet has been updated for the modern guest. Behind a symmetrical facade lie two storeys comprising reception hall, library, bar and dining chambers. Sporting original geometric concrete floor tiles on the ground floor and teakwood boards above, two fabulous turnaround staircases, ample windows with pastel-painted shutters as well as period furniture, the décor echoes that of a domestic interior in Malacca around 100 years ago.

Retro-style suites and rooms with heavy teak furniture — think four-posters, capacious desks and old armoires — and bathrooms sporting both claw-foot tubs and modern facilities, as well as a world-class spa, are housed in the modern ten-storey tower behind. As if that weren't enough, there's a sweet swimming pool with loungers and a convenient gym as well. If the original owner, Canton-born rubber baron Leong Long Man, were to walk into the house today, I am sure he would have been delighted with the transformation of his family home!

Opposite and right *Sweet pastel shades, so beloved by the Peranakans, dominate the colour palette at The Majestic Malacca. Floor tiles in the library were made in Vietnam.*

A Polyglot of Styles

Malacca's Architectural Heritage

rchitecturally, Malacca is a fascinating town as it has a plethora of extant buildings left by the various different nationalities that made the port their home over a period of 600 years. Some are intact, others have been renovated, adapted and built on to over the years (for example, The Majestic Malacca), while a few have been preserved as close to their origins as possible. For centuries, this eclectic mix of styles has intrigued visitors, and, in 2008, Malacca was granted UNESCO World Heritage status.

Once a small fishing village, Malacca began to rise to prominence in the 14th century under the leadership of a fugitive prince from Sumatra named Parameswara. By 1403, it was an established trading centre with sea-going vessels unloading in its deep-water river. It attracted the attention of both Chinese fleets, who visited the Sultanate no fewer than seven times, and Europe's colonial powers: the Portuguese arrived in 1511 and they were succeeded by the Dutch in 1641 for a century and a half, before surrendering the region to the British in 1795. The Dutch took power again in 1818 to 1824 before returning Malacca to the British in exchange for territory in Sumatra. Naturally, these successive imperial powers — along with local Malays, overseas

Chinese from Fujian and Guangdong provinces who settled in Malacca, and other traders from Arabia and India — left a lasting architectural legacy in both Malacca and the surrounding areas.

A wander around Malacca's town centre is a rewarding experience: the Portuguese introduced stone construction to what had predominantly been a town of timber buildings (see Malay house opposite, bottom right); also, at some point during their rule, they instigated rudimentary town planning, the manufacture of tiles and use of local laterite in their buildings. The only remnant from their time, however, is the pentagonal fort on the south side of the Malacca river; called *A Famosa*, it was razed to the ground by the British in 1803, but nonetheless its gate still exists as do parts of its walls (see opposite, bottom left).

While the Portuguese mainly built fortifications and religious buildings, the Dutch moved into the residential sphere with brick manufacturing and tile construction — for both floors and roofs. Dutch heritage is to be seen in the form of the red Christ Church (opposite, top) and the old *Stadhuys* or Governor's residence, as well as west of the river in the area known as Kampung Belanda or "Dutch Village". Its streets, set out on a rectilinear plan, are lined with row houses built from brick with tiled roofs. Constructed

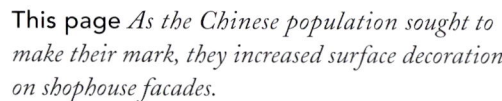

This page *As the Chinese population sought to make their mark, they increased surface decoration on shophouse facades.*
Opposite, clockwise from top left *A variety of roof forms; elaborate exterior of the Chee family ancestral mansion or* rumah abu *of a Straits Chinese household; fine examples of beautifully carved Chinese character signage; chien nien frieze using shards of ceramics along a roofline.*

from the early 18th century onwards, they were usually narrow and long, as residents were taxed on the width of the house frontage, and the facades were fairly plain.

After the Dutch were ousted, Malacca came to be dominated by the growing population of prosperous Chinese: intermarrying with local Malays, these Straits-born Chinese modified many of the terraces to suit their eclectic tastes and burgeoning wallets. Combining Classical, Chinese and Malay elements with a plethora of surface decoration, the downtown streets changed significantly in the 19th century. This was almost certainly because craftsmen from China were employed in the building works and this new breed of Chinese merchant wanted to express his wealth and dominance in an overtly conspicuous manner.

Isabella Bird, the inveterate Victorian traveller, visited Malacca in the late 1870s and wrote about the Chinese in Malacca thus: "Malacca is to most intents and purposes a Chinese city. And it is not, as elsewhere, that they come, make money, and then return to settle in China, but they come here with their wives and families, buy or build these handsome houses, as well as large bungalows in the neighbouring cocoa groves, own most of the plantations up the country, and have obtained the finest site on the hill behind the town for their stately tombs.... They love Malacca, and take a pride in beautifying it."

As with the other Straits Settlements and Chinatowns in South East Asia, the Chinese built shophouses or townhouses in town and rather larger stand-alone mansions out of town. Both were based

on the archetypal Chinese courtyard house, a type that varied from region to region but had many shared features. The most important is that all constructions had adjacent open and closed spaces — courtyards of various shapes and sizes and surrounding rooms or buildings. In southern China, the term *tianjing* or "skywell" was coined to describe them: in addition to improving ventilation, bringing light into the dark interior and facilitating the collection of rainwater, they shaded areas as the sun moved overhead and provided an outdoor social space for residents.

All Malacca shophouses have either one or two *tianjing*: in addition to providing the practical benefits mentioned above, they had cosmological significance as well. Similarly, as with

Above left and below *Five foot way and facade decoration in auspicious red and gold (1911).*
Above *Five foot way, an original well in a back court, tiles, furniture and a window cupboard.*

the Chinese courtyard house, the "front" room was used for entertaining visitors or for commercial purposes and the next room after the *tianjing* was commonly used as the ancestral hall — here the family altar and shrine dedicated to the ancestors was housed. Behind this were the kitchen and the back *tianjing*, the latter containing a well before the advent of plumbing. Upstairs, rooms were used for sleeping and storage, while out front was the ubiquitous "five-foot way", a continuous covered walkway that protected pedestrians from both sun and rain. Isabella Bird described these as "long shady alleys" where "crowds of buyers and sellers chaffer over their goods, the Chinese shopkeepers asking a little more than they mean to take …".

Beyond the organisation of space, most Chinese residences in Malacca sport some auspicious imagery, both inside and outside the building. This rich symbolic vocabulary is another feature of the archetypal Chinese building: be it a wooden plaque with Chinese characters extolling virtues; an ornamental ventilation panel with characters symbolising longevity; wall paintings of fruit with symbolic significance; or simple Chinese couplets of four-character phrases pasted to the wall, this type of signage is one of the most enduring traditions of Chinese visual culture. Whether the building is a simple home, a large ancestral hall, palace or temple matters not a jot.

As some Peranakan families grew more prosperous, they moved out of town, erecting stand-alone mansions backing on to Pantai Klebang or somewhere inland. A few remaining *towkay* villas in a mix of styles remain in a very dilapidated condition along Jalan Klebang (see above). Others built family homes in town. The hotel we feature on the following pages is one such example: an early 20th-century Peranakan mansion turned boutique lodge, it retains the spirit of the past, yet contains all the necessities for the present age.

THE PAST REBORN

A Heritage House turned Hotel

Malacca is a busy town — vibrant, colourful and visually arresting, but hot, humid and hectic nonetheless. All the more reason to step out of its busy streets and seek sanctuary in the cool confines of today's The Majestic Malacca. Located only a 15-minute walk from the Jonker and Heeren heritage area, the hotel offers respite from the teeming streets outside.

Thoughtfully restored to showcase the city's multi-faceted history, the building has been designed in a manner that beguiles with both old-world charm and no-nonsense modern convenience. The reception hall and bar, with comfy sofas, plantation stools and chairs, and help-yourself peanuts and cookies, is convivial and cute, while upstairs the Mansion restaurant serves meals as multi-cultural as Malacca itself: sample Portuguese, Dutch, English and *Baba-Nyonya* dishes, redolent with the aromas and spices of the Orient.

Even though it isn't really necessary in a 54-room hotel, there is a sweet swimming pool and gym situated behind the old house. Cleverly sandwiched between the new and old wings, they add an extra dimension to the food and beverage service and various excursions offered by staff.

Opposite *Much of the character of the original building comes from the carefully re-organised floor tiles, salvaged by architect Zaidan Tahir.*
Above *Motifs in the spa, such as this traditional "dog-bone" window, add authenticity to the décor.*
Right *Examples of Straits Chinese cuisine: Kuih pie tee or "top hats", a popular veggie or seafood snack, and ayam pong teh, a type of chicken stew.*

The spa at the hotel is another plus in this boutique hotel. Offering truly world-class therapies mainly devised by a Traditional Chinese Medicine doctor, it uses fresh ingredients more commonly found in *Nyonya* cuisine — think fermented tapioca, chopped guava leaves, fragrant pandan, as well as the local palm sugar or *gula Malacca* and the saliva of swifts from birds' nests highly prized by the Chinese.

Painstakingly designed in Straits Settlement style with the pastel colours so prized by the Peranakans (see above and opposite), the spa features dark wood Chinese day beds, cubicles accessed by *pintu pagar* or saloon-style doors, colourful floor tiles, and floor-to-ceiling windows with louvres and fantail vents. The relaxation lounge is an airy space filtered by layered light, while treatment rooms include carefully thought-through details such as soft kingfisher blue and turquoise batiks, porcelain wall tiles and custom-crafted wood detailing. All in all, the rich culture of the Peranakans is skilfully evoked.

Marrying Straits Chinese architecture and therapies, specialised service and unique treatments is a first in Malaysia — if not the world. As such, the spa has won numerous awards both locally and globally.

Below *A floor plan of the first floor shows the relation between the main house and the tower behind. The flat roofed building is the gym, the adjacent rectangle the sweet swimming pool.*

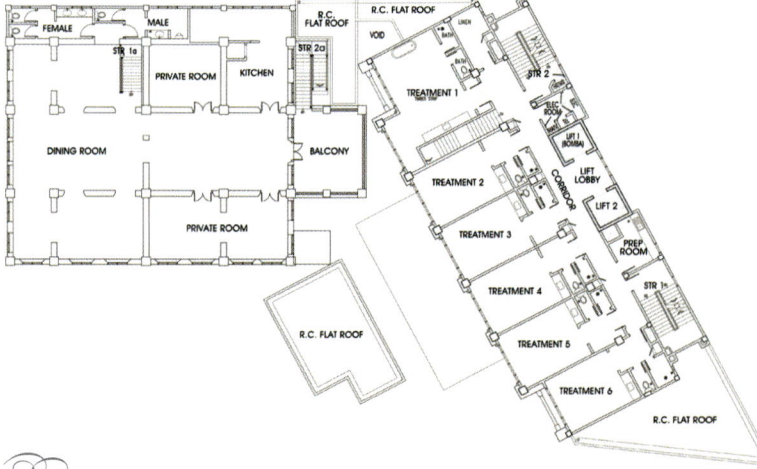

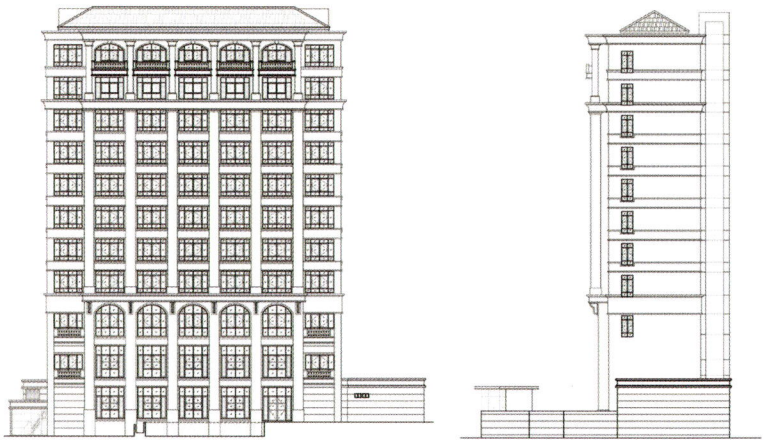

When tycoon Leong Long Man built his family home in 1927, he spared no expense. His 150 acres of rubber had yielded a vast fortune to the self-made entrepreneur and he wanted to show off his wealth. So, even though the exterior of the hotel was quite simple, inside was a different matter. Imported Victorian tiles, stained glass windows and expensive furniture and fittings were all incorporated into a home that took two years to build.

Sadly, he fell ill only two years after moving in and died in 1931. Later, his son squandered his inheritance and was forced to sell the family mansion to a businessman named Lim Heng Fang. Fortuitously, Mr Lim preserved the building and converted it into a hotel — the Majestic — with a clientele that mainly comprised British planters. In the 1950s and '60s, it became quite *de rigueur* to stay at the Majestic if one was visiting Malacca. Malaysia's first prime minister even stayed here when he announced the former British colony's independence in 1957.

Before it closed its doors in the year 2000, the hotel had taken a turn for the worse, operating as a budget guesthouse with a dilapidated air. Luckily, the acquisition by YTL Hotels and the no-expense-spared renovation resulted in a luxury lodging when it was fully restored and reopened in January 2008. The new ten-storey tower (elevations above) house the suites and rooms (left and right) and, once again, visitors can appreciate everything it, and Malacca, has to offer.

CONCIERGE

Take a Guided Walking Tour

The UNESCO World Heritage Site of Malacca is home to numerous historic buildings — Portuguese, Dutch and British, as well as those left by other early traders and settlers, namely the Chinese, Malay, Indian, Javanese and Bugis. The hotel's complimentary guided tour takes guests along the river and through numerous narrow alleyways to see many prominent historical landmarks, age-old religious institutions and the architecturally interesting shophouses. Guests will be sure to receive unusual insights into seemingly ordinary sights as well as in-depth information about the various architectural styles. Not to be missed are the Baba & Nyonya Heritage Museum and the Straits Chinese Jewellery Museum (right): both are on Heeren street in beautifully restored and well-maintained shophouses.

Take a Trishaw Ride

The only place in the world that has this particular design of trishaw with the driver cycling alongside his passenger rather than in front or behind (not to mention flashing lights, blaring music and a canopy likely to be decorated with love hearts or flowers!), a Malacca trishaw ride can be a hilarious experience. For starters, you may be accompanied by music from popular 1960s Malay movies — and, secondly, many of the drivers are real characters with fascinating stories to tell. Go on .... live dangerously!

Visit Spa Village Malacca for a Peranakan-inspired Treatment

The beautifully appointed spa at The Majestic Malacca begins every treatment with a unique head and hair cleanse that has its roots in Peranakan wedding culture. Key ingredients are a floral tonic and a zesty lime and flower combo. Then, a specially prepared questionnaire indicates whether you are a "heaty" or "cool" person — and a ritual of therapies, devised with the help of a TCM doctor, follows. Don't miss the opportunity for a once in a lifetime experience not offered at spas anywhere else in the world. Of course, all treatments use 100 percent natural products — expect exotic tropical fruits and even the elixir taken from swiftlet birds' nests, a speciality of the area.

CONCIERGE

Go on a River Cruise

Every half an hour you may spot a small boat making its way up the once-busy Malacca river that runs its course at the front of the Majestic. Today, lined with the backs of shophouses gaily painted by local students with murals that depict the history of both Malacca and Malaysia, the river allows guests to see the town from a different perspective. A commentary provides information on the various trade wars, rulers and settlers, so you'll come ashore a little more educated about Malaccan history as well.

Take a Peranakan Cooking Class

The women or *Nyonyas* of Peranakan families were well known as highly accomplished chefs, with the kitchen in Straits Chinese homes known as the *perut rumah* or "stomach of the home". It was here that these women honed their skills to produce a distinctly eclectic cuisine based on Chinese recipes but using Malay ingredients. Learn how to incorporate the local palm sugar or *gula Malacca* into *ayam pong teh*, a totally authentic recipe that translates as "Nyonya chicken stew". Other dishes using local ingredients such as fermented shrimp paste, pandan, coconut and more are also on the menu.

Explore Malacca's Dying Crafts Scene

Along with Penang, and to a slightly lesser extent Singapore and Kuala Lumpur, Malacca is home to some of South East Asia's last remaining craftsmen and women well versed in the dying arts of lantern making, wooden signboard carving and painting, *popiah* skin making, the construction of funerary paraphernalia and more. Visit the few remaining ateliers to see how these skilled crafts continue to flourish — even if not for much longer. The women and men involved are happy to show visitors what they do; it gives a fascinating insight into the artistry of these individuals, all the while showing how fleeting some of these professions may be.

MUSE Bray Cottages

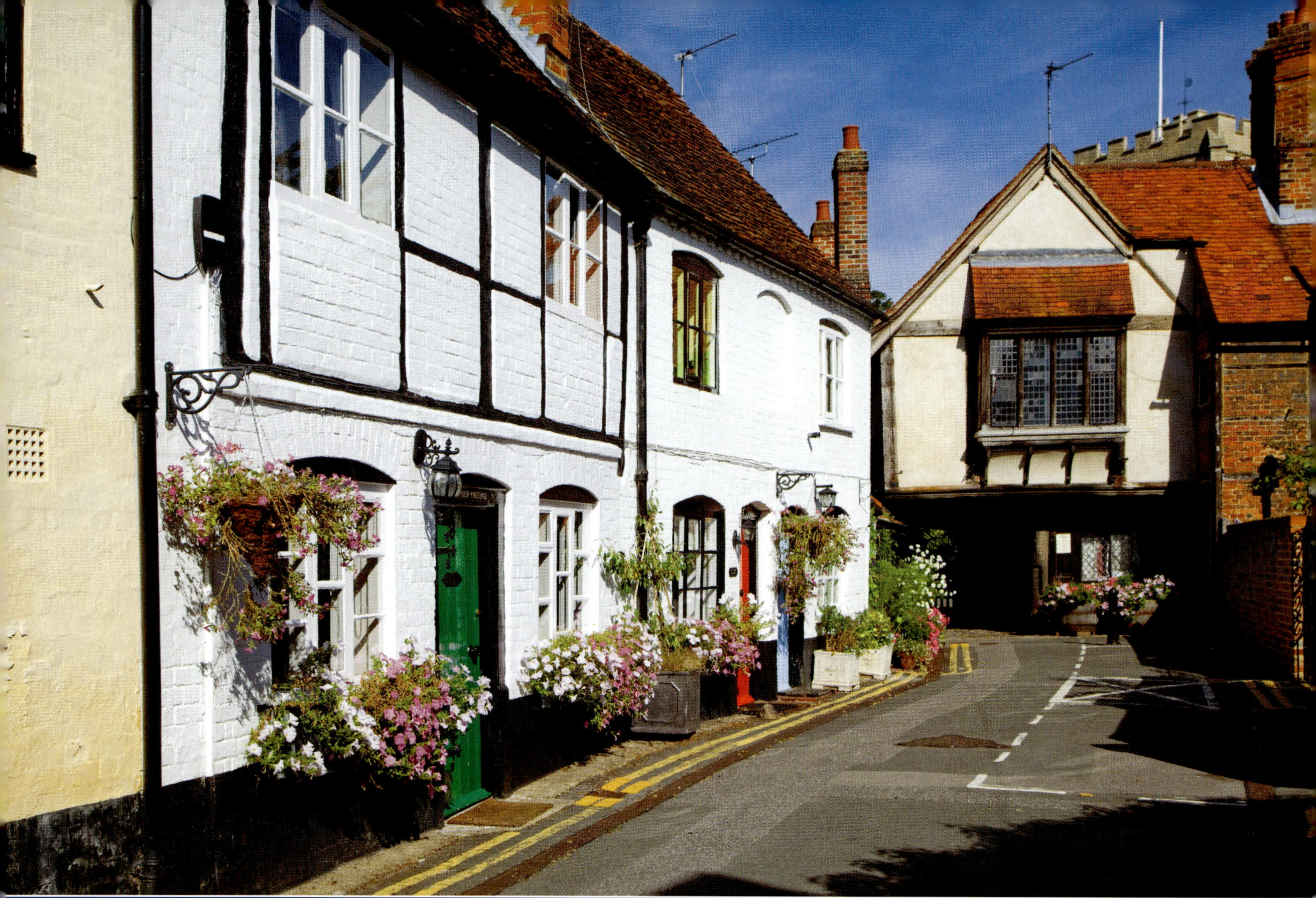

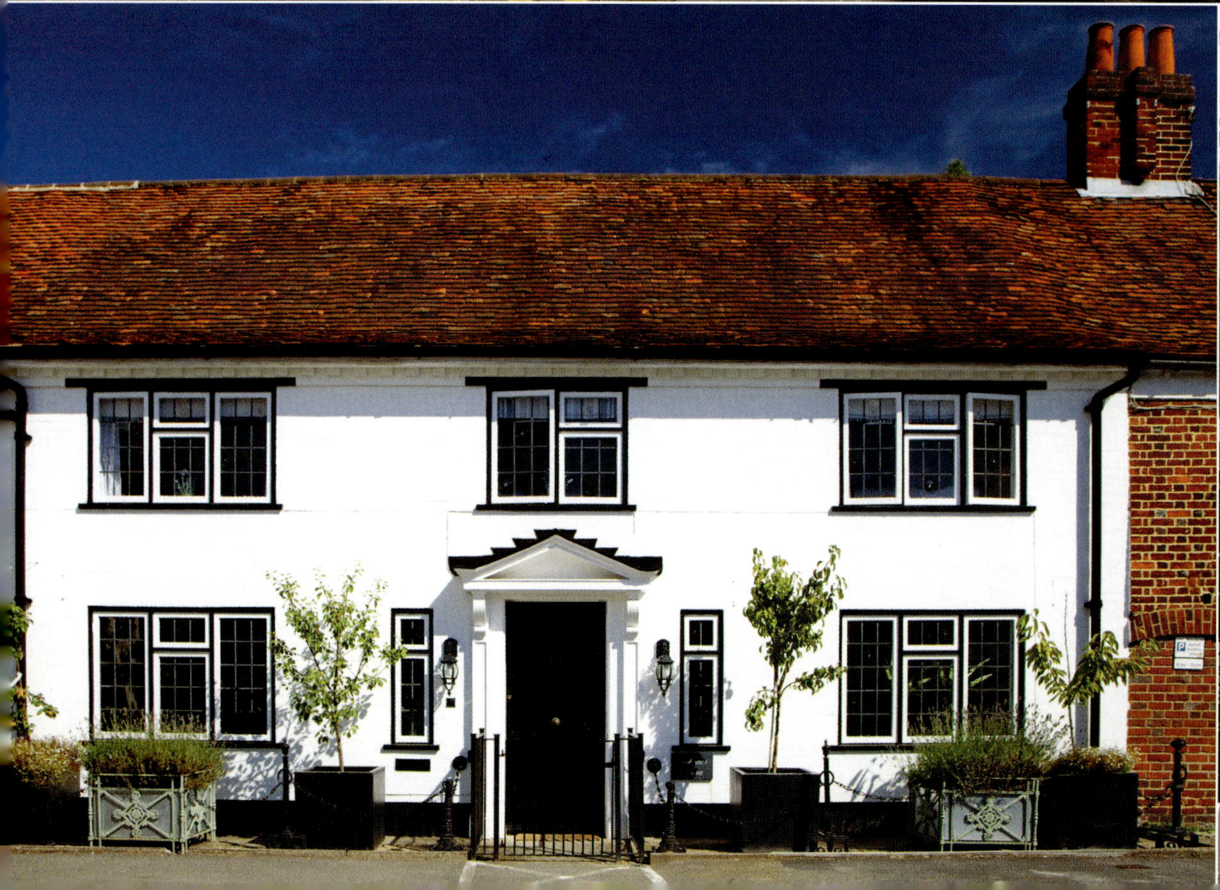

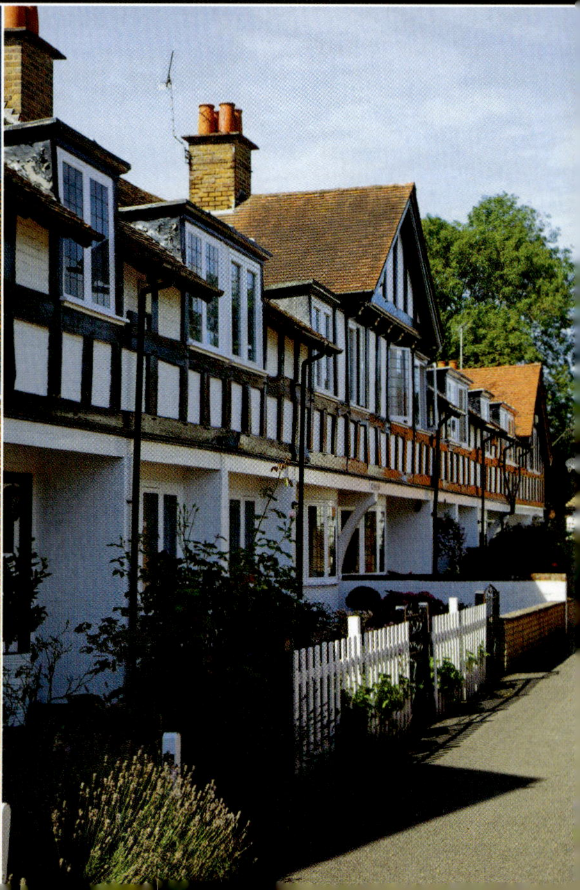

MUSE Bray Cottages

Bray-on-Thames

 England has long been known for its traditional village life set amidst tracts of serene green countryside, with many people opting for a holiday or long weekend in an English country cottage. Often a pretty rough-and-ready affair, such a break usually involves self-catering, mucking in and generally doing quite a bit of work. Hardly a holiday really!

Recently, all that has changed with some companies now offering tailormade holidays and mini breaks in authentic country cottages, along with five-star facilities, private chefs, personalised service and the like. Our three heritage cottages in Bray are not only wonderfully situated in the heart of a quintessential English country village, they are equipped to an extremely high standard and come with the benefit of a concierge service, up-market provisions, and as much or as little catering as required. Think of it as a private home, but one with deluxe hotel service.

In addition, the cottages are situated in the village of Bray-on-Thames, a sleepy Berkshire village in the Windsor Forest that has experienced a revival of sorts in recent years: Well known for its Waterside Inn, the English outpost of the Michelin-starred Roux brothers, it is now home to Heston Blumenthal, a British chef who has been making waves in culinary circles with a molecular gastronomy approach. The Fat Duck, a restaurant he opened in 1995, received three Michelin stars in 2004; since then, Blumenthal has gone on to add the adjacent Crown and Hind's Head pubs to his coterie of eateries. As if that were not enough, Bray has other upscale dining establishments as well.

So, if long country walks, a trip along the River Thames, haute-cuisine dining and super service tick your boxes, a weekend in Bray could be just the answer. Bespoke concierge company, the super efficient Private Label, organises everything for you; all you have to do is turn up.

BRAY-ON-THAMES

The Story of an English Country Village

ith mention in the Domesday Book (1086), ownership by the Royal family, an idyllic location in the Royal Windsor Forest on the banks of the River Thames and picture postcard charm, the village of Bray has a long and illustrious history. Luckily for visitors, strict planning laws ensure that its heritage remains intact.

Bray's story is inextricably bound up with the Thames — used for fishing, trade, transport and, more recently, for recreation. Its earliest incarnation was as a Saxon settlement with a church around a river crossing; then in the 11th-century Domesday Book it is depicted as a large area in Berrochescire (today's Berkshire) centered around the "vill" of Brai with "King's manors and holdings". By the 13th century, there was a tannery, a mill and a wharf for receiving goods transported by river — the charge at Bray Wharf was 3 old pence per load. Work on the present-day church began in the 13th century, and it is safe to say that the

beginning of today's village on Church Lane and the High Street dates from the 13th to the 16th centuries.

As with all early settlements, the first roads radiated out from the church, so Church Lane was probably the first road in Bray. In the 16th century, when it was known as St Thomas's Street, it began at the Lych Gate just off the churchyard and stretched out some 200 metres or so to the High Street. Lined with tiny half-timbered cottages, thatched-roofed terraces built from a timber frame filled with wattle and daub, it contained homes for local families who served the estates and larger houses in the area. These houses remain to this day: Even though they now sport brick facades, tiles have replaced the thatch of old, and they benefit from the addition of modern plumbing and electricity, their character remains essentially the same.

Other additions in the village before the 16th century were the 15th-century Hind's Head public house, Vicarage Cottage, Stuart Cottage and Shottery for foresters, the Crown Inn and the Chauntry of the Blessed Virgin or Bray's town hall. The year 1628 saw the addition of the Jesus Hospital, a charitable almshouse venture (see opposite), and in 1682 Bray's first school, housed in the Old Schoolroom, was built. The cottage that houses today's

Opposite, clockwise from left *The Jesus Hospital for the poor and elderly; Hind's Head pub; a statue of William Goddard, the benefactor of the Jesus Hospital; rows of Tudor-style cottages.*

Fat Duck restaurant used to be an inn called The Ringers. All these buildings are extant today.

By the 18th century, today's main road or High Street leading off Church Lane stretched from Chauntry House at the northern end of the village to the Jesus Hospital in the south. Then as now, it was lined with "Tudorbethan" cottages and terraces, the timber painted black and the rendered surfaces white. As the village grew, other roads were built parallel to Church Lane and at right angles to the High Street. Leading down to the river, they were (and still are) lined with half-timbered cottages.

Ferry End, parallel to Church Lane, is one such street. It contains a terrace of such cottages built between 1875 and 1912, many of which were leased out as "clubs" between the two world wars. In fact, Bray was quite famous for these establishments. Serving liquor, they provided entertainment in the form of bridge, gaming tables and congenial company for a nominal membership fee of five shillings. Bettoney Vere, another row of cottages built slightly later in 1906 on the site of an old orchard, served a similar function. Although fairly uniform on the exterior, these houses were not identical internally; yet each had a living room entered by the front door and a staircase leading to bedrooms above.

Recent alterations have been mainly at ground level, with modern kitchens and bathrooms either incorporated into the original buildings or added as extensions out the back.

Somehow it seems fitting that the village, well known in the past as a lively entertainment venue, is now highly regarded as a gourmet haven. Containing two of the UK's four three-Michelin-starred restaurants as well as a few other excellent pubs and restaurants, it attracts foodies from all over the world. Naturally, after a gastronomic meal in one of these venues, it is far more congenial to walk home to your cottage lodgings than get a taxi or train back to accommodation elsewhere.

This is where the following pages come into their own: view three beautiful "homes from home" in Bray. Not only do they offer salubrious surrounds for a long weekend, they give guests a taste of heritage and history to boot.

Above left *An old farmhouse known as Old Dutch House sits behind the War Memorial. The Crown public house, now operated by Heston Blumenthal.* **Opposite** *The street leading up to and interior of St Michael's Church. The lych gate (1448).*

LAVENDER HOUSE

ituated just down from the Fat Duck and looking out towards the Hind's Head pub in the heart of Bray, Lavender House manages to be both modern and traditional at the same time. Believed to date back to the early 1700s when it comprised a terrace of three cottages, the residence has been substantially remodelled over the years. Today, it offers accommodation over two floors and has an extensive rear garden.

From its impressive black and white double-fronted facade to its airy, spacious interior furnished with a contemporary feel, Lavender House is welcoming in the extreme. The ground floor, with limestone floors and a huge modernist conservatory that stretches the width of the building, is truly integrated with the garden, thereby making this the perfect space for summer entertaining. With light streaming in through extensive glass walls and skylight, the relaxing space works well during the colder months as well.

Assuming it is a hot summer's day, the wall-to-wall patio doors open out to a partially walled garden that is also laid with the same limestone tiling. The outdoor seating area merges seamlessly with the comfortable lounge space and open-plan kitchen inside. Along with a pizza oven and unique green egg barbecue, there's a stretch of lawn, an assortment of fruit trees

Opposite *A trestle table separates the kitchen from the lounge section in the conservatory.*
Right *The exterior of Lavender House. At the end of World War II, the three cottages were patriotically painted red, white and blue.*

and a small structure, adapted from a utility shed, at the end of the garden given over for private massages. What could be more indulgent, one asks oneself?

In addition to the conservatory with semi-industrial modern kitchen and clever use of mirrors, breakfast bar and lounge seating, the ground floor also contains a cinema room and a bold, contemporary study. The former, decorated in hues of silver and purple, features a large screen with an impressive surround system, while the latter pays homage to the publisher Penguin Books with a wallpaper montage of classic book covers.

Upstairs contains a master bedroom suite and two further bedrooms, all tastefully furnished in a palette of cool grey with lavender accents. What better place to return to after a world-class meal in one of Bray's famous eateries?

Previous page, clockwise from top left *View into the cinema room; the unique study; a classic English summer's day in the garden; the stylish kitchen hob looks out to the garden.*

Opposite and this page *Upstairs comprises a harmonious whole with a grey and lavender theme: the master suite's bathroom includes a claw-foot tub in deep purple, while lavender accents punctuate the soft grey elsewhere.*

DORMER COTTAGE

ituated just down Church Lane from Lavender House, Dormer Cottage comprises sweet one-bedroom lodgings that are cosy, quaint and welcoming. Surprisingly roomy for a terraced cottage, it contains everything the archetypal English cottage should have: a black and white facade with a sturdy wooden door; exposed wooden beams inside; an open fireplace with log burner; as well as a sweet walled garden behind.

As an added bonus there is a decent-sized dining area, a kitchen with all mod cons and a gorgeous bedroom and dressing room above. Done out with slate flooring, Stephani rugs, burnt orange silk wallpaper and subtle lighting, the interior is sumptuous, even slightly decadent. Yet the original features and character of the low-ceilinged abode keep it anchored firmly in its historical milieu.

In fact this terraced row, known as Church Cottages (as opposed to Lych Cottages opposite), is one of the earliest terraces in the village. Probably built around the time of the Lych Gate and the Hind's Head, both dating from the mid 15th century, it would have housed a family who worked on one of the large estates nearby. Today it provides succour to weekend visitors, honeymooners and anybody requiring peace, comfort and an intimate place to stay.

Opposite and top *The surprisingly roomy ground floor of Dormer Cottage combines a strong burnt orange decorative theme with original beams on walls and ceilings.*
Right *The exterior with green front door.*

This page and opposite *Characterful touches in the cottage include original architectural features, as well as sturdy wooden doors and an open hearth. Nevertheless, modern comfort and convenience is fully incorporated.*

BRAY HOUSE

Taking pride of place along the High Street next door to the Hind's Head is the pleasant residence known as Bray House. Previously called Green Shutters, this comfortable home was converted from what used to be the stables and coach house of a manor house on Church Drive. Retaining some of the original features, as well as substantial modification, its present incarnation comprises a three-bedroom home with airy living spaces and a sweet terrace garden.

History melds with modernism in the interior: there's a handsome living room with an eclectic mix of 1920s' furniture; a cute bar done out in bordello-style with Art Deco flourishes; a large open-plan kitchen that opens out onto the courtyard; as well some original features such as a stable door that dates from the 1780s. Of particular note in the courtyard are the clever landscaping and a tranquil water feature, both of which give the illusion of space.

Upstairs, three very different bedrooms offer stylish accommodation for six. The master suite is set beneath the pitched roof as if to embrace the original wooden beams, while its adjoining bathroom features a modern scroll bath, a walk-in shower and twin vanities. The other two bedrooms are direct opposites — one is cool, calm and serene in gauzy white, while the other sports a dramatic combination of dark wood, crimson walls and Italian silks.

Oposite *The Art Deco style bar room is cosy and warm — perfect for cocktails.*
Top *Breakfast in the garden.*
Left *The exterior with window boxes.*

Whether it is a celebration or a chill-out, a party or a quiet gathering, Bray House delights with both its layout and amenities. Special touches, like original 1920s china and glassware, add a special authenticity. In fact, it is this feeling of authenticity that contributes much charm to the cottage as a whole; despite the alterations and adaptations by various different owners, each modification has taken care to keep the original character intact. Between 1969 and 1971 the stable and sitting room were opened out to create a bigger space and the open staircase was added. Specially-made bottle glass was used for the front windows. In its most recent alteration, the upstairs was enlarged and the modern kitchen added, thereby modernising the residence substantially.

Above left *An old carriage clock attached to the wall in the courtyard adds a characterful touch.*
Above right *The open–plan kitchen/diner has everything the modern cook requires. It looks out over the courtyard which is accessed through a stable door.*

Above *Early evening in Bray is a particularly lovely time. Traffic has reduced, and the village slips back into a quieter mode. Because of the UK's strict conservation laws, its architectural heritage has been carefully conserved; as a result, it isn't difficult to imagine the village as it was many centuries ago.*

Visit the Parish Church of St Michael

This substantial church was originally built in 1293 by Queen Margaret, the wife of King Edward I. Being a royal foundation close to the royal family in Windsor, it was a large and expensive building for the size of the population of the parish. Its massive embattled tower made from flint dates from 1400 and has stood virtually unchanged for more than 600 years, although the church itself has been remodelled many times. The tower contains a ring of eight bells, the earliest dating from 1612. The church's 18 stained-glass windows date from between 1858 and 1890 and are fine examples of Victorian workmanship. A wander round this spectacular church and peaceful grounds is a must.

Indulge in a Gastronomic Experience in the Village

Surprisingly for such a small village, Bray contains two of the four three-Michelin-starred restaurants in the United Kingdom — the Waterside Inn and the Fat Duck — along with a number of other first-class eateries. In fact, this is the reason many people visit Bray in the first place! Whether it is updated pub grub courtesy of Heston Blumenthal's kitchen, a seasonal Italian meal, or something altogether in the haute cuisine stakes is irrelevant: all options are available seven days a week in Bray.

Go on a Nature Walk

As the village itself is so small, it is very easy to find oneself in open country in only a short space of time. Head towards the river on one of the small lanes leading off the main high street and you'll soon find yourself in fields and woods or along the banks of the river Thames. Follow the signs to Monkey island and explore this small island in the middle of the Thames: it still houses two amusing structures built by the 3rd Duke of Marlborough, one of which is furnished with paintings of monkeys. Otherwise, take in England's green and pleasant countryside along one of the many bridle paths in the area.

CONCIERGE

Enjoy a Picnic along the River Thames

Champagne and strawberries, fresh vine tomatoes and a diverse selection of English cheeses, freshly baked bread and any number of terrines, patés and spreads — what could be more enticing than an English picnic on a cloudless summer's day? Even better if it is offered on the banks of the Thames after a scenic cruise along this most iconic of British rivers. Such a scenario is easily arranged by the folks at Private Label — make sure you put an afternoon aside for it.

Arrange a Bespoke Spa Treatment

The concierge service of Private Label, the friendly folks who welcome guests, organise their meals and generally cater to visitors' needs, are more than happy to arrange a bespoke spa treatment. At Lavender House this takes place on a massage bed in the little structure at the bottom of the garden, while guests at Dormer Cottage or Bray House can be transported to nearby Maidenhead for the treatment of their choice: think scented facials and sensual massages with oils and fragrances redolent of an English country garden.

Take a Trip to Windsor

Just up the road from Bray is the town of Windsor, best known for its eponymous castle, the home of the British royal family. In addition to the castle, there are the magnificent surrounds of Windsor Great Park to explore, or take in a trip to the theatre, visit Legoland or Windsor Safari Park or simply benefit from Windsor's great selection of shops. Every September sees the Windsor Festival, a wonderful two weeks of music, theatre, film, literary events and the like. Originally founded in 1969 with Yehudi Menuhin and Ian Hunter as Artistic Directors, it has gone from strength to strength and continues to attract distinguished guest speakers, actors, musicians and more from around the world.

YTL Hotels

THE GAINSBOROUGH BATH SPA
Beau Street,
Bath BA1 1QY, England.
Tel: +44 1225 358 888
www.thegainsboroughbathspa.co.uk

THE SWATCH ART PEACE HOTEL
23 East Nanjing Road (Bund 19),
Shanghai 200002, China.
Tel: +86 21 23298500
www.swatch-art-peace-hotel.com

THE MAJESTIC MALACCA
188 Jalan Bunga Raya,
75100 Melaka, Malaysia.
Tel: +60 6 289 8000
www.majesticmalacca.com

THE MAJESTIC HOTEL KUALA LUMPUR
5, Jalan Sultan Hishamuddin,
50000 Kuala Lumpur, Malaysia.
Tel : +60 3 2785 8000
www.majestickl.com

CAMERON HIGHLANDS RESORT
By The Golf Course,
39000 Tanah Rata,
Cameron Highlands,
Pahang, Malaysia.
Tel: +60 5 491 1100
www.cameronhighlandsresort.com

MUSE BRAY COTTAGES
Chartam House,
16 College Avenue,
Maidenhead,
Berkshire SL6 6AX, England.
Tel: +44 1628 583 517
Email: bray@muse-hotels.com
www.muse-hotels.com/braycottages

For reservations or enquiries, please contact:
YTL Travel Centre
Tel: +60 3 2783 1000 | Fax: +60 3 2148 7397 | Email: travelcentre@ytlhotels.com.my | www.ytlhotels.com

ACKNOWLEDGEMENTS

The publisher, author and photographer would like to thank YTL Hotels, in particular Dato' Mark Yeoh Seok Kah, for the opportunity to produce this book. In addition, our thanks go to Tracy Khee for her wonderful organisation and members of staff at all the hotels for their help during the photography, writing and production of this book.

A Spirit of Family

The first fifty years
of Princethorpe College

Nick Baker & Alex Darkes

*Ours is a spirit of family
and a spirit of brotherhood
formed by kindness and understanding
by compromise and mutual forgiveness
by gentleness, humility and simplicity
by hospitality and a sense of humour*

JULES CHEVALIER

ISBN 978-1-5262-0449-3

First published in 2016 by
The Princethorpe Foundation
Princethorpe College
Princethorpe
Rugby
CV23 9PX
www.princethorpe.co.uk

A catalogue record for this book is available from The British Library

Printed and bound in the United Kingdom by
Tadberry Evedale Ltd
Units 1-4
1A Philip Walk
London
SE15 3NH
www.tadberry-evedale.co.uk

Printed on 170gsm white silk art paper from sustainable sources

Design, typography and origination by
Debbie McLaughlin
Dam Design Creative Limited
Warwickshire
www.damdesign.org.uk

Foreword

Princethorpe College has a fascinating history and I am extremely proud to have been given the opportunity to lead this wonderful school. Arriving in 2009, I was the last member of my family to enter the College; my three children were already at the school and Tracey, my wife, was firmly established in the History Department. As a parent, I had already experienced the Princethorpe "magic" and knew the positive effect it had on my children's development.

It is difficult to put it into words, but the ethos which we value here so deeply is firmly derived from the values of Missionaries of the Sacred Heart, who founded the College in 1966. The "spirit of family" which we continually strive for is firmly underpinned by the human values of kindness, compassion, friendship and love which I believe have always been at the very heart of the Princethorpe community.

Of course, we are blessed with a stunningly beautiful campus created by the Benedictine nuns, who founded the original priory at the start of the 19th century and this has been sympathetically developed over years. We are incredibly fortunate to have such fine buildings as the recently restored Round House alongside the latest major teaching wing, The Limes. Important though the buildings are, it is the people which are at the heart of any true community and *A Spirit of Family* manages to capture so many of the characters who have played a part in shaping the development of Princethorpe College.

I am delighted that, in the year of our Golden Jubilee, we have this commemorative book to enjoy. My sincere and heartfelt thanks go to Alex Darkes and Nick Baker for their painstaking efforts on producing this record of the first fifty years of Princethorpe College and its people. It has been a real labour of love and I am sure that the reader will agree, it captures the unique qualities which make Princethorpe what it is.

Benedic, Domine, Collegium nostrum; per multos annos floreat.

Ed Hester MA
Senior Head
The Princethorpe Foundation

Acknowledgements

This book, like many others, exists only because of the generosity of others. Indeed, there would be no publication if had it not been for the hard work of Debbie McLaughlin of Dam Design Creative, who has managed to arrange text and images in the attractive layout you see before you. We are also grateful to Tim Edgelow of Tadberry Evedale who, along with his colleagues Alan and Ricky Hurle, was responsible for printing copies of the book and who guided the authors through the process from beginning to end.

The support of Princethorpe colleagues, past and present, has been a boon and each and every one has contributed something to the book. Particular thanks are due to Debs Brookes, Graham Bullock, Melanie Butler, Patrick Carrington, Steve Doherty, Sue Francis, Peter Griffin, David Hare, Ed Hester, Tracey Hester, Paul Hubball, Emma Litterick, Neil McCollin, Adrian Moore, Denise Morgan, Karen O'Connor, Margaret-Louise O'Keeffe, Simon Peaple, Gwilym Price, Vanessa Rooney, Celia Scott, Sarah Stewart, Rachel Taylor, Eddie Tolcher and Fr Alan Whelan MSC. Likewise, Robert Duigan, Angela Barnard and Anna Bond of Crackley Hall have supplied the authors with ideas and much needed pieces of information.

As Princethorpe's story includes many different institutions, the generous assistance offered by past pupils and staff has been vital. For St Mary's Priory School, we thank Biddy Allen, Beatrice Gaspard, Maria Cecilia Cordoba Good, Janet Haynes, Marianne Horne, Mary Wheildon and the late Beryle Peeke. We are also indebted to Sr Mary Bernard OSB, Sr Mary Lawrence OSB, Sr Mary Lucy OSB, Sr Mary Stephen OSB and the late Sr Mary Placid OSB. For assistance with the chapter about Abbotsford, we are very grateful to its former head Barbara Chitty.

There are many others who have also provided support, ideas and expertise in their respective fields: Gretchen Ames, Curator, Stoneleigh Abbey; Stella Beer, Archivist, New Hall School; Meg Boulton, Research Associate in the History of Art, University of York; the late Len Bowers; Alison Day, Archivist, Douai Abbey; Bernard and Françoise Fleury; Javis Gur, Archive Licensing Officer, Historic England; Jonathan Hall, proprietor, Arnold Lodge School; Phil Hibble, Deputy Editor, Rugby Advertiser; Alex Miller, Manager, Wigan Archives Service; Charlotte Paxton, Syndication Executive, BPM Media (Midlands); Rt Rev Geoffrey Scott OSB, Abbot and Librarian, Douai Abbey; Rev Dr John Sharp, Archivist, Birmingham Archdiocesan Archives; Jenny Smith, Archivist, Union of the Sisters of Mercy GB; Leo Tomson and Alex Walker, Digitisation Consultant, TownsWeb Archiving. The authors are grateful to the following for allowing us to reproduce copyright images in the book: BPM Media (Midlands), Historic England, Leo Tomson, the Rugby Advertiser and John Wright Photography. Every effort has been made to contact the copyright holders of other photographs, where known, and if any omissions have been made, please inform the authors and the necessary amendments will be made in a subsequent edition. The information in this book has been provided to the best of our knowledge and we would welcome any corrections which should be made.

It is clear that the story of Princethorpe is a fascinating one and there is a great deal more to be told. We hope that a fuller, and more scholarly account will emerge in due course and shed some light onto the many who have contributed to our very special 'Spirit of Family'.

Nick Baker and Alex Darkes

Feast of the Visitation of the Blessed Virgin Mary
31 May 2016

Contents

01

Introduction

From France to England

As the 18th century drew to a close, France's costly involvement in the American Revolution and lavish spending by King Louis XVI and his predecessor had left the nation virtually bankrupt. Not only were the royal vaults depleted, but years of poor harvests, drought, bovine disease and soaring bread prices had kindled unrest amongst peasants and the urban poor. The rioting, looting and striking by the labouring classes was an expression of their resentment towards a regime which levied heavy taxes and yet failed to provide relief.

Had it not been for the watershed of the French Revolution, beginning in 1789 and ending in the late 1790s, this book, with certainty, would have not been written. During the Revolution, French citizens radically changed their country's political landscape, uprooting established institutions such as absolute monarchy, the church and the feudal system. Without these radical events in France at the end of the 18th century, there would be no Princethorpe College.

On 29 October 1789, just days before the nationalisation of church property, France's new Constituent Assembly heard that two women in a nearby convent were being forced to take up the religious life. The Assembly made a proposal to bring to an end the taking of solemn vows, paving the way for the closure of France's monasteries and the departure of their inhabitants. It was hoped that the rapid sale of monasteries and their assets would help to prop up the nation's finances. The announcement was met with loud protests; the new French state had not only taken control of the church's revenue and property, but also appeared to be redefining the boundaries between church and state.

It was against this background, that a group of Benedictine nuns fled the reign of terror and sought sanctuary elsewhere. They followed a peripatetic existence in England for the best part of forty years, during which they inhabited various properties and eventually settled at Princethorpe where they built their own priory.

"Had it not been for the watershed of the French Revolution, beginning in 1789 and ending in the late 1790s, this book, with certainty, would have not been written."

ST MARY'S PRIORY

J. Branston

Publd. by J.Arthur

The Library, Leamington.

Radcliff, London

"*Prior to her departure from Montmartre,
she received a vision, not of the Virgin,
but of Christ, who held a cross on which
there was a bleeding heart with three nails
surrounded by a crown of thorns...*"

From Montargis to Wigan

The Benedictine nuns responsible for establishing Princethorpe priory originated at the house of Montmartre in Paris. This monastery had been a royal house for many years and was located on a site of immense religious significance. The hill on which it stood, the Mount of Martyrs, was so-called because it had witnessed the execution of the first bishop of Paris, St Denis, along with other Christians in the 3rd century. A small chapel was raised shortly afterwards and a church dedicated to St Peter was constructed at the summit by 750 AD. Although it was under the protection of the Montmorency family, who were involved with the house until its close, members of the French royal family also played their part in this monastery's affairs. Its fortunes changed over time, often affected by external events such as the Hundred Years' War, which impacted on the discipline and regularity of the community. Marie de Beauvilliers was made its abbess in 1598 and set to work on reforming the order at Montmartre, which included the restoration of regular meals and reinstitution of the famous black habit; financial affairs improved, too and more women were professed.

As a result, the reputation of Montmartre grew, so much so that bishops called on this community to assist with the reformation and foundation of other houses. This led to the creation of a new convent (and school) at Montargis, a small town situated south of Paris and to the east of Orléans. It was established by Marie Granger, the daughter of John Granger and Catherine Gaudais, who had pronounced her vows at Montmartre in 1620 and, following a period of ill health, became its Mistress of Novices. After various negotiations, and with support from the archbishop of Sens, Marie was selected to found a community in that town and she, along with a small band, left Montmartre on 13 May 1630 and reached Montargis on the 19th of the same month. Marie decided to pledge the new foundation to the Blessed Virgin and so the convent's church was dedicated to Our Lady of the Angels. However, prior to her departure from Montmartre, she received a vision, not of the Virgin, but of Christ, who held a cross on which there was a bleeding heart with three nails surrounded by a crown of thorns; this became the community's emblem.

All went well for many years but this period of peace and devoted prayer was not to last. In 1792 the nuns of Montargis decided to leave France and seek asylum elsewhere. The prioress noted that a direct journey to their intended destination, Flanders, was probably too dangerous, and decided to find a passage to England instead. After a little time at Rouen, the sisters reached Dieppe on 9 October. They were transported across the Channel by Captain Burton of the *Prince of Wales* and suffered many hardships, not least the storm they encountered, which meant that a ten hour crossing took twenty-four.

The nuns were impoverished and had only four pennies in their purse, yet were fortunate that they had landed at Shoreham in Sussex. It was a happy chance that the Prince Regent (later King George IV) was in the nearby town of Brighton with Mrs Fitzherbert, and they despatched a number of carriages to transport the Benedictine sisters to join them. They were housed in a hotel and visited by the Prince and Mrs Fitzherbert on a number of occasions. Indeed, one sister, Placid, was shocked by the opulence of the royal silverware when the community dined with the Prince! It was at one such meeting that the Prince urged them to abandon their original plan, which was to carry on to Flanders, and remain in England; Flanders was considered to be too dangerous and there was still much uncertainty in other parts of Europe.

The community followed the Prince's advice and followed a somewhat peripatetic existence until it settled at Princethorpe. The sisters' first port of call was London, where they rented two houses, Numbers 1 and 2 Duke Street, which provided living accommodation, together with spaces for a chapel, infirmary and school room. They received considerable help from French priests who had arrived in England beforehand and offered spiritual and pastoral support; leading Catholic families helped to fund the nuns' venture and paid for food, clothing and other necessities. Unfortunately, these two houses were too small and such cramped conditions made it difficult to live out the regular life. In the end, alternative accommodation was acquired at Bodney Hall in Norfolk, nine miles away from Brandon. It was offered to the nuns at a pepper-corn rent, which was welcome because the cost of the London houses had swallowed the funds kindly donated by Mrs Fitzherbert. The financial situation made the establishment of school an imperative, just as there had been a school at both Montmartre and Montargis. And there was space for a Catholic establishment, bearing in mind that until that point only two communities had defied the Penal Laws by setting up such institutions.

"It was a happy chance that the Prince Regent was in the nearby town of Brighton with Mrs Fitzherbert, and they despatched a number of carriages to transport the Benedictine sisters to join them."

The school was a great success, despite local anti-Catholic opposition; French émigré priests joined them and the number of postulants increased. After eighteen years, Bodney Hall, like the houses in London, had become too small for the community's purposes and alternative accommodation was needed. So in 1813 they rented Heath Hall, a large Elizabethan house near Wakefield in Yorkshire, owned by the widow of the Honourable John Smyth. The stables were utilised as school rooms and a glass passage constructed between them and the main house provided a sheltered walkway during inclement weather. Once again, further space was required and the community purchased Orrell Mount, near Wigan, in 1821. It was a magnificent Georgian house, surrounded by parkland, just the sort of place where an enclosed order hoped to find the peace and privacy needed for their work. In this case, its location was a problem. A number of mineshafts littered the surrounding area which made the sinking of foundations, necessary for future building work, impossible. The decision was made to look elsewhere.

Orrell Mount today

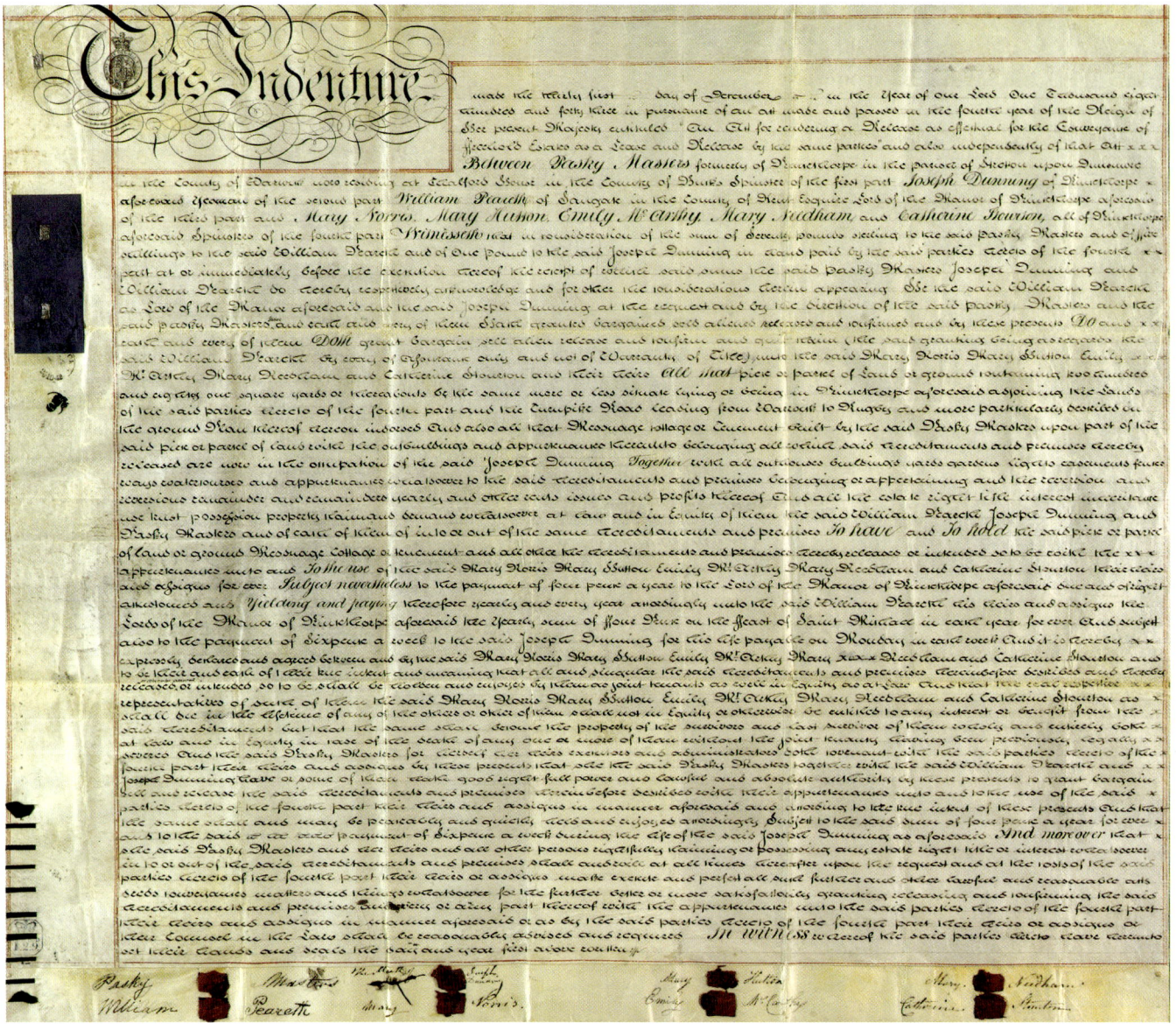

The indenture recording the sale of two-hundred-and-eighty-one square yards of land from Pasky Masters, Joseph Dunning and William Peareth to the Benedictine community, 31 December 1843

"It is not known where the funds for this project were obtained, though some financial support must have come from the sale of Orrell Mount."

St Mary's Priory

It is not clear why the Benedictine nuns chose Princethorpe but it had many advantages for a new monastic complex. There were wealthy families in the area and a strong Catholic presence too. Although St Anne's in nearby Wappenbury was not constructed until 1849, mass had been offered in local houses centuries before. There was an important historic link too. Land in Stretton and Princethorpe had belonged to the Benedictine nuns of Henwood Priory, Solihull, between the 14th and the 16th centuries. (This priory was dissolved in 1535 and the land passed to other hands). Yet, the site at Princethorpe had attractive natural features: it was raised up, surrounded by woodland and hills, and therefore offered the seclusion required by an enclosed order. Natural springs emerged to the north and provided a valuable source of water; there was good farmland and clay soil. This clay was eventually employed to make the bricks used in the priory's construction. By this time, too, many of the Penal Laws had been repealed and therefore allowed the building of religious houses like Princethorpe.

It is not known where the funds for this project were obtained, though some financial support must have come from the sale of Orrell Mount. In any case, sections of land were purchased over a number of years and from different owners in the area, such as Benjamin Russell in the 1830s and George and Pasky Masters in the 1840s. The foundation stone, laid in July 1832 by Thomas Walsh the Titular bishop of Cambysopolis, bore part of the prayer used for the evening service of Compline:

Visit, we beseech Thee, O Lord, this house and family, and drive from it all the snares of the evil one; Let they Holy Angels dwell therein, may they keep us in peace, and may Thy blessings be always upon us.

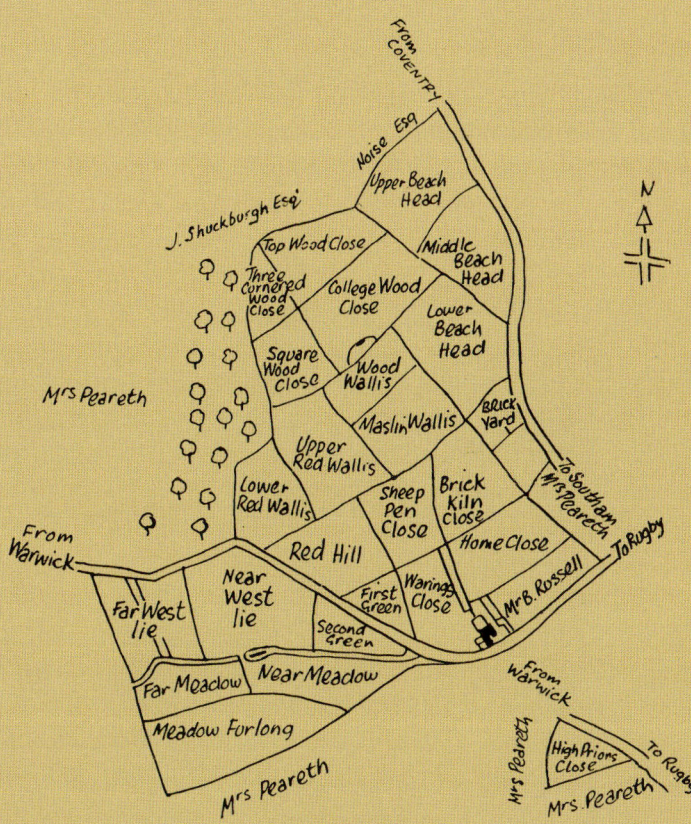

Plan of the Princethorpe estate, showing the names of fields. The bricks used for the construction of the priory were fired on Brick Kiln Close

View of the cloister garden (now The Quad), shortly before 1900, showing the Old Church, consecrated in 1843 and its wooden spire, which came down in a gale and was never replaced

The construction of the priory began in earnest in 1833 and attracted a great deal of outside interest – up to eight hundred people wandered over the construction site to see what was going on. And a number of individuals were involved in the design and building work before the main monastery was completed. Although Nicolas Pevsner states that Mr Craven was the designer of some of the earliest structures, it is more likely that he supervised the development, or acted as Clerk of Works, at the start of the project. (He had past experience of religious structures elsewhere, chiefly in Spain). But the first individual who had an impact on the design was John Russell, best known for the Congregational Chapel, Spencer Street in Leamington, in 1836. Regardless of the individual input, the overarching plan was to create something akin to the original house at Montargis. Indeed, Craven had been presented with a pasteboard model of the French priory, and he in turn passed it to an old woman in the village for safekeeping. She hung the model with string to the ceiling of a ground floor room and allowed visitors to look at it through an open window for a shilling a peep. Once Craven had heard about this entrepreneur, he complained to the prioress who ordered that the model be removed; the old woman had collected ten pounds of silver as a result of her labours!

View of the sanctuary of the Old Church from 1837

The Round House

"Craven had been presented with a pasteboard model of the French priory, and he in turn passed it to an old woman in the village for safekeeping. She hung the model with string to the ceiling of a ground floor room and allowed visitors to look at it through an open window for a shilling a peep."

Russell and Craven worked mainly on the oldest buildings at the priory (1833-5), chiefly the north wing but they also started on the west wing and first church. Around five-hundred men were employed for the work and many dug the clay for the bricks from the fields to the north known as Wood Close and Wood Wallis; the bricks were fired in Brick Kiln Close. (The excavations for the clay left a hole that later filled with water and became known as Switzerland; it reminded people of that country as the terrain looked distinctly alpine). One of the oldest buildings was the first church, constructed between 1835-7 at the centre of the complex, just as it had been at Montargis, and faces south (its liturgical east end); it was consecrated in 1843. Originally the square turret, bearing a clock and three specially commissioned bells, supported a wooden steeple; this collapsed in 1900 and was never replaced. The church, which features lancet or y-traceried windows, was later adapted by Joseph Aloysius Hansom. Best known for patenting the *Hansom cab*, this architect had been responsible for Arundel Cathedral, amongst other prestigious projects. Hansom most likely became involved with the Princethorpe project in or around 1837 when Russell was ill, and he also accelerated the rate of progress. He returned to Princethorpe a number of times to work, firstly on his own and later in partnership with his younger son Joseph Stanislaus; the latter continued to be involved with the priory after his father's death.

Apart from finishing the original chapel, which included beautiful stained-glass by Hardmans of Birmingham, Hansom was also responsible for completing *Le Tour*, or guest house, which was started in 1836 and finished in 1840. This unusual feature is constructed of brick and resembles a gate house, complete with crenulations and Georgian-type windows. It was used to accommodate visitors in a separate area because the nuns lived an enclosed life. Many of the guests lodged for lengthy periods of time, like the French priest, M. Carpue from Arras, who was given a suite of rooms for himself and two maiden sisters. Other features, too, have contributed to the significance of Princethorpe in the history of 19th-century architecture. One of these is the Round House, a circular room with brick walls and arches pointing heavenward; the roof was once made of turf and a central opening exposed the interior to the ravages of the elements. It was constructed as the nuns' cemetery and remains the resting place for ninety sisters and four or five lay people; a new burial ground was opened in 1910 to the west of the New Church at Princethorpe. The construction of the Round House began in 1835, but it was razed to the ground and rebuilt by Hansom. And near to this circular structure, and again the work of Hansom, is the mortuary chapel finished in 1843. It is of Neo-Norman design and built in the Rundbogenstil style, an idea Hansom may have picked up during his travels through Europe. It boasts a splendid west doorway, vaulting and chancel arch, and the space was used for the funeral services prior to burial in the Round House. In addition to these, Hansom was also responsible for the extraordinary *La Mère Dieu* Chapel on the first floor of the north range. It has a decorated ceiling which is similar to Bishop Nicholas West's chantry chapel at Ely Cathedral.

Le Tour, *with Pugin's lofty tower as a backdrop. This building is now the main College Reception and accommodates administrative offices*

The statue of Our Lady Abbess at the rear of the New Church

The choir of the Old Church showing gothic-style wood carving and Pippet's mural the 'Death of St Benedict'

The school was enlarged between 1875 and 1876. A new gothic wing was added and it contained new schoolrooms, music and day rooms; this desire for more accommodation may have sprung, in part, from the arrival of new pupils after the Franco-Prussian War of 1870. Hansom died in 1882 and his son, Joseph Stanislaus, returned and completed various projects including the church. In 1891 it received wooden stalls, and a magnificent mural depicting the 'Death of St Benedict' was painted by Joseph Pippet, who was related to one of the sisters. The most significant addition to Princethorpe, which had nothing to do with the Hansom family, was that of the New Church by Peter Paul Pugin, third son of A W Pugin, on the site of the former laundry and kitchens. Begun in 1897, and funded by a substantial dowry, its tower dominates the sky-line – it would have been higher but the cost would have increased. It possesses a nave, transepts, polygonal apse and boasts a highly elaborate ciborium altar. When the New Church was completed in 1901, the Old Church was handed over for parish use.

"The most significant addition to Princethorpe, which had nothing to do with the Hansom family, was that of the New Church by Peter Paul Pugin, third son of A W Pugin."

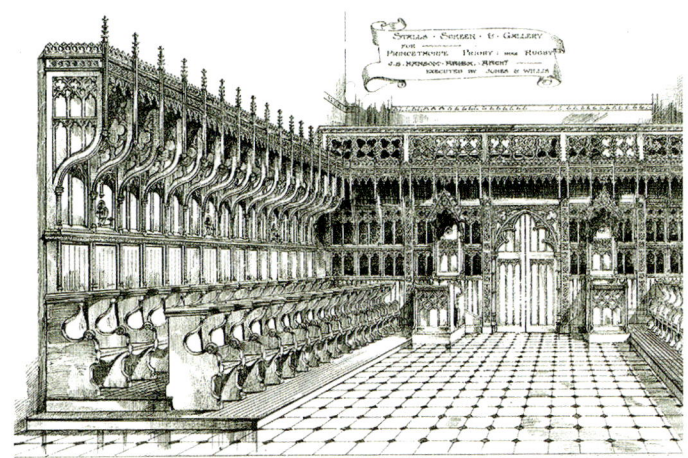

The stalls in the Old Church as depicted in The Building News *of December 1892. The stalls later made their way to the New Church*

Princethorpe College

The school developed. Unfortunately, fewer postulants joined the community and by 1965 there were only around thirty-three nuns left. Similarly, the numbers of pupils fell. The community decided to sell the priory and no one was sure who would buy such a place: some said that it would be occupied by a religious sect, or turned into a psychiatric hospital. In the end, it was purchased by the Missionaries of the Sacred Heart (MSC), an order founded in the 19th century by Jules Chevalier, who sought larger premises; their boys' school, St Bede's, established in Leamington in 1958 had fast run out of space. They successfully purchased the priory, two hundred acres of land and twelve to fifteen tied-houses, for £160,000. The community of Benedictine nuns departed. For the sisters, many of whom had never left the confines of the convent before, it must have been a distressing moment. They established a new house at Fernham, Oxfordshire, and continued as a community. Numbers eventually declined so much that this house was dissolved in 2002 and its members found new homes with other communities. Only one year previously, in 2001, some of the Princethorpe nuns returned and celebrated the one hundredth anniversary of the consecration of the chapel with a mass celebrated by Archbishop Vincent Nichols.

Jules Chevalier, founder of the Missionaries of the Sacred Heart

"The Missionaries of the Sacred Heart (MSC), an order founded in the 19th century by Jules Chevalier... successfully purchased the priory, two hundred acres of land and twelve to fifteen tied-houses, for £160,000."

The Fernham Benedictine community with Archbishop Vincent Nichols at the centenary anniversary of the New Church in 2001. Vincent Nichols is now the Cardinal Archbishop of Westminster

Under its first headmaster, Fr John Kevin Fleming MSC, Princethorpe College flourished. The transition from St Bede's to the new College took a number of years - the last attendance register for St Bede's dates from 1976. And like all institutions, the College enlarged organically: a new sports centre, called St Bede's Hall after the original school, was completed in 1979. The Old Church was adapted: a dividing floor was placed in the centre to separate the space into a study hall (now the library) above and gymnasium (now the theatre) below. The community's life was altered too.

By 1975 there was a co-educational Sixth Form and the College eventually became a co-educational day school. Being a world-wide federation, the MSCs decided to withdraw from Princethorpe and a lay trust was established. The College also merged with St Joseph's School, Kenilworth, now known as Crackley Hall and is the junior school; a further merger with Abbotsford School followed in 2010, but its buildings were sold. In 2007 a new Sixth Form Centre was sympathetically added to the Princethorpe campus and a new teaching and learning wing, The Limes, was completed in 2014 with state-of-the-art computer suites and a modern home for the IT, Modern Languages, English and Sports Departments. A new and exciting chapter has just opened with the addition of Crescent School to the Princethorpe Foundation.

Despite the years of change, Princethorpe's past is still very much a part of its future. The strong Roman Catholic ethos, practised by both the nuns and priests, whose prayers have soaked the walls, continues to this day and strengthens the school for those adventures yet to come. The chapters which follow chart the history of this place, from a priory school to a co-educational college, and records the people who have made a contribution to its fascinating story.

St Mary's Priory in the Twentieth Century

Pugin's Chapel

The death of Mother Mary Evangelista (Marie Lucie Delphine Doussin du Breuil) on the 15 October 1923 marked the end of one of the most significant periods in the life of the priory. She had been elected prioress of the community in 1895 and guided it into the new century. It was her vision which led to the successful completion of two projects, both of which contributed to the mission and witness of the Benedictine sisters. The first was the erection of a small convent in 1897. Situated at the end of the priory's drive, leading to the Banbury Road, it was built to house members of the Sisters of Mercy who had been sent from St Anne's Convent in Birmingham. At the suggestion of the priory's chaplain John Caswell, they had been invited by the Benedictines to run a school in the village and offered education for children in the 'outside' world, something which the enclosed community was unable to provide.

The other construction, and one which has become an iconic one for Princethorpe, was the lofty Gothic chapel. It is much larger in scale than the first church, but it met Mother Evangelista's plan for a grand building fit for the worship of the glory of God. Peter Paul Pugin, third son of the famous Augustus Welby, acted as the architect and Foster & Dicksee were chosen for the construction work; stained glass was added over the years and much of it, along with the other furnishings and fittings, was the work of Hardman & Co. of Birmingham, the company responsible for a great deal of ecclesiastical decoration in the 19th and 20th centuries. This huge project was funded by a dowry brought to the community when Hilda, daughter of Sir Humphrey and Lady Annette de Trafford, entered the religious life, the building rose; its tower would have been higher had additional funds been available.

"It is much larger in scale than the Old Church and met Mother Evangelista's plan for a grand building fit for the worship of the glory of God."

The new tower takes shape

The Convent built in 1897 for the Sisters of Mercy who all worked in the village school

The west end of the Pugin church

The high altar with the relics of St Fructuosa below

This magnificent chapel was finished in 1901 and consecrated with great solemnity on 8 May that same year by Bishop Ilsley, who was assisted by his own clergy and choir from St Mary's College, Oscott. The sermon was preached by Fr Vaughan SJ, on the words: 'this is the will of God, even your sanctification' (I Thes., iv, 3). The church was dedicated to Our Lady of the Angels, the high altar to Our Lady of the Angels and St John the Evangelist. The community received significant relics to sustain them in its work and those of St Fructuosa, long removed from the catacombs by Urban VIII and sent to Princethorpe from a church in Rome, were placed under the high altar. Additional altars dedicated to Our Lady of Compassion and that of the Holy Child were consecrated on 23 October 1903; the stone altar of the Sacred Heart, given to replace a wooden one, was consecrated on 13 January 1904. Under the latter were placed the relics of Saints Laurence, Blaise, Fructuosa, Cecilia, Francis of Assisi and Jane Frances de Chantal. Joseph Pippet, who was responsible for the painting on the north wall of the Old Church at Princethorpe, was responsible for the decoration in the Pugin structure too.

The Lime Walk, which when planted, had a lime tree for each of the nuns at the Priory

The Priory School

Acommunity is much more than the structures which house it, however impressive they may be, and the priory's life was devoted to prayer and service to God. A major part of that service was the education of girls, who were chiefly boarders, though the occasional day pupil was accepted for various reasons. Being enclosed, the nuns lived and died at the priory. Indeed, those who had passed away were buried in the circular cemetery until 1910 when a new graveyard was opened to the west of the new chapel, and so even in death the community remained a part of the present. And that community was a varied one, consisting of choir nuns and lay sisters: the former, who were educated and well-versed in Latin, performed the liturgy, whereas the latters' responsibilities centred on manual work, such as cleaning rooms and washing the laundry.

The pupils were taught by a combination of teachers, religious and lay, some of whom remained at Princethorpe for many years, even up until the departure of the nuns in 1966. In the middle of the 20th century, a number of schoolmistresses made their mark, including Miss Beryle Peeke, Miss Gill Cowling, Miss Kay Cummuskey, Miss Nora Cooke and Mrs Pargetter, to name but a few.

Sr Mary Scholastica, Gill Cowling, Kay Cummuskey and Sr Mary Walburga outside the school wing in 1965

"A major part of that service was the education of girls, who were chiefly boarders though the occasional day pupil was accepted for various reasons."

Beryle Peeke

1916 to 2013

Beryle Peeke was one of the greatest living authorities on St Mary's Priory. Miss Peeke - as she was known to everyone - arrived at Princethorpe in 1942, having responded to an advertisement for a history teacher in a Catholic newspaper. She recalled how the taxi driver had thrust his visiting card into her hand on dropping her off at the Priory, certain that she would call him, as he thought it unlikely that she would want to stay. Nothing could have been further from the truth and it was only when the school closed in 1965 that she was forced to leave, ultimately taking up another teaching post at the Ursuline Convent in Westgate-on-Sea, where she remained very happily until retirement.

Those whom she taught recall an inspirational, charming woman who treated her charges as adults, whilst remaining mindful of her own responsibilities and their youth. History was her passion and former pupils attribute their love of the subject to her graphic and exciting commentaries. The subject, too, had perks: visits to Canterbury, London, Oxford, Cambridge, Stratford and abroad also featured. She was naturally at home in France and Germany where she spent many school holidays, being fluent in their languages. Both of the schools were boarding, so she was able to live on the premises and contribute fully to their extra-curricular lives. *Scrabble* was a favourite: "such a lovely way to extend one's vocabulary and improve spelling." At times she found herself teaching English, German and French as well as history; one former pupil commented that "it was hard to think of a subject which Miss Peeke would not be able to teach!"

After retirement her mind would constantly revert to her days at Princethorpe where she had clearly been so happy. She continued to attend all school re-unions and would frequently take the train to Victoria to have lunch and share with "her girls" what really went on behind the scenes, missing only one meeting shortly before her death. She was fiercely independent and brave, kept her own home and maintained a razor-sharp intellect and strong sense of humour right to the end. She defied all medical science and never needed medication until shortly before her death. Her strong faith was central to her life and it tempered the way in which she interacted easily with others: she was always fair, kind and had high standards, never appearing to have favourites amongst her pupils.

The Hockey Field

St Mary's Priory china plate

The Refectory became the Art Room in 1966 and is now a Technology workshop

The Dormitory (now S1, S2 & S3)

The Junior School Room which is now part of the History & Poitics Department

The first fifty years of Princethorpe College

27

> *"Public transport was rare in that part of Warwickshire, with only one bus a week which travelled from Rugby to Leamington via Princethorpe."*

St Mary's Priory was a unique place in which to live, work and play. One of the reasons why the Benedictine community secured this site was most likely due to the seclusion which the place offered; it was separated from large towns, surrounded by some beautiful woodland and was self-sufficient in terms of water sources and farmland. Such a location had an effect on the activities of the girls and teachers, in which they were almost as 'cocooned' as the religious community itself. Public transport was rare in that part of Warwickshire, with only one bus a week which travelled from Rugby to Leamington via Princethorpe; taxis were even rarer. So when the girls and staff went for a 'walk in the world', it was just that, a walk down the drive and into the countryside. Moreover, the girls were not completely isolated because regular visiting Sundays allowed family members to take pupils off the campus (for the day) after that morning's church service. Motorised vehicles were a rare site at the priory, though Gill Cowling had a *Lambretta* and slowly upgraded to a series of small cars. The farm manager, Mr Baines, also drove members of the community to various destinations as required.

End-of-term shoe cleaning

Fancy dress competition on the occasion of the marriage of HRH Princess Elizabeth in 1947

Access to the outside world was limited and there were restrictions within the priory too. Sections of the complex were strictly off limits to the pupils and lay staff because they were part of the 'enclosure', a space only inhabited by the Benedictine sisters. The cloisters were restricted on the whole, though part of it was accessed to reach the nuns' library run by Sr Mary Emmanuel, always known as 'Birdie'.

The priory benefited from good quality land and had a farm (which continued into the time of the MSCs) with cows for milk, and there was a garden which offered a constant supply of fresh vegetables. Like many aspects of school life, the food was either hated or loved and former pupils have varying opinions, yet all recollect a particular pudding with a pastry lid known as 'Father Dwyer's Bashed Hat.' Miss Peeke remembers Sr Mary Bernard taking all the fresh vegetables from the garden to the kitchen door. Pupils were also allowed to pick fruit, such as gooseberries and blackcurrants, but were not permitted near the strawberries or raspberries.

Visit by the Portuguese Ambassador, His Excellency Pedro Pereira

Teaching & Learning

The curriculum was a varied one with music and sport playing a major part. At one time Miss Peeke taught three subjects at Princethorpe, including history, her favourite, but the headmistress Mère Walburga asked her to add a third, something that Miss Peeke commented upon because a school inspector might very well have delivered a poor report if such a situation was encountered. As it happened, the inspector passed the priory's school. Sometimes dramatic means had to be taken so that the public examinations could take place. One O-level science test required fish and the priory had none to give the students. It was true that someone could have travelled all the way to Rugby to purchase a number, though Mère Walburga suggested that a few fish could be removed from the lake at Switzerland and replaced after they had been used. Gill Cowling, assisted by Miss Peeke, took a wooden pole with a net to catch fish, though they were not successful. In the end, Kay Cummuskey had to go to Rugby for some specimens from the fishmongers.

Life at the priory was exciting for the girls and like all pupils they had their fun. On one occasion the pupils decided to have a midnight feast in a field, one where a cherry tree grew, and they all thought that they had kept their plans a secret from the headmistress. However, when they were in their pyjamas, ready to go out, Mère Walburga turned up and gave the girls a bottle of squash for their party. Life was also hard work. Cleaning tasks included assisting in the kitchen, laying the tables in the refectory, washing up, tidying the garden shed and dusting the office of the headmistress.

Mère Mary Walburga, 1946

Switzerland: the small lake to the north, formed when clay was hewn to produce bricks on the site for most of the early building work

"Mère Walburga suggested that a few fish could be removed from the lake at Switzerland and replaced after they had been needed. Gill Cowling, assisted by Miss Peeke, took a wooden pole with a net to catch fish, though they were not successful."

The Recreation Room also doubled up as a gymnasium; now a chemistry laboratory

The West Door

The Plantation (or Plan), now known as the Mile Walk, although it is considerably shorter than a mile

"Sport was a popular pastime at Princethorpe, and included the famous 'jog trot', a run around the Plan."

Sport was a popular pastime at Princethorpe, and included the famous 'jog trot', a run around the 'Plan', now the 'Mile Walk'. Games were normally held immediately after lunch at twelve o'clock, followed by lessons at two and tea at four. Although the girls changed after games into a different shirt, there was no opportunity to wash. Indeed, the boarders only took two baths a week! They could wash themselves with a jug of water in the morning, but if it had been a cold night, the ice had to be broken at the top first. To start, the bath water came from the spring at Switzerland, and it was soft rain water and sometimes leaves made their way down through the pipes. The water was eventually supplied from Rugby, which meant that the quality was different but at least it did not have to be treated at Princethorpe.

The priory's living and working environment was a bit gloomy because electricity was not installed until the early 1950s. Before that the nuns manufactured their own acetylene gas, which did not project particularly good light. On one occasion Miss Peeke took a pot of what she thought was Yardley's face cream from a cupboard, smeared it on her face and later discovered that it was blue shoe cream instead. The lighting was so bad that Miss Peeke failed to notice her error until breakfast time.

All the doors would be locked up during the holidays and the girls accompanied to Rugby Station, most often by Miss Peeke, in order to catch their trains to London or elsewhere. Miss Peeke oversaw return journeys from Euston Station when they were separated from their parents. When they came back from their holidays, the girls first arrived with their trunks in the Recreation Room with sacking on the floor. There was a small door to this room, complete with a tiny grille, which allowed people to see outside the enclosure. It was in this playroom that the trunks were opened, contents removed and carried to the allotted dormitory; your particular sleeping quarters could change from time to time.

> *"On one occasion Miss Peeke took a pot of what she thought was Yardley's face cream from a cupboard, smeared it on her face and later discovered that it was blue shoe cream instead."*

Closure

The decision to close the school came as a terrible shock to everybody. For Miss Peeke, Mère Benedict sat in her room and gave her the bad news; Gill Cowling knew beforehand. It is clear that the full story of events leading up to the sale, and the sale itself, has still to be told. In any case it was a great surprise, particularly to an enclosed community who had remained within the walls for many years, and one nun had never left the priory for nearly thirty five years. Father John Kevin Fleming, headmaster of St Bede's and first to take charge of the newly created Princethorpe College, even asked Miss Peeke to remain and teach; she declined the offer having never taught boys before.

The community founded a new home at Fernham, near Faringdon in Oxfordshire, where it opened a small Montessori school. This eventually closed and the remaining members of the community departed to other religious houses including Boarbank Hall (Cumbria) and Minster Abbey (Kent).

The end of an era

St Mary's Priory, Fernham with the new chapel and additional nuns' cells

"The community founded a new home at Fernham, near Faringdon in Oxfordshire, where they opened a small Montessori school."

Aerial view of St Bede's College in Leamington.
Photograph ©Historic England (Aerofilms Collection)

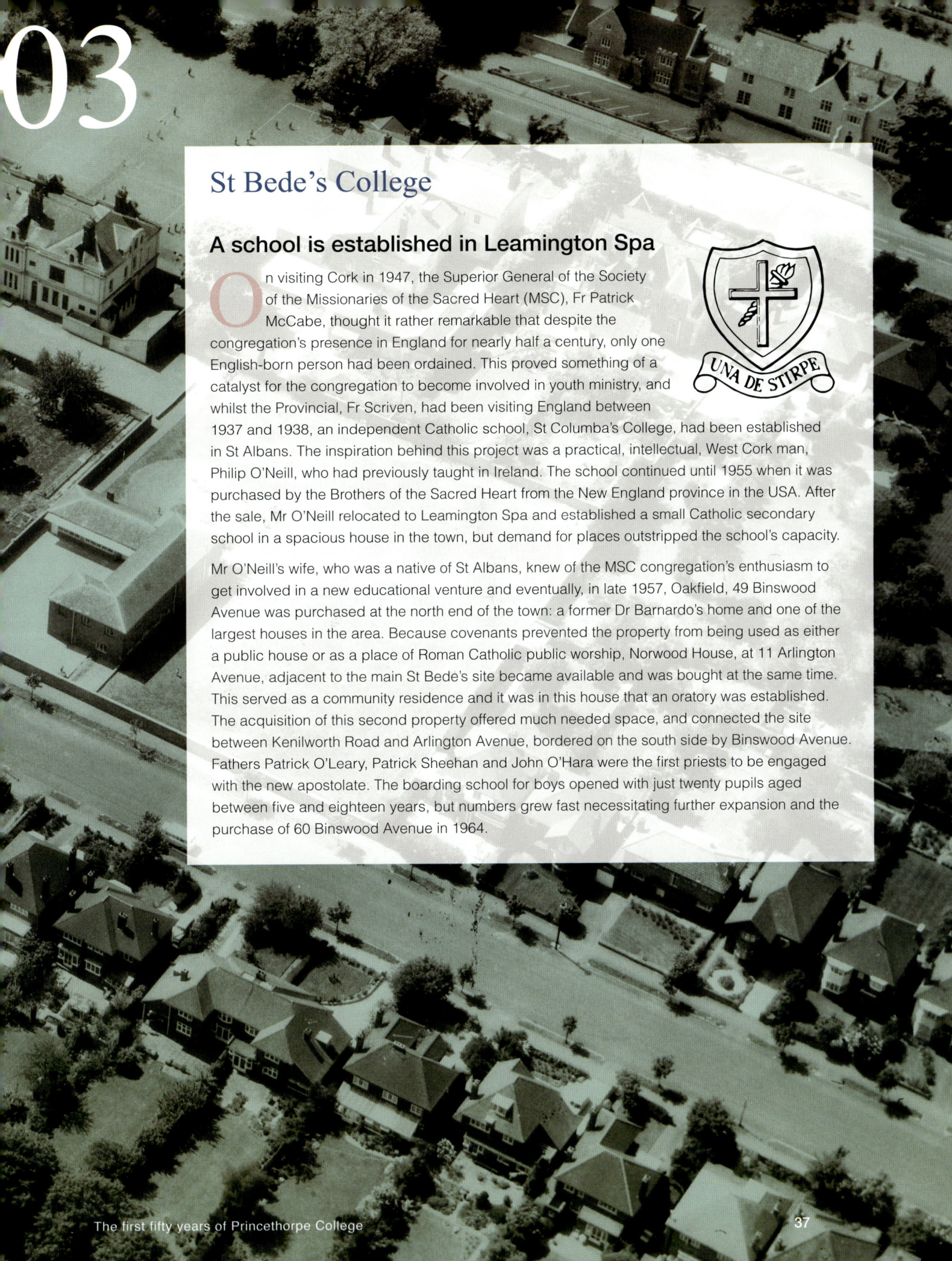

03

St Bede's College

A school is established in Leamington Spa

On visiting Cork in 1947, the Superior General of the Society of the Missionaries of the Sacred Heart (MSC), Fr Patrick McCabe, thought it rather remarkable that despite the congregation's presence in England for nearly half a century, only one English-born person had been ordained. This proved something of a catalyst for the congregation to become involved in youth ministry, and whilst the Provincial, Fr Scriven, had been visiting England between 1937 and 1938, an independent Catholic school, St Columba's College, had been established in St Albans. The inspiration behind this project was a practical, intellectual, West Cork man, Philip O'Neill, who had previously taught in Ireland. The school continued until 1955 when it was purchased by the Brothers of the Sacred Heart from the New England province in the USA. After the sale, Mr O'Neill relocated to Leamington Spa and established a small Catholic secondary school in a spacious house in the town, but demand for places outstripped the school's capacity.

Mr O'Neill's wife, who was a native of St Albans, knew of the MSC congregation's enthusiasm to get involved in a new educational venture and eventually, in late 1957, Oakfield, 49 Binswood Avenue was purchased at the north end of the town: a former Dr Barnardo's home and one of the largest houses in the area. Because covenants prevented the property from being used as either a public house or as a place of Roman Catholic public worship, Norwood House, at 11 Arlington Avenue, adjacent to the main St Bede's site became available and was bought at the same time. This served as a community residence and it was in this house that an oratory was established. The acquisition of this second property offered much needed space, and connected the site between Kenilworth Road and Arlington Avenue, bordered on the south side by Binswood Avenue. Fathers Patrick O'Leary, Patrick Sheehan and John O'Hara were the first priests to be engaged with the new apostolate. The boarding school for boys opened with just twenty pupils aged between five and eighteen years, but numbers grew fast necessitating further expansion and the purchase of 60 Binswood Avenue in 1964.

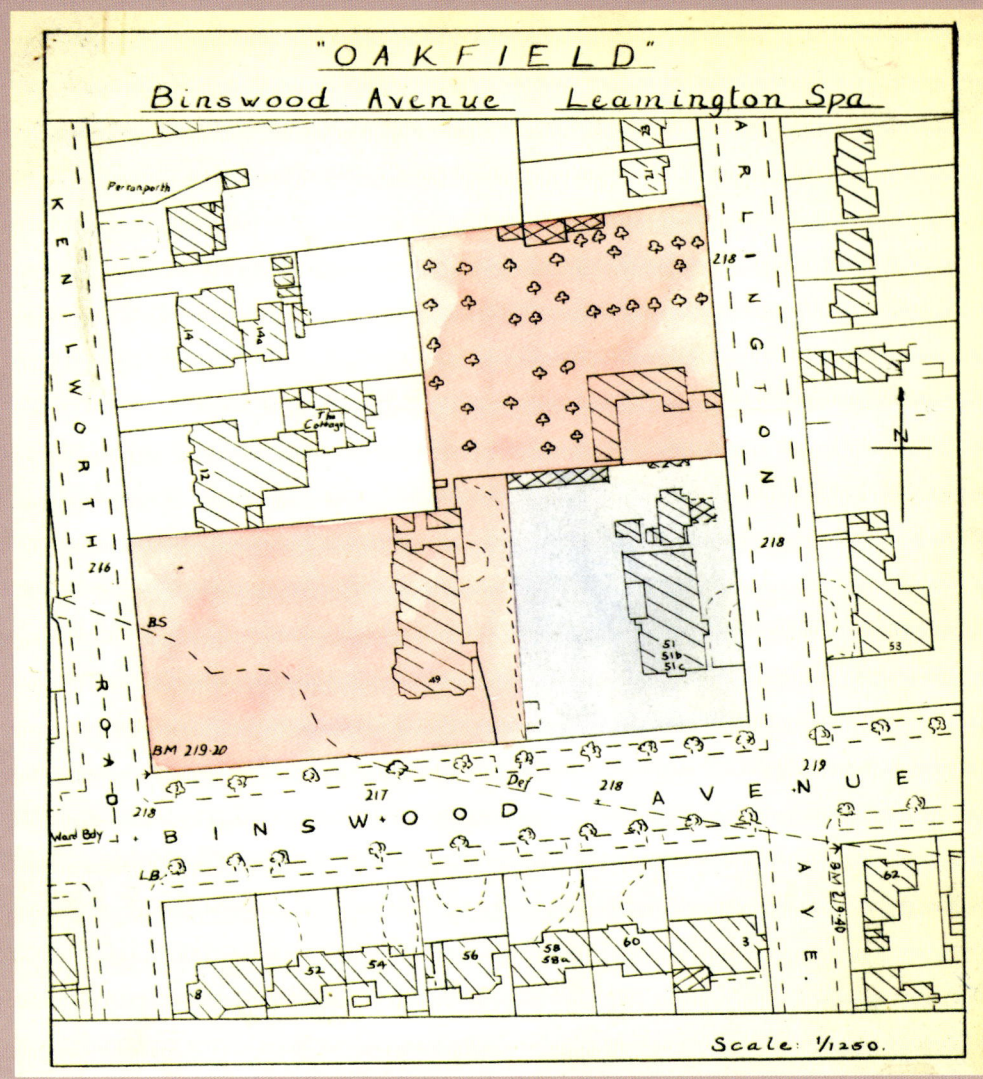

Oakfield (shaded in red) and Norwood House (shaded in blue)

Oakfield: the main house at 49 Binswood Avenue which had been a former Dr Barnardo's home

The Binswood Avenue site in 2016: only Oakfield's gate posts remain

Fr Patrick O'Leary MSC was appointed as the school's first headmaster and remained in post until he was succeeded by Fr John Kevin Fleming in 1962. The school continued to grow and soon the MSC congregation was forced to look for larger premises, resulting in the purchase of St Mary's Priory at Princethorpe from the Benedictines in 1966. Fr Fleming was now head of the newly-formed Princethorpe College and the senior pupils, aged between eleven and eighteen, moved from Leamington to Princethorpe in September of the same year. The recently ordained Fr James McManus (always known as Seamus) took over the helm at St Bede's, which became solely a preparatory school. He remained in post until 1972 when he joined the community at Princethorpe and was replaced by Fr Jim Mannix, then Head of Art at Princethorpe.

The decision was taken in 1976 to close St Bede's and the buildings were subsequently sold, with the eldest boys (Junior 6) completing their final year of Junior school on the Princethorpe campus. The sports centre at Princethorpe was later named St Bede's Hall to commemorate the school's beginnings in Leamington.

Oakfield remained empty for some years until 1983, when an application was made by Target Housing to demolish the Victorian mansion to make way for modern flats, linking it with Norwood House. Despite numerous objections, including the Leamington Society, Warwick District Council's Planning Officer, Geoff Wilson, recommended that demolition should be allowed.

The official opening of St Bede's College in 1957. The girls from St Joseph's School in Kenilworth were invited as guests and a Mass was celebrated

The Society of
The Missionaries of the Sacred Heart (MSC)

Humble beginnings…

The MSC Congregation was founded in Issoudun, a small town some 250 km south of Paris, a little over 160 years ago, on the 8 December 1854. The vision of its founder, a thirty year-old priest, named Jules Chevalier, was to establish a missionary society which would have as its purpose to bring an experience of the compassionate and merciful love of God to all people as the one remedy for the evils which afflicted society. This was the vision which had captivated him since his seminary days: a dream he would quickly share with a small band of other young, enthusiastic men. The beginnings were humble, but perseverance and complete trust that their project was indeed the will of God, led to a flurry of vocations and early missionary expansion.

Jules Chevalier was a man of his time. His life spanned most of the 19th century. It was a century which saw radical changes in western society, often torn apart by war and revolution, especially in France. In the midst of such turmoil, Chevalier was captivated by the reality of God's love, revealed in the human heart of Christ. His one desire was that the whole world would come to the same experience and understanding of God.

Rapid early growth and a first foothold in England and Ireland

The growth of the Congregation was rapid and by the spring of 1876, just twenty-one years after its foundation, one of Fr Chevalier's original companions visited England to explore the possibility of acquiring a house and establishing a community. In August of the same year, Fr John Neenan, a young Irish priest from the Diocese of Cloyne in Ireland, travelled to France to enter the MSC novitiate. So began the inseparable link between the MSCs in the little town of Issoudun and the countries of Ireland and England. The first house in these islands was opened in Madely in Shropshire, England in 1882 and by 1909 the first foundation in Ireland had been established on Western Road in Cork.

A vision still very much alive

Since those first footholds, the missionary charism and vision of the MSC has spread beyond Ireland and England to the other three territories which now make up the Irish Province. Over 150 years after being founded, the Missionaries of the Sacred Heart work in fifty-four countries and number 2,000 priests and brothers. The Society's vision inspires new generations of MSCs as they work among the people and train future ministers in South Africa, Venezuela and the Southern United States of America, as well as in Ireland and England. The vision of Jules Chevalier in 1854 is still central to the MSC's mission: that all people, in every place, circumstance and stage of life, may know the transforming love of God revealed in the human heart of Jesus Christ.

Norwood House in Arlington Avenue: the priests' first residence in Leamington

High jumper, Nicholas Doyle

Fr Fleming hands out the awards at sports day

Heads of House

PE lesson with Fr Jim Mannix

"The school continued to grow and soon the MSC congregation was forced to look for larger premises, resulting in the purchase of St Mary's Priory at Princethorpe from the Benedictines in 1966."

Is everyone listening?

Mrs O'Donohue accompanies a music lesson

Fr Bill Clarkson with senior St Bede's boys

Science lesson

The four heads of St Bede's

Fr Patrick O'Leary MSC
1957 - 1962

Fr John Kevin Fleming MSC
1962 - 1966

Fr James McManus MSC
1966 - 1972

Fr Jim Mannix MSC
1972 - 1976

Fr James F McManus MSC

1935 to 1999

When Fr Mac died suddenly in January 1999, aged only 63, the sense of shock and grief in the whole College community was palpable, an indication of how greatly he was loved and valued.

Tributes were published in a special issue of *The Tower*. One read: 'Father McManus was a kind, gentle and good man...He brought out the best in people... You could always trust him and you could always talk to him and he always listened. He would always go out of his way for you, for anything'.

Another Year 7 wrote: 'He had a very good memory. He would walk up to Year 7 students and would know everyone's names... He also knew everyone else's names...He was always happy and everyone else around him was happy too. He would even go round Princethorpe and pick up all the litter which other people had dropped. He always did his duties and he had a lot of responsibilities, but he did them for Princethorpe College and for us.'

He was called James, but typically, accepted the name Seamus from his Irish confreres, and was also simply known as Fr Mac. Born in Dublin in 1935, educated in Sligo and Cork, he entered the MSC novitiate at Myross Wood, West Cork. After studying philosophy and theology for six years, he was ordained at Moyne Park, Galway on 21 September 1961.

Thereafter, he worked at St Bede's in Leamington before taking a B.Ed in Education at Warwick University. Headmaster of St Bede's from 1966-1972, he moved to Princethorpe where, from 1975, he held various positions including Deputy Head. From 1993 to 1994, he was in Dublin as Provincial Secretary and Archivist before returning to the place he most loved, Princethorpe, as Dean from autumn 1994.

He was involved in so many areas of school life: showing prospective families round the school and writing meticulous notes on each; chairing the Marketing Committee and initiating Fun Days for feeder schools; supporting extra-curricular activities with a passion. A keen follower of Formula 1, he travelled miles to support pupils in motor sports, karting and equestrianism. As a spiritual priest of deep faith, he loved all of God's creation equally. He savoured every experience, from the Buckingham Palace garden party he attended with Fr Whelan in July 1998 to the hard work involved in clearing up the playground after horseboxes had been stationed there during a rained-upon event. His phenomenal knowledge was matched by his humility and sense of humour. Asked to recall one pupil, he replied; 'Ah yes, fine chap. Father drove a Volvo. Mother wore those dreadful hats. Nuneaton, I believe.'

Fr Mac's generous spirit and selflessness, combined with the twinkle in his blue eyes and his warm smile, made him unforgettable.

The Extended Family

St Joseph's School and Crackley Hall School

As a result of repeated requests by the Coventry-based Benedictine Fathers at St Osburg's to the Sisters of Mercy in Chelsea, a founding party from London, led by Sr M Elizabeth Vincent Watkins, was sent in May 1862 to take possession of a Victorian mansion overlooking Gosford Green. The need for a house to be established arose principally from the large numbers of young girls and children employed in the silk mills, who were without proper instruction or protection.

A day and boarding school was opened shortly after the sisters arrived which continued to flourish until the outbreak of the Second World War when sisters and pupils were obliged to evacuate to nearby Stoneleigh Abbey, the Warwickshire home of Lord and Lady Leigh and the move was completed by 16 October 1940. The air raids increased in intensity and in April 1941 the convent was destroyed beyond any hope of repair.

The search for a suitable house to replace St Joseph's in Coventry now began. With the help and support of Archbishop Williams, Mother Magdalen Pennington purchased Offchurch House in October 1941 for £16,000. In December, five sisters moved there with the senior girls, to start a boarding school. The rest of the sisters remained at the Abbey with the junior school because Lord Leigh was keen for them to stay there until the war was over. The schools at Offchurch and Stoneleigh grew. Large donations from parents, friends and benefactors were received which helped towards the purchase of the house and school furniture for Offchurch. War damage compensation together with the money from the sale of the bombed site in Coventry, paid off the debt on Offchurch House.

As there were signs of the war coming to an end, Mother Magdalen began to look around for a suitable place to buy before moving the sisters and children from the Abbey. In June, John Siddeley, Lord Kenilworth, offered Crackley Hall with forty acres of land for £20,000. This sum seemed quite impossible, so the offer was at first refused, but Lord Kenilworth invited Mother Magdalen to go to Crackley and look over the house and generous purchase terms were agreed. All legal matters were arranged and in September 1944 the keys were handed over.

St Joseph's Convent, Kenilworth

Animal Antics November 2011, Will Robertson (l) & Jamie Smith

In January 1945, Crackley Hall became St Joseph's Convent. The children transferred from Stoneleigh Abbey, while the boarders continued at Offchurch, where they remained for the next five years, before moving to Kenilworth. By September there were 140 pupils at St Joseph's. As the numbers continued to rise, the community purchased a large house, The Gables, which stood in the grounds and had formerly belonged to Sir Bernard Docker, Chairman of Daimler Cars. New buildings soon became necessary to accommodate the ever-rising numbers of children. The building programme continued over the next twenty years giving the school every modern amenity.

The school went from strength to strength and was highly regarded – not only by the people of Kenilworth, Coventry and Warwick - but farther afield and it enjoyed a reputation of successfully placing girls in higher education and launching them along life's journey.

The Sisters of Mercy, however, were becoming more and more conscious of the "cry of the poor" for whom the Order was initially founded. In 1988 the Chapter drew up a Mission Statement, in which the sisters committed themselves to those ministries which directly enabled them to be with the poor and powerless today. Consequently, a decision was reached to withdraw from the independent schools' arena and also from the Hospital of St John and Elizabeth in London. St Joseph's was transferred to lay trustees in 1991, thereby ending a long tradition of service to education in the Coventry area.

Crackley pupils at Princethorpe with Head, Jane Le Poidevin & Sarah Lammas (later Mansfield)

Lloyd and Bethan Ellis won a competition to run the school for a day (Lloyd Ellis is Head Boy at Princethorpe for the Golden Jubilee year)

Teaching & learning, Mary Kelly (l) & Alexandra Kennedy, 2007

School photograph, 2005

First Communion, June 2016

Cricket A & B teams, 2015

Neil & Patricia Starkie, PTA Ball, 2008

Nursery children, 2005

Robert Duigan & Martha Harris, Nursery celebrations, 2001

Due to falling numbers in the senior school, it was decided to merge St Joseph's with Princethorpe College in September 2001, under the umbrella of Warwickshire Catholic Independent Schools' Foundation. Senior pupils are based at Princethorpe and Junior pupils, from nursery to 11 years, are taught in Kenilworth. Jane Le Poidevin was the first Head of St Joseph's Crackley Hall from 2001 until 2008 and the school was renamed Crackley Hall in 2004. Paul Ryan took over in 2008 when Jane Le Poidevin was appointed as General Secretary of ISA. Robert Duigan became Head in 2011 and £1m developments at the west end of the campus in 2012 provided a new art room, two further classrooms, toilet & changing facilities and a new science laboratory. The Gables, providing a 250-seat multi-purpose hall, two classrooms, a music room, learning development room and peripatetic music teaching rooms, opened in spring 2016 at a cost of £2m.

Hard at work, 2005

In 2010, Crackley Hall merged with Abbotsford School, also in Kenilworth. Seven staff and forty-five pupils transferred from the Abbotsford site. In 2016, there are 245 pupils on roll.

Miss Debbie Texeira by Amy Gordon, March 2008

FELDON SCHOOL

Feldon School

Including a section on Feldon School, which had no direct connection with Princethorpe College may seem a little strange, yet when it closed, many pupils and a few staff transferred to Princethorpe. In the south cloister, a Feldon School photograph – procured at a local car boot sale – is on display and carries many familiar faces from Princethorpe's past.

Feldon School was set up in Leamington by Dr J L and Mrs S A Matthews in the summer of 1950. In September 1948, they had taken over a small private school, Ardmore, based at 69 Willes Road on the corner of Leam Terrace.

In a matter of two years, increasingly successful under Dr and Mrs Matthews, the school outgrew the space at Willes Road. The Matthews, meanwhile, had acquired Walpole a large Victorian villa on Milverton Hill. This became a boarding house for boys aged 9 and above, and later the junior department of the school, for girls and boys aged 5 -10. The school moved to Milverton Hill and was renamed Feldon, eventually occupying five villas, from Victoria Lodge, Coach House and stables at 2 Portland Place, up the hill to Feldon at the junction with Warwick New Road. It housed Dr Matthews' study, the school office and the dining room. The gym and assembly hall were in the coach house at Victoria Lodge, with changing rooms in the basement of the main house, next to the boiler room.

The gardens of the five houses offered ample recreational space, but organised school games and matches were played on Victoria Park, across the river. John Matthews, an Oxford classicist and rower, also introduced rowing.

Under Dr Matthews, all sports were encouraged: inter-school matches were played, as were tennis matches against Leamington's *Yorkshire Society* and inter-house sports days were held on the "big lawns". The school colours were navy and gold, and when 'colours' were awarded, boys had scarves representing the four school Houses: Fleming (yellow), Lincoln (maroon), Murray (green) and Shaftesbury (blue.) Uniform was supplied by Messrs Francis & Sons Ltd of Bath Street.

FELDON SCHOOL

MILVERTON HILL, LEAMINGTON SPA

Principals:

J. L. MATTHEWS, M.A. (OXON.), PH.D. (LONDON)

SUSAN A. MATTHEWS, B.SC. (EDIN.), Cambridge Teachers' Certificate

Assisted by a qualified and experienced Staff

Day and Boarding Pupils.

Boys prepared for General Certificate of Education and various special examinations.

Football, cricket, swimming, tennis, rowing, boxing.

JUNIOR SCHOOL (for Boys and Girls aged 4-9) at

VICTORIA LODGE, 2 PORTLAND PLACE

Enquiries to the Principals at Walpole, 1 Milverton Hill. Tel. 26995.

Dr and Mrs Matthews and family made their home at Walpole. Dr Matthews taught Classics and Mrs Matthews Physics and Chemistry. Art was taught by Roger Johnston, who went on to become a head of department at Leamington College for Boys for the rest of his teaching career (and also refereed many a rugby match at Princethorpe).

The school flourished under the Matthews' leadership, producing a number of talented stars: Leon Vitali is a well-known RADA-trained British film actor; David Warner of the Royal Shakespeare Company, film and television, is another celebrity actor whose talent was fostered at Feldon. George Dick, cricket aficionado and local travel agent, whose late son James was Head Boy at Princethorpe, was a Feldon pupil

Once Dr and Mrs Matthews retired, Feldon, bought by George P Bidder, seemed to lose impetus under the weight of educational reforms and health and safety concerns. Mr Bidder had held a high government post in Africa, but perhaps lacked the drive and charisma of John Matthews. In 1968 the school moved to Radford Road to the Southlands School premises. As well as taking over the premises, it also took over Southlands' pupils. The school closed in 1970 and the Milverton Hill site lay empty and vandalised until razed to the ground and redeveloped as their headquarters by the Royal Leamington Spa Building Society (which on merger, became the Bradford & Bingley).
For the last quarter of a century the building, renamed Riverside, has been home to Warwick District Council.

Alan O'Grady (Mathematics & Sport), Jock Davies (Mathematics) and Sid Spanner (Chemistry) all formerly employed at Feldon, took up posts at Princethorpe, with Alan O'Grady remaining in post until his retirement.

Feldon: section from a school photograph dated 1952

Abbotsford School

Abbotsford School, which joined the Princethorpe Foundation in 2010, was founded in 1909 by a Miss Hodsman in Waverley Road, Kenilworth and had about nine boarders. In 1912, Miss English became the Headmistress and five years later she moved the school to its familiar location in Bridge Street. At that time the building was rented from a Mr Harry Wells Lawrence and had been known as Bridge House. Arnold Lea was the first boy pupil to attend the school from 1916 to 1919.

In 1924 the school was taken over by Miss Williams and Miss Burton, who lived on the upper floors of the house and shared quarters with young boarders. They were affectionately known as Willy and Burty. They started with twelve pupils and grew to approximately ninety when they left in 1946. They were followed by a Mrs Janet Higginson, who had taught for some years in India and the Far East. One of her first jobs was to install electricity throughout the house and to increase fees to 6 guineas (£6.30) for the Kindergarten (boys and girls from 5-7 years) and 11 guineas (£11.55) for girls up to 17 years. Weekly boarders were charged 20-24 guineas per term!

Mrs Higginson later remarried and became known as Mrs MacLaren. It was in 1952 that she decided to buy the school from the sons of Mr Wells Lawrence for £2,000. During her time at Abbotsford, Mrs MacLaren increased the numbers to 160 pupils. There were ten classes and it was one of the largest independent schools in the area, taking children from as far as Southam and Meriden. Extra rooms were rented in St Nicholas' Parochial Hall, where the children took their PE lessons.

Winifred Bowden became Headmistress in 1958 and changed the emblem in 1961 to two crossed abbot's croziers and blue wavy lines to represent a ford across a stream – hence Abbotsford. The school motto *Nostra Res Agitur* means: 'We answer for our own actions'.

In 1963 the school became an educational trust in order to secure a measure of relief from rates and taxes. The stables and coach house, which had been used as a builders' yard, were also purchased from Mr Wells Lawrence. In 1969 it was decided to close the school because the scope of critical maintenance work exceeded the funds available. However, the parents provided money to meet immediate needs, agreed an increase in fees and the trustees decided that the school would continue with pupils only up to the age of 13.

Bridge House, which is a listed building

Early days: the schoolroom

The kindergarten, Christmas 1947

Music day at St Joseph's School

The extension, which provided further classrooms, a space for the nursery and specialist teaching rooms for science and art, 1987

"Winifred Bowden became Headmistress in 1958 and changed the emblem to two crossed abbot's croziers and blue wavy lines to represent a ford across a stream – hence Abbotsford."

It was at this time that Miss Bowden retired and Mrs Norma Cooke-Davies (later Kittendorf), who was a teacher at the school, became the next Headmistress. At first she concentrated on preparing pupils for entrance examinations to local senior schools, with extremely good results.

Mrs Barbara Chitty, who joined the school in 1973, taught a class of sixteen pupils part-time, ranging from 8 to 13 years-of-age, a position which she shared with Mrs Brown, who had taught at Abbotsford since the early 1940s and who finally retired in 1975, well into her seventies. Mrs Robson took over Mrs Brown's post and together, under Mrs Cooke-Davies' leadership, the Junior Department was built up and gradually senior girls joined. During this time the old stables and coach house were converted into a gymnasium, which was opened by rugby player David Duckham, whose daughter was a pupil.

Mrs Cooke-Davies retired in 1982 and Barbara Chitty became Headmistress. A great deal of modernisation was needed and the gymnasium was extended in 1984 at a cost of £25,000.

The senior department closed in 1985; there were too many financial demands from a small department of 26 girls and the number of junior pupils was increasing. Space was needed to meet the demands of a broader curriculum in the Junior Department.

In 1987 a large extension was built, which connected the school to the hall. It consisted of two classrooms and a nursery unit on the ground floor and a classroom, science laboratory and art room on the first floor.

The school was fortunate enough to benefit from the William Edwards Charity – an educational trust - which provided the school with extra equipment, including a demountable stage, a kiln, computers and a minibus.

Abbotsford School, 1998

Barbara Chitty's retirement party, 1998

Staff in Edwardian costume for the 80th birthday celebrations, 1989

Children in the new extension, which was completed in 1987

Close relationships were established with other independent schools in the area including St Joseph's School, which acted as host for a music day for several years, during Sr Philomena's headship.

The school celebrated its 80th birthday in 1989 with an Edwardian theme; everyone was dressed in period costume for lessons. Mrs MacLaren, now in her eighties, but still lively and impressive, was guest of honour. On retirement in 1998, Barbara Chitty handed on the headship to Joan Adams (later Jarvis), who had previously worked at a junior school in Dunchurch. Barbara Chitty's farewell was marked by a party at the DeMontfort Hotel in Kenilworth with friends from Abbotsford and from other schools.

Nine years later, Joan Jarvis moved overseas and the headship passed to James Skuse, who was in position for 15 months.

Dominic Cook, then aged 37, a former deputy head and educational advisor from Berkshire, joined the school in 2008 to become Headmaster, and along with the Board of Management, was instrumental in the successful merger with Crackley Hall two years later, when most pupils and some staff transferred to the Coventry Road campus, just up the road. The two schools realised that they had much in common in terms of shared goals and a similar ethos. Although the Bridge Street site held the most memories in the school's history and was home to a supremely interesting and historic house, the lack of owned playing fields and a somewhat land-locked campus at a busy road junction, meant that it was sensible to consolidate the two schools at Crackley Hall.

The Bridge Street house was sold for development shortly after the merger and at the time of writing remains empty.

Crescent School

The most recent addition to the 'Princethorpe Family' began life at Troy House, 12 Hillmorton Road, Rugby, in 1946. The building was at that time essentially a "waiting house" for boys entering Rugby School. However, it was a happy chance that Mrs Eve Mortimer, whose husband had been appointed a wood and metalwork teacher at Rugby School, and an experienced teacher in her own right, took over the education of some of the children of Rugby School staff who also met at Troy House. It soon became apparent that space was tight and Mrs Mortimer's pupils relocated in 1947 to the Old School Sanatorium building at the corner of Horton Crescent and Barby Road.

Numbers swiftly increased and the pupils were engaged in the usual occupations such swimming at the 'Tosh'. Not surprisingly, new buildings had to be constructed to accommodate pupil numbers. A new annexe was built in the 1950s and other work followed in the subsequent decade. By the time Mrs Christine Barrett became Head Teacher in September 1971, numbers had increased so much that there were eight classes, one for each school year. Pupils continued to use a number of the Rugby School facilities, like the 'Tosh', together with the playing fields and Chapel.

The lease on the Sanatorium was due to expire in the 1980s. Unfortunately, Rugby School decided to take back the building and so a committee was established to consider other possibilities. By lucky chance, the old St Mark's School in Bilton, which had been left derelict for the previous eighteen months, became available. A successful bid was submitted and Crescent School prepared to move to its new home at Bawnmore Road; this took place in the summer of 1988, assisted by two tractors obtained from Rugby School. Under the leadership of Ian Wren, who became Head Teacher in 1992, the school celebrated its Golden Jubilee in 1996. Wren was succeeded by Mrs Christine Vickers in 2000, who changed the plain green ties to striped ones (thereby depicting the colours of the three houses); she was followed by Huw Marshall in 2002.

The school has changed considerably since the time when Mrs Mortimer gathered with the pupils in Troy House. However, its ethos and concern for the welfare and development of each and every pupil remains the same. The Princethorpe Foundation is pleased to welcome Crescent School to the 'extended family', and a new chapter in the life of this trust is about to be written.

Huw Marshall, Headmaster; Pat Lines, Chair of Governors - Crescent School; Mary O'Farrell, Chair of Trustees - The Princethorpe Foundation and Ed Hester, Senior Head

Crescent School in Bawnmore Road

Buildings and places

Those who made the transition in 1966 from St Bede's must have been astonished by the sheer space on offer at Princethorpe. In St Mary's Priory days, most of the building had been used by the nuns, rather than by the school. The guest house was effectively separated off from the enclosure, as was the school, the latter occupying a single large wing at the east end. After 1966, the MSC community used the guest house for their living accommodation and the ground floor housed administrative offices and reception rooms. The community's refectory was at the far side of the New Church, close to the West Door.

Suddenly, with the MSC's arrival, much of what had been part of the nuns' enclosure became the school and about sixty acres of the estate were turned over to playing fields; a far cry from the urban surroundings of Oakfield and Norwood House in Leamington. An open air swimming pool was constructed next to the Orchard wall and provided great entertainment during the warmer months, though many will remember the icy-cold water!

In the early days, with relatively small numbers, the school rattled around a bit with so much space to spare. If you needed a room for a hobby, then it was a matter of finding somewhere empty which was suitable and putting a name on a door. Laurence Armitstead had a large cupboard for his electronics, near the former mortuary chapel; Anthony Bennett commandeered a room near the original tuck shop for making model aeroplanes and the Wildlife Club had their cellar under the priests' refectory.

The first staff room (complete with a television set) was in the room currently used for Food Technology theory; moving at the end of the sixties to the two rooms which now make up G10. During John Shinkwin's tenure as head, because of sheer numbers, staff moved to F10 and F11, where they remain today.

Some rooms and places took on their own special character. The Chemistry Lab, which was the former girls' recreation room and gym, is still the Chemistry Lab (G4) and is probably the most frequently visited part of the school for those who come back to reminisce. It was the preserve of teachers such as Sid Spanner, Fr Bill Clarkson MSC, Mrs Helby, Dr Lipscomb, Harold Crossley and John Miller for so many years. A single storey extension, forming a further Chemistry laboratory (G5), was added as part of major science reorganisation in the early 1980s.

The former school room next door (G6), which provided the first assembly hall, was quickly divided into two classrooms and subsequently became another laboratory (G6) and science preparation area. Much the same happened to the two rooms on the floors above; as more classrooms were needed the large rooms were divided into two. The top floor of the main school, now S1 and S3, were junior dormitories well into the seventies, separated by a room which was Matron's (S2). Later the sinks were removed and two classrooms were constructed which are occupied today by the Mathematics Department, who utilise most of the top floor of Main School.

Form E1 occupied what is now one end of the Dining Room (incorporated in the late 1960s) and Fr Bill Clarkson was delighted that his form had the largest classroom in the school. Outside was the main cloister, of which Fr John Kevin Fleming boasted it was so wide that a car could be driven down it! In those days, the north cloister had a few wooden pigeon holes which were the preserve of boarders and where tins of *Nesquick*, jars of *Marmite* and personal napkins (how civilised!) were stored for meal times. Just across the way is The Quadrangle, which underwent considerable restoration in 2014.

Priory cemetery with French rooms and woodwork workshop in the background, 2006

Pupils in the Lime Walk, 1966

Anthony Rudge canoeing on the lake at Switzerland, 1969

Rapid expansion of the school in the run up to 1970 meant that classroom space was short and so various portable buildings were erected beyond the West Door, with greenhouses and potting sheds being demolished to make space. The two most familiar classrooms were the French Rooms, occupied at the outset by Mrs Hilda Crosby and Madame Marguerite Jones. Beyond was a larger room, used initially for drama and for a while as a common room, but ultimately converted into a Biology Lab with adjacent preparation area. With the arrival of Frank McGreevy in the mid-seventies, a further building, parallel and near to the Gas Works, provided a woodwork shop. Many years earlier, in 1969, Alan O'Grady had commandeered a cellar under the kitchen and this was set out as a workshop where boarders could learn skills with wood.

The buildings outside the West Door were razed to the ground in 2007 to make way for the Sixth Form Centre, which was the inspiration of head, John Shinkwin and Bursar, Paul Shaw. The two-storey building, designed by *Peter Manning Design Group*, was opened in 2008 by former Deputy Head, Margaret-Lousie O'Keeffe and provides a Sixth Form common room and dining room, a number of teaching rooms, offices, a large multi-purpose atrium and a 100-seat lecture theatre. Further upgrades in 2014 resulted in a Sixth Form study library and resources centre.

'Alan O'Grady's window' is still untouched at the end of the corridor by the Physics Lab (G23); this room remains used now for the same purpose as it was in the very early days, though in 2003, the corridor outside G23 was incorporated into an additional laboratory (G22), which extended into The Quad. The staircase opposite G23, giving access to the first floor area near to the Study Hall (now the New Library) was closed off some years later and access was changed to an opening near the kitchen door, where a rather gentler and safer staircase was added.

Lunch in the Refectory before the room was enlarged to incorporate the neighbouring E1 classroom, c.1968

Sixth Form Common Room (G1),1980

Cleaning Switzerland, 1966. On the left is the late John Mitchell, who for many years was Sacristan. His wife, Miriam, attended the priory school, and his three grandchildren, Harriet, Robert and William Phayer went to Princethorpe

Singing lesson with Christina Rex in the Music Room (former sacristy), 1970s

Paddy Nunn, Kevin Reeves, Michael Lee and John Wheildon with Fr Dan O'Connor in the Sixth Form Common Room, former mortuary chapel. (Photo courtesy of John Wright Photography)

With the end of boarding in 2004, the Geography Wing became an IT centre and Upper and Lower Pugin (the old top and bottom boarding corridors) were reassigned as teaching rooms, studies and offices, as they are today. The kitchen and dining room are much as everyone remembers them, though both have seen modernisation over the years and a cafeteria system operates at mealtimes, with breakfast offered daily in the Sixth Form Centre. The Medical Centre is now part of the sports centre, having moved in recent years from its original site near to the chapel in the room which was originally used as the nuns' apothecary.

As part of the major 1980s work, the courtyard, which accommodated the lunch queue, was covered over between what was then the Technical Graphics Room and the corridor adjacent to the kitchen, to form a light and airy room for Food Technology which has seen colossal popular use.

Technology was firmly established as a subject in the early nineties and by 1992 a new suite of rooms had been adapted in the part of the school previously occupied by Art and the original boot room! This provided a large resistant materials workshop, an electronics laboratory and a room for textiles all near to Food Technology. Art moved to the former games changing rooms and the original laundry areas, with later developments to increase the size of the accommodation into loft spaces as well as providing specialist areas for ceramics and Sixth Form work. A new darkroom and photography suite was opened in 2011, when A-level Photography was added to the Art curriculum.

The original mortuary chapel had ceased being a common room and became a classroom by 1968, used as Form A1 with Fr Chis Coleman MSC in charge; a row of pegs outside provided the youngest pupils with somewhere to hang their caps and games kit. The adjacent 'Crystal Palace' which was a suite of smart toilets - in the best Victorian gothic style - with a glass roof, was demolished in the 1980s to make way for the new Biology Lab (G8) and two classrooms above (F10 and F11). The ground floor bathrooms and the staircase which connected the areas outside G7 with the landing adjacent to the Dean's living quarters were removed at the same time, as part of a scheme started by Fr Brendan Kennedy MSC, to widen the main corridor which snaked around the tuck shop and created something of a bottle neck. Adjacent to the old tuck shop was the book shop and also the laboratory technician's room which, from 1972, was the domain of Roy Lucas.

In the early seventies, the school's ATC had a number of cellars under the dining room and one of the rooms in the tower was used as a common room, but these arrangements were short-lived as there was limited escape in case of fire.

Early during the MSC's tenure, it was decided that there was no need for two chapels, so the original 1835 chapel was deconsecrated and divided into two in 1968: the top half becoming the very memorable Study Hall and the lower half a lofty gymnasium, used for PE lessons and basketball games. For many years the sanctuary end was home to a rowing machine and the storage of sports equipment, but the former sacristy, adjacent, became the first library and the senior prefects commandeered a room nearby as their office.

Gerry Lovely (l) and John Miller after a session repairing the clock

Physics lesson with Mr Bolton in the former nuns' library, 1970s

Temporary classrooms craned into position, summer 2006

The swimming pool built in 1968 adjacent to The Orchard. It was later demolished in the late 1970s because of problems with the foundations

Basketball game in the gymnasium, formerly the original church. (Photo courtesy of John Wright Photography)

Restoration of the New Library mural, 2007

The library later moved to the sacristy of the New Church, with vestments being stored in smaller rooms which were once part of the Chaplain's rooms. This was a vast improvement: the room was much larger and lighter and became the preserve of the new librarian, Mrs Bessie deVries, who had recently retired from teaching. When John Shinkwin arrived in 1998, his ambition was to move the library to a central and more impressive part of the school and one of the millennium projects was the transformation of the Study Hall into a glorious library, befitting the school's heritage. Naturally, the floor had to be strengthened to cope with the weight of the books. Paul Shaw was also keen to restore the ceiling, the mural depicting the 'Death of St Benedict' and the stained glass. The plasterwork of the original sanctuary was also reinstated and decorated as it would have been originally.

When St Bede's Hall (the sports hall) opened in 1979, the old gymnasium was quickly converted to a theatre, as it is today, though a lighting control balcony was added in the eighties. The New Church was used for daily worship - as it is now - and for Sunday Masses, and on the last Friday of each month, for Benediction.

The estate seemed to be freely accessible to the boys, even if parts must have been technically out-of-bounds. Adjacent to the woods on the west boundary, the 'Mile Walk' was well-trodden and formed an attractive place for strolls at break times and a hideout for smokers who hoped to remain undiscovered! Bill Clarkson bought an old *Austin A35* which was driven around 'The Walk' by boarders during evenings and weekends. A decaying old car immediately behind the Orchard wall provided another secret escape. The Lime Walk remains much as it ever was, flanked now by sports centre extensions from 2005 and the Orchard for many years has been a games area. The north car park was enlarged in the 2000s to provide additional staff parking.

View of the Round House from the tower during restoration

The Round House interior, post-restoration

The north bay and tower in the snow from Switzerland, 2013

Bird's-eye view of The Summer Art Show in the Sixth Form Centre, 2009

Lew Baines, who had looked after the estate for the nuns, farmed those parts of the grounds which were not utilised as sports pitches or as gardens and he had various helpers, including Br Donal Hallisey MSC, Br Pascal McKenna MSC and latterly Howard Enstone, who also helped back-stage with the theatre productions. Boarding pupils also got involved with the farm in their spare time. When Lew Baines retired and moved to St Joseph's on the Leamington Road, the farm land was leased to a tenant and the farmhouse and buildings were sold for development, now forming Priory Court. Many pupils must remember the occasional games lessons which were devoted to potato picking in the Orchard in order to keep the school self-sufficient and even fields on the far side of the Leamington Road were cultivated for vegetables.

The tied houses on St Benedict's Terrace (Coventry Road) were gradually sold off, the last going when Alan O'Grady moved away after retirement. The Leamington Road lodge was bought by the Weir family in the 1980s, but the Coventry Road lodge is still owned by the MSCs, as is Gardener's Cottage. The Convent, which has also been variously called Alban House and The Retreat Centre, was purchased by the MSCs from the Sisters of Mercy in the 1970s and still forms part of the estate.

Foundation Bursar, Paul Shaw, surveys the new Sixth Form Centre, summer 2007

Astroturf construction begins, autumn 2007

The late Andrew Varah, furniture designer, with Eddie Tolcher, Foundation Bursar. The furniture in the reception hall and in the Headmaster's office was designed and made by Varah, summer 2009

Premises Working Group during a visit to Denstone College, November 2011. Dr Michael Tideswell (3rd from r) has made a huge contribution to the curriculum, timetable & premises development

Headmaster's office, 2012

Gutter cleaning time with Tom Knowles, 2012

Sixth Form Centre takes shape, autumn 2006

Student Hub opens, with Julie Satchwell in charge, September 2010

New Tuck Shop, September 2005

Main drive resurfacing, summer 2016

The first fifty years of Princethorpe College

David Hodgkinson, former Archivist (foreground) with Eddie Tolcher and Librarian, Celia Scott, 2013

Librarian, Celia Scott and Assistant Librarian Karen O'Connor help Peter and Sandra Garman from New Zealand with some family history, 2013

By 1966, The Round House had become a large store and over the years fell partly into disrepair. The trustees generously supported its restoration incorporating the room into the Music Department, with a new conical roof with clerestory windows. The project was completed in summer 2011, providing a beautiful teaching, meeting and reception area.

By 2012 with around 800 pupils on roll, there was urgent need for further teaching accommodation and planning started for a 14-classroom wing on the back of the Sports Hall. After 12 months of building, the state-of-the-art concept which was evolved by Leamington's *AT Architects* was completed at a cost of £4.5m and in September 2014 The Limes was formally opened by the Most Rev Bernard Longley, Archbishop of Birmingham.

At the time of writing, a new 1,000m^2 Science centre, The Close, providing seven further laboratories is about to go into the planning process as part of the College's drive to make facilities the best which they can possibly be.

Any chapter on the building would be incomplete without mentioning some of the schoolboy myths which go back as far as we can remember. The ghost story of the half-nun, who wafts along the cloisters by night, is still alive and well, though few are able to qualify whether it is the top or the bottom half! There has always been chatter about the secret tunnel which extends from Switzerland into the New Church, though nothing has even been found to substantiate this!

Catterall's coaches after the morning drop-off, December 2014

The Mile Walk (formerly The Plantation), 2013

Judy Vick

Judy Vick, who has worked for the College for 42 years, holds the record as the longest-serving full-time member of staff and started whilst Fr Bill Clarkson was Headmaster. Colleagues at the time were Flo Bush, Kath Mercer, Mrs Flavell (sister of Michael O'Flaherty) and Maureen Vick, all of whom held similar long-service records. Matron was Maria Lawless (then Maria Martin) and Judy remembers Maria being smartly dressed in a nurse's uniform.

Boarding was in full swing when Judy joined and together with other colleagues was responsible for looking after the top and bottom boarding corridors (Upper and Lower Pugin), which in those days were lined with wardrobes and also had a row of sinks running along one end. Judy remembers the younger boarders on the Geography Wing, many of whom left teddy bears sitting on their beds as they went off to school for the day. She recalls that in those days many of the boys had parents serving with the military overseas, frequently in the Army and Air Force. Many would go off to far-flung and unusual places in the holidays.

Particular memories are of the Christmas parties where there were lots of humorous moments and plenty of cheerful banter, with the priests and nuns also invited. Fr Teddy O'Brien was usually in charge of the bar!

When boarding closed in summer 2004, Judy hung up her duster and transferred to work in the laundry (now the ceramics room), as there was still a need to look after the residents and to launder items such as sports kit and linen. Coffee time was always a sociable part of the day when Gerry Lovely would join the girls and catch up on the news.

When major building work took place in the Art Department in 2011, it was decided to close the laundry and contract the work out. Judy was offered general cleaning duties and particularly looking after staff offices, something which she has done ever since with close colleague and friend Cynthia Carpenter.

When she is not at work, Judy enjoys her house in the village and a spot of gardening, though admits that she is better looking after the grass than the flower borders!

Although Judy has seen the school change and grow she is quick to point out that the soul of the place remains as it always was and this is something which has kept her happy and contented. "This has been a marvellous place to work", she said. "There has never been a dull moment and it has been a wonderfully cheerful and good-natured place where everyone looks after each other," she added.

Starting work on The Limes, 2013

Tony Pugh (AT Architects), Jeremy Wright MP and Ed Hester inspect plans for The Limes and The Close projects, 2012

Neil McCollin and Debs Brookes visit The Limes building site, November 2013

Sixth Form Resources Centre, September 2014

The Limes, September 2014

First IT lesson in The Limes with David Smith, September 2014

Gerard Starling

I moved from St Bede's to Princethorpe in 1967 when it was in its second year of existence. I had boarded at St Bede's since I was seven and knew Fr Fleming and Fr Clarkson well.

Looking back, those early years must have been a steep learning curve for our guardians. Moving from a tight inner town 'campus' to wide open spaces, both in terms of buildings and grounds, must have been something of a challenge. We (the boarders) ran wild at times, canoeing on the lake in the middle of the night, shooting rats in the old Chapel tower, climbing all over the roofs of the buildings and so on. As Fr Clarkson once memorably advised us, we could be "utter tugs!" He was excited at the time and the accent got a bit strong!

However, the memory I remember best was the walking home through the snow in 1968. I often went home for weekends, as did quite a few boarders, and on this particular Friday it had started to snow around midday and kept going. We gathered as normal, along with the day boys, for our buses into Leamington, where we could catch trains and buses onward. It was a considerable group, normally three or four bus loads, even in the early days of the school.

At the usual time for the pick-up, no buses! In those days there were no mobiles and it took a while to establish what was happening. Someone nice at Hill Farm Cottages, situated on the Leamington Road, eventually let the bus drivers telephone the school to say they could not get any further than the bottom of the steep hill at Wappenbury. After a short wait it was decided that we should walk to meet them (about 1.7 miles *Google* tells me) but this was through what was now quite deep fresh snow and it was still falling. This decision indicates how much the fathers wanted to get a quiet weekend and, I fear, that 'us' boarders might get funny about not getting home as well!

So off we set in a crocodile through the snow. I remember being encouraged to sing as we went. Initially this was fun but I have to say that the last half began to get a little grim; it was hard walking through the fresh snow and we did not all have wellies. We were a very cold and wet group when we eventually caught sight of the buses at the bottom of the hill. We eventually reached Leamington around 6.30 pm, and those who took the train from there had to deal with the inevitable railway disruptions. I recall getting picked up from Solihull station by my Dad at around 9.30pm.

Obviously we were supported by about four priests on our walk, one at the front and one at the back of the 'crocodile' with two going up and down the line. These four then had to walk back to Princethorpe, and so they had a round trip of over three miles through pretty awful conditions - it was dark when we reached the buses. I regret I cannot recall the priest's name, but he already had a cold and after this trek he was seriously ill with pneumonia.

School life

When Princethorpe College opened in 1966 and the senior boys transferred to the new campus, St Bede's became a natural feeder school for well over a decade, until its closure in summer 1976, when all of the Year 5 pupils moved to Princethorpe for their final year of primary schooling.

Princethorpe College has always drawn its pupils in fairly equal numbers from both the independent and maintained sectors, keeping a relationship in 2016 with just under 200 feeder schools. Many have featured for a very long time, including Arnold Lodge, Bilton Grange, Crackley Hall, Crescent School, The Croft, Knightlow, Milverton House, Our Lady's Princethorpe, The Revel, Ruckleigh, Spratton Hall, St Augustine's, St John Vianney, Telford and Warwick Junior School. In the past, Abbotsford, Emscote Lawn and Tower Lodge also featured strongly.

Entry has always been traditionally at 11+, with two forms in the early years (A1 and A2), plus twenty or so coming from the preparatory schools at age 13. Recent years have seen six forms of entry at 11+ as the school has gained in popularity and it has now achieved its optimum size of 865 with a Sixth Form of 200, a far cry from about 180 across the school when it opened.

In the early days, all boys wore caps in their first year up until 1969 and everyone was required to change into 'house shoes' and then back into outdoor shoes when they left the building. The main pupils' entrance was off the playground, through a green lean-to, which went into the boot room, now part of the Technology Department.

The curriculum was fairly traditional; the three sciences were offered from the beginning, with Chemistry in G4 and Physics in G23, as they both are today. Biology found a home nearby in G1, but today this is part of the History Department. G2, next door, which had been the head's office in the days of the nuns, doubled up as a Sixth Form teaching room and preparation area for Biology. Latin was offered until 1969, and was taught principally by Fr Chris Coleman, but made a permanent return to the curriculum just after the millennium, under the subject leadership of Rachel Taylor.

Teaching was carried out largely by MSC clergy. Fr Dominic Duffy who arrived as Bursar in 1968, also taught English and Religious Studies (RS). Fr Clarkson was responsible for senior Chemistry, but also taught RS. Fr Nick Harnan had French and careers in his portfolio and also taught RS to the Sixth Form. Fr Martin Mitchell was Maths and RS, Fr Liam O'Callaghan was Head of Physics and coached rugby. Fr Michael Buckley earned a reputation as an erudite historian and had his inimitable style of delivery; Fr Dan O'Connor as the ablest mathematician was also a first class rugby coach; his humility and commitment won the respect and hearts of everyone; those who got to know him well soon realised that the bark was much worse than the bite. Fr T J Boyle was affable and friendly, commanding a great deal of respect and his English teaching was inspiring. Outside lessons, he was keenly involved with sport and much of the early basketball success was down to his commitment. Fr P C Horgan taught French and RE and always wore his black habit and sash. The trick in a lesson was to get someone to way-lay him with a complicated question and whilst he was helping the puzzled learner, someone else, out of sight, would tie the end of the sash to a desk or chair… Fr Byrne, a humble and gentle man, was school secretary and remained in post until Helen Jackson arrived in 1970. Fr John Mannion joined in the early seventies and taught Biology.

The clergy from St Bede's frequently ate their evening meals with the Princethorpe community and when Fr Jim Mannix became Head of St Bede's, Fr James McManus moved to Princethorpe, where he remained until his death in 1999, other than six years spent in Dublin working at the Provincialate.

Fr Jim Mannix was calm and avuncular with the natural pace of a schoolmaster; he took full advantage of the grounds for drawing and painting lessons and frequently played a soothing record in the background during art lessons; one might expect that by now pupils would all be quite adept at penning cows and farm machinery! He was also responsible for the design of the school crest. Additionally, Fr Mannix took charge of singing lessons, which always followed games and naturally many pupils faced the consequences of arriving late. In those days, talking between lessons was also prohibited; those who were naturally loquacious dreaded the Friday form assemblies when the punishments were meted out!

As Headmaster, Fr Fleming appeared as a calm and holy captain of the ship, with a clear sense of vocation; he knew everyone by name and where they lived, about which we all used to marvel! Fr Clarkson, who as Dean was Fr Fleming's right-hand man, had huge presence; he connected easily with everyone and there was no mystery when he was appointed to succeed Fr Fleming in 1969. Mathematician Fr Teddy O'Brien, took over from Fr Clarkson as Dean and as well as teaching, put huge energy into co-ordinating a variety of stage performances, before moving on in the early eighties to work as a prison chaplain, later becoming parish priest of Wappenbury.

Lay staff were certainly in the minority in the late sixties. Bessie deVries had joined from St Bede's and taught Geography; Gerry Ferguson was at home teaching Latin and a wide variety of other subjects. Sid Spanner (Chemistry), Jock Davies (Mathematics) and Alan O'Grady (Mathematics) had all joined from Feldon when it closed in Leamington. Alan O'Grady became something of an institution, and those in his lessons, remember his natural ability to teach, his consistency, fairness, sense of humour and the fact that he was missing two fingers on one hand! His annual trips to Wimbledon, tennis coaching and overseeing "bowling for a pig" at the Summer Fête, became legendary!

John Sutton spent his spare time helping out on the College farm

John Wheildon on his appointment as Deputy Head Boy, 1972

Sixth Form group with Fr T J Boyle MSC, 1972

The Year of 1975; Sixth Form group

Fr Clarkson set up the Parents' Association around 1972 and the Christmas Fair, Summer Fête and a wide variety of social events were born. For many years, the association had staff representatives and in 2013 it was a natural development to change its name to the Parent-Teacher Association. Ken and Mary Bainbridge offered support for over three decades, with Di Downes also being one of the longest-serving members. The late Anne Davey joined the association in 1995 and spent so much time helping that it was a natural progression for her to become College Bursar, a rôle which she carried out with great wisdom and humour under Foundation Bursar Paul Shaw and later his successor, Eddie Tolcher.

Herbert Wright taught English. Peter Wilks taught Biology and was responsible for PE and games. Those who were sportily challenged, remember his cross-country runs along Burnthurst Lane, when he would make circuits periodically in his *Morris Minor* traveller to check that the boys were not slacking. As the car disappeared into the horizon, they were free to throttle back into a gentle walk once more, until he later reappeared on another lap, when naturally the pace quickened!

All pupils had an afternoon of games each week and a single lesson of PE. Fixtures were, as they are now, on Wednesday afternoons and Saturday mornings.

The curriculum grew in the seventies, when Dave Drew took charge of Economics and was replaced in 1978 by Peter Griffin, who remained in post for the next thirty-seven years! Barry Weenen set up Engineering Drawing, which later became Technical Graphics and occupied the room now used for Food Technology.

Peter and Christina Rex arrived from Huddersfield in the late sixties; Peter quickly established a reputation as a disciplinarian. Christina taught English and Music, and Peter, History and Politics. Peter had always been enthusiastic about writing and it was retirement in 1994 which gave him this marvellous opportunity, producing a total of seven books, all of which have become revered texts.

Pat and Moira Weir were not far behind, both teaching English and living at the Leamington Road lodge which they ultimately bought from the College. Pat took over from Fr T J Boyle as head of department and as their children grew older, Moira became more and more full-time, ending up as Head of Sixth Form, when the amiable Paul Norris retired. Moira had an astonishing ability to write plays, spanning from the moving *Friedrich* to the hilarious *Cinderella*, where she also wrote the lyrics for the songs. They ultimately retired to France and Margaret Robinson became responsible for the Sixth Form, as well as teaching French. Margaret rightly earned a reputation for being able to understand young people exceptionally well and many Princethorpians have been successfully launched along life's pathway by her wisdom and support. She retires in December 2016.

Madame Crosby and Madame Jones shared transport from Coventry and were close teaching colleagues and friends, though never ever appeared to call each other by their first names! They were both exceptionally hard working; Hilda Crosby had a down-to-earth, organised, industrious and no-nonsense approach, whereas Marguerite Jones relied to some extent on routine, dry humour, eccentricity and shock: "The more I shout at you the more I love you," she would say to her charges!

Lew Baines managed the home farm for the priory and also for Princethorpe College. He was still working on the grounds well into his nineties and always referred to Princethorpe as his "bit of heaven on earth"

Sue Harris, Paul Hubball and Christopher Hunt inspect the new printing press in the Art Department

Governing body, Bursar, clerk and heads, 2007. Professor Brian Ray (f, 2nd from r), was the first Chair and is the longest serving member

The multi-talented Lou Skiffington replaced Fr Jim Mannix in Art when he took up the headship of St Bede's in 1972. Lou made an immense contribution to Princethorpe, not only in the Art Department but on the stage as an accomplished producer and a capable musician. He was joined later in the department by his wife Barbara. Mary Woodward then headed Music; Peter Jewel stepped in when she became unwell and Sue Francis ultimately served for twenty-eight years from 1982 and led many overseas choir tours.

In 1978, St Paul's College at Newbold Revel was sold and the Sisters of Charity of St Paul moved to new apostolates, including a very memorable group of nuns who came to live at Princethorpe for the next decade. The core of this group was made up of Sr Julian Burrows, Sr Helen Morgan, Sr Alban Neale, Sr Mary-Josephine Shine, Sr Marguerite Shine and Sr Eileen O'Gorman. Most taught, except for Sr Julian who looked after pupils' accounts and boarders' pocket money, (succeeded on retirement by Trish Simmons) and Sr Eileen who was a matron. They all aligned totally with the ethos of the College and brought great warmth, support and humour.

South African polymath, Stannard (Stan) Silcock joined in 1979 and there was little to which he could not turn his hand. An inspirational teacher and raconteur, he kept his classes (and colleagues) spellbound and was equally capable on the sports field.

Fr Bill Clarkson's appointment as Provincial Deputy in 1981 came as something of a shock and a replacement needed to be found. Fr Brendan Kennedy, who joined in the mid-seventies, looked after The Convent when it was used as a boarding house, was Head of Religious Studies and was appointed as Fr Clarkson's successor. He had a good sense of creativity and during his headship a considerable number of building enhancements and alterations took place to improve the campus. He also introduced the popular summer school for Spanish children, which was staffed by Princethorpe teachers and visitors and run by the late Vincent Hamilton, who had come to Princethorpe as a Mathematics teacher and who also found himself with a summer holiday job!

Form AD, 1980

Brendan Kennedy moved to parish work in 1984 and Fr Dan O'Connor became the fourth Headmaster in the College's history. Although in many ways, and by his own admission, he was a reluctant head, he was someone who communicated easily with all members of the Princethorpe community. Hard work came easily to him and as well as keeping his hand on the tiller, he continued to teach a fairly busy timetable and played squash and rugby enthusiastically. He had a natural affinity for meeting parents, a keen sense of proportion, was fun, good-humoured and strong in his faith, all of which made him a respected leader. A heart attack – which was successfully treated – brought his headship to an unexpected end and his pace slowed whilst he fully recuperated.

Computers started to play an increasingly important rôle at around this time; a couple of early *Apple Europlus* computers were bought and initially evening classes were run by a parent, Keith Cuthbert; Sr Julian was one of the first attendees. Computing became a curriculum subject when Colin Morgan joined the school and *Research Machines 380z* and *480z* computers were added to the inventory, much to John Hopwood's delight, as a capable programmer. Some years later, Steve Hunt, who had arrived from South Africa, ably computerised much of the school's administration system; a database handled the pupil ledger and the first computerised printed bills had arrived! Colin Morgan, who also taught Mathematics, moved across to be head of that department and Tim Machin joined the school solely to teach computing and IT, with G7 becoming the first computer room. The department moved to the old Geography Wing when boarding finished in summer 2004 and then to The Limes in 2014.

Father Charles Sweeney, who had arrived and taken over the Bursar's job from Finbarr Barry, had quickly settled into Princethorpe was seen as a natural successor, taking on the headship in 1986 for the full term of six years. He taught Religious Studies and games, had a clear sense of vocation and was an enthusiastic sportsman, having gained representative honours in volleyball. He was popular with parents and pupils alike and seen very much as a mentor and motivator by the Sixth Form. He was modern in his thinking and the curriculum evolved with A-level Theatre Studies being added. It was during his stewardship that Technology was really established, with Frank Gahan taking over from Frank McGreevy, when he moved to another school. Later, Food Technology and Textiles were added, both taught for many years by Lesley McGaw and Sarah Sellars.

The late Matthew Jacoby who came to Princethorpe from Crescent School and was a pupil from 1982 until 1987. An award in his memory is made each year at Prize Giving to a pupil who has displayed courage, cheerfulness and spirit

Time capsule buried under the floor of The Limes by the History Society, February 2014

The late Anne Davey (who became College Bursar) with PA Chair, Val Midgley (r)

As well as being a Biology and Games teacher, Bob Cooper was traditionally always the starter of races at Sports Day

Bessie deVries taught Geography and moved with the school from St Bede's. She was also a qualified nurse and later became school librarian

The late Rosie Neal, well known for her inspirational teaching and love of the theatre. She also wrote the words of the College anthem Christus Regnet

John Lafferty with his form, c. 1997. (Photo courtesy of Leo Tomson)

Hilda Crosby with Form BC, 1980

ATC parade at the top of the drive, c. 1969. (Photo courtesy of John Wright Photography)

Retirement of Betty Waddoups from the kitchen in 1994 after 23 years' service

Matrons in the early days were Mrs Condon (blue Matron, on account of her uniform) and Miss Margaret Black (white Matron, on account of her white coat!), with Miss Hannah Lyons (who became Mrs Hannah Minehane when she married Pat) and Miss Maria Martin from 1974 (later Mrs Lawless), who became one of the longest-serving members of staff when she retired in 2014. Ann Grant joined the team from Bishton Hall in Stafford in December 1984 and maintained a rôle with the school well into retirement, including keeping in touch with all of the former Spanish boarders. Over the years, matrons were helped by Mrs Anne Healy and Mrs Greta McGovern, both of whom had children at the school.

In the early days, catering was managed by Miss Long; when she left, the capable and cheerful Br Kevin McAteer took on the rôle, ably helped by the wonderfully friendly Molly, who lived at the hospital in Weston. Not long after, various catering companies were employed. Janet Griffin joined the team as a teenage school leaver, putting in several decades of sterling service. Eddie and Sue Keeley were similarly very long-serving and loyal; Colin Jamie has just completed thirty years, having worked in the kitchen at Princethorpe and at Crackley Hall. Catering managers in recent years have been Margaret Fuggle, Lesley Topham and now Maureen Kennedy.

Michael O'Flaherty (known to everyone – pupils included – as Michael) worked as the maintenance engineer and handyman for the nuns and was retained when the MSCs arrived. He had an encyclopaedic knowledge of the plant and his wife, Kathleen, worked in the laundry. They had two daughters and lived in the Coventry Road Lodge. Michael stoked the coke-fired heating boilers three times a day; these were converted to oil in the seventies and then to mains gas during Paul Shaw's time as Bursar. Shortly before Michael died in 1978, Gerry Lovely and Donal Murphy headed up the maintenance team, joined afterwards by plumber Max Banzolzer; Gerry is still working at the College one day a week, where his seasoned knowledge, skill and wisdom are still much in demand. Fr Jim Mannix (and some of the older boarding pupils) somehow found time to cut lawns; Jim Keegan later joined the grounds staff and was helped by Lew Baines and finally Donal Murphy transferred over from maintenance.

Fr Alan Whelan MSC, who joined Princethorpe in 1981 had found himself doing most jobs in addition to teaching, including being Director of Boarders; a job which he shared with Sean Philpott and they made an excellent team. Sean Philpott, who is also a past pupil, went on to become Head of the Junior School. Desmond Jack and Jo Purkiss-Small also served as Directors of Boarders. When Fr Charles Sweeney moved to parish work in 1992, Alan Whelan was asked to take on the headship, which he did for the following six years. He had an excellent team with Peter Griffin and Fr Joe McGee as his deputies, both of whom understood the school and its community well. Both Peter and Joe stepped down from their rôles in 1994 and Peter's wife, Liz, who taught Geography took up a new post of responsibility in Coventry, with Peter concentrating on Economics & Business Studies and Joe McGee returning to Ireland as Director of Formation for the MSCs.

Bernie Moroney became one of the longest-serving members of staff, having been Head of Biology and Year Head for Years 10 and 11 until retirement in 2012. He was someone who was able to solve difficulties with a rational and reassuring approach and guided innumerable sporting teams to excellence as a gifted rugby coach.

Christmas time with Fr Teddy O'Brien MSC and Sr Marguerite

Considerable changes came in this period under Alan Whelan's fair, honourable and thoughtful leadership. Margaret-Louise O'Keeffe was recruited in 1994 as Deputy Head and one of her first tasks was to prepare a plan for admitting girls to all years, but she also had a fairly full timetable teaching English, RS and Art History. Her razor-sharp intellect, warmth, decisiveness, astonishing memory and empathy with staff, pupils and parents alike, meant that she made an awesome contribution to the school's development over thirteen years.

Josephine Kenning had joined the school as the first girl Sixth Former in 1978, but in 1995 girls were admitted throughout the school, with Jenny Welch and Rosie Davey being amongst the first to be signed up. Year 11 had just one girl: Nicola Morton, whose late brother, Andrew, was also a member of the school. The atmosphere seemed to become more civilised overnight and teachers quickly saw that girls generally work harder than boys!

By 1998, Alan Whelan had completed his six-year term as Head and was happy to take sabbatical study leave in the USA, returning to Princethorpe to head up the RS Department. With falling vocations and calls to new apostolates in needier parts of the world, the MSCs felt that they were unable to offer a natural successor as Head, so recruitment had to come from elsewhere. John Shinkwin, an Oxford physicist and keen sportsman, who was a member of the senior team at Prior Park College, was appointed in September 1998 as the first lay head of the school. John successfully carried out a careful and sometimes stressful balancing act of preserving all that was good, yet modernising systems, raising its academic profile and making the school an even more credible player, something which he did very successfully over an eleven-year period; his gentle persuasion, immense hard work, strong faith, kindness and persistence won the day. John Shinkwin's expertise also came into play when St Joseph's School merged with the College in 2001, with girls transferring to Princethorpe and the junior school consolidated at Crackley Hall. It was also at this time that Psychology, Sociology and Academic PE were added to the curriculum.

Like father like son! Sean Kerrigan (l) Head Boy 1971-1972, Michael Kerrigan Head Boy, 1999 - 2000 and Headmaster John Shinkwin

Irene Minehane who taught Mathematics before moving to the Chaplaincy full-time

John Shinkwin receives a cheque to the school presented on behalf of the Parents' Association by Di Downes, October 2000

John Harwood with his form. John is remembered as Librarian and for all his charitable work

Woodwork shop, 1979. (Photo courtesy of John Wright Photography)

Edmund House with Fr Tom Mulcahy MSC, c. 1970. The house colour was white and formed the fifth house, which was later abolished, with members redistributed to the other four houses: Austin, Benet, Fisher and More. (Photo courtesy of John Wright Photography)

With a decrease in parents' appetite for sending their children away to school, boarding ended in summer 2004 after thirty-eight years, during which time there had been fifteen Directors of Boarding and students from throughout the world, including Hong Kong, Malawi, Nigeria, USA, Spain, Germany and France. The space which boarding liberated was quickly used up as the number of day pupils grew.

John Shinkwin was appointed to the rôle of General Secretary of the Catholic Independent Schools Conference in 2009 and was replaced as Foundation Head by Ed Hester, who at the time was an Assistant Head at Rugby School. Having studied engineering at Oxford and gained a Blue for cricket, he had a wide variety of teaching experience at home and overseas in maintained and independent schools. Ed quickly won the hearts and minds of all the Princethorpe community and with the backing of trustees, has taken the school to a new height, including gaining membership of HMC in 2012.

Ed Hester was immediately able to build a strong leadership team, with the advantage of already having Sue Millest in place as the pastoral Deputy Head and Digby Carrington-Howell as the academic deputy (later taking on staffing responsibilities). Sue Millest was the architect of vertical tutoring which was successfully introduced in 2015 and few will have been unaffected by her keen sense of purpose, motherly care, kindness, concern and drive. Sue Millest contributed outstanding and unstinting service over a period of nine years, before retirement in summer 2016.

As part of the drive for consolidating academic standards and to celebrate all which is good, the College has found a way, under the leadership of English teacher Helen Pascoe-Williams, to stretch students to excel in subjects and to raise aspirations across the school. The da Vinci Programme identifies and recognises excellence through an approach which engenders a sense of independence, hard graft, and personal responsibility. Any individual can be gifted or talented if they work hard and are committed to knowledge. The initiative is named after Leonardo da Vinci, because of his undisputed status as the archetypal Renaissance man. The Renaissance Ideal considers man to be boundless in his capacities for development. It champions the notion that people should try to embrace all knowledge and develop wide ranging capabilities as fully as possible.

A considerable programme of building expansion, continued emphases on the sound bases of teaching and learning, and the merger of Crescent School into the Foundation, have all benefited from Ed Hester's expertise, collaboration, sensitivity, vision and strong sense of direction as the Princethorpe family enters the next fifty years of its memorable journey.

Head Boy, Adam Sturt, with OPs Paul Byrne, John Beauchamp & Colin Byrne, c. 1989

The kitchen at a time when cooking was done using solid fuel AGAs, 1969

Princethorpe's first laboratory technician, Roy Lucas who was responsible for very significant improvements to the Science Department. (Photo courtesy of John Wright Photography)

Ann Grant (driving) and (l to r) Luke Welch, Edd Robertson & Tom Probert

Fr David Nixon MSC, who ultimately went on to take charge of MSC new vocations

Sixth Form field trip with biologists Wilks and Jones in the first minibus, 1970. (Photo courtesy of John Wright Photography)

(l to r) Sr Julian, Kate McElwain, Liz Griffin and Jo Purkiss-Small (who was for many years a stalwart of the Parents' Association and also Director of Boarders)

Mrs Greta McGovern (who worked for a time as relief matron) & Mrs Olive Doherty (r)

Prep time in the Study Hall

Puppeteers Bob Cheshire & Ben Kelly

Chess players planning the next move.
(Photo courtesy of John Wright Photography)

Sister Alban with her form, 1980

Staff Room, 1973 (l to r) John Miller, Harold Crossley, Geoff Clarke, Fr Michael Buckley, Sr Linda, Hilda Crosby, Richard Whittle & Marguerite Jones

Bernard Moroney (l), Moira Weir & Mick Kitterick enjoying the Parents' Association Ball

Maths lesson with Alan O'Grady. Alan taught at Feldon School in Leamington prior to joining the staff at Princethorpe in 1968

Magdeburg hemispheres. Steve White & Evie Ratcliffe, Open Evening, 2009

ISA Art Compeition winners, Richard Revill (l) and Roderick Spollon

Registrars, Elaine Warwick (l) and Loretta Curtis, 2012

Crackley Hall Technology workshop, organised by Paul Scopes, with pupils making a vibrobug

Catering team, 2009

Tastes good! Food Technology with Charlotte Hetherington, April 2009

Astonished! Digby & Sue, 2012

Sixth Form Leavers' Ball, 1999

Fr William Clarkson MSC

1932 to 2009

William Joseph Clarkson was born in Collooney, Co Sligo in 1932. He was educated by the Christian Brothers, whom he held in great esteem. A dedicated student, he also excelled on the hurling and football field. He came from a devout Catholic family and his uncle, Fr Willie Clarkson, was already a member of the MSCs. It was no surprise that Bill entered the novitiate of the MSCs in August 1950 to begin his religious training, and was ordained on the 29 September 1956. After the completion of his theological studies he went to Cork University.

A naturally gifted schoolmaster, with a real sense of vocation and duty, he graduated in chemistry, which he taught to A-level, alongside religious studies. Saturday mornings would see him on the touchline supporting the first XV and he was an accomplished and enthusiastic golfer.

Equally at home with pupils, colleagues and parents, 'The Boss' as he was universally known, commanded instant respect and was someone who managed to combine being a strict disciplinarian with a strong sense of compassion, humour, kindness and great humility.

Bill's faith played the largest part in everything he did and the ethos which is central to the College today is in no small way due to his leadership and example. Pupils who had failed at other schools triumphed when Fr Clarkson gave them a second chance and few of them let him down.

The early part of his ministry was served at St Bede's College in Leamington Spa and he transferred to Princethorpe in 1966 to become Dean, when the new school opened under the leadership of Fr John Keven Fleming. In 1969 he was appointed as Fr Fleming's successor and his twelve years in the post make him the longest serving head.

Bill Clarkson left Princethorpe in 1981 to become the Deputy Provincial of the Missionaries of the Sacred Heart, where his fine administrative skills were used to look after the well-being of the province. He travelled extensively in this rôle and after a brief sabbatical, was appointed as Superior of the USA section, though the climate was never terribly to his liking.

In 1996, ill health forced Bill to return to Ireland and to Galway where he exercised his skill as a spiritual director. In 1998, he found himself back only a stone's throw from Princethorpe, with responsibility for the parish of Wappenbury.

On retirement, he returned to Ireland and was involved with retreat work in Waterford before taking life easier in Galway. Those who knew him well will remember that was never a great one to relax for too long!

Princethorpians from all round the world kept in touch with Bill Clarkson and many would divert their journeys to call in and see 'The Boss' for a cup of tea and to chat over old times. The fact that so many past pupils returned to renew an affectionate friendship, reinforces the profound influence which Bill had on their lives.

He died on March 3 2009 aged 76; a memorial mass was later held at Princethorpe on 19 April.

Helen Pascoe-Williams mentoring student Kaya Nightingale, 2013

Sarah McKeever and her A-level Maths group visit the tower, May 2009

Carnegie Reading Group, summer 2009

Anne Healy, who as well as serving as relief Matron, was also the first parent governor

Barbara Carpenter with her form, 1980

John Shinkwin presents Certificates of Achievement to (l to r) Callum Channing, Ed Statham & Niamh Kelly, summer 2009

Education-Business Partnership workshop, summer 2009

The first fifty years of Princethorpe College

Book Quiz winners, December 2010

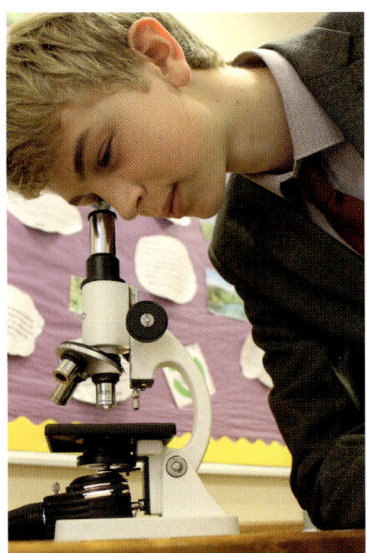

A-level scientist Jake Sheridan

Head, Fr Dan O'Connor MSC congratulates Mark Cannon on his appointment as Head Boy, 1984

Abi McGaw and Hugh Bissett, Heads of School, 2006

Food Technology lunch, summer 2006

Tim Douglas and Kim Maxwell, Heads of School, 2003

Music maestro! John Shinkwin makes a presentation to top pianist Daniel Leung, summer 2008

Prefects, 2004

(l to r) Ian Power (Membership Secretary, HMC), Ed Hester & Chris Ramsey (Head of The King's School, Chester) during the HMC validation visit, 2012

John Shinkwin in conversation with Rachel Glanville, Art Show, July 2006

Heads of School meet Heads of School! Ed Hester welcomed as Senior Head, September 2009

Angela Hales, former school shop manager

Kathryn Price exhibiting her work, Summer Art Show, 2007

Prefect body, 2013

Matt Farr with the ISA prize-winning portrait of his grandfather

Form MAW with tutors Kristina Grosser and Ben Packwood, 2016

Jeremy Peacock

It was 1967, the year when the world's first heart transplant took place, the year the breathalyzer was introduced to England and the year the Beatles released *Sgt Pepper's Lonely Hearts Club Band* album. It was also the year that a shy, small skinny child from a military family - Jeremy Peacock – was deposited at Princethorpe College to become a full time border for the following five years.

At that time Fr Fleming was the headmaster and Fr Clarkson was responsible for the boarders and their pastoral care. I was shown to the dormitory, which I initially shared with two weekly boarders. The lights went out and tears were silently shed under the blankets! The morning dawned; it was a new beginning and I never looked back.

My trunk was placed underneath my bed and within it were homely goods such as fruit cakes and biscuits to sustain one before the arrival of half-term when it could be replenished. Unfortunately a week passed and all was gone. Sustenance was relied thereafter by the food from the school refectory. But a growing and active child cannot live on fresh air alone – so the kitchen was surreptitiously visited in the late evenings, and stale bread with butter and sugar soon provided the necessary fuel!

Boarding obviously played a big part in my time at Princethorpe. It was a special time and only now, with a wise head on, do I realise that the school report mantra "must work harder" applied. Academically it was a disaster, but sporting successes, the discipline, the character building, independence, a sense of belonging and the kindness of the Missionaries of the Sacred Heart priests and brothers will always be with me.
These life skills were to come to the fore in my future career whilst 'catching villains' during my time with the Metropolitan Police! I was caught many times at Princethorpe! I recall the momentous embarrassment, and loss of house points, when Hani Daniel and I stood on a pedestal in front of Monday morning assembly having been caught on the previous afternoon racing pedal cycles around the 'circuit de cloister' by Fr O'Connor. The temptation of experimenting with the first cigarette resulted in capture and six of the strap, only to be increased to seven having withdrawn my hand at lightning speed! A late return back from an Air Training Corps meeting in the village meant that all entrances to the school were locked so a necessary 'burglary' style entry was made through the unlocked Geography classroom's sash windows.

Memories of assisting Farmer Baines to bring in the potato harvest; cutting the cricket creases with a monster ATCO lawn mower; driving around 'The Mile' in a 1950s Austin car and many, many more adventures. But the overriding memory is of the Missionaries of the Sacred Heart priests and fellow college peers, some of whom have long departed but not forgotten, and who made my time at Princethorpe an experience that was safe, friendly, exciting at times, but above all memorable. Thank you.

Science Matters Lecture with Les Duckers, October 2013

Senior team. (l to r) John Gallagher, Sue Millest, Ed Hester, Digby Carrington-Howell and Greg Hunter, February 2015

Sixth Form Physicists observe the solar eclipse, 20 March 2015

Handing over the keys. Heads of School changeover, March 2016

There's always one! Head takes a selfie, school photograph, September 2014

Successful ISA inspection, spring 2014

New prefects with Margaret Robinson & Ed Hester, spring 2016

The first fifty years of Princethorpe College

Liturgy and Music

One of the earliest buildings to be constructed for the Benedictine community at Princethorpe was the Chapel, now the School Library and Theatre. This setting for prayer and worship altered when the current Chapel, designed by Peter Paul Pugin, was completed in 1901. The core Christian values, practised by both the Benedictine sisters and MSCs, beat at the heart of the school. This ethos, rich and varied, emphasises love, kindness and is expressed in prayer, worship and action.

The liturgical life of the College is important because it brings staff, pupils, family and friends together to praise God in a fitting way, to pray for the needs of Princethorpe and the world, and to spur individuals on to do good in the wider world. The Princethorpe community gathers together in both joy and sorrow. Just as the academic year is punctuated by events like examinations, house competitions and prize giving ceremonies, the liturgical calendar marks significant feasts such as Christ the King and Ash Wednesday. In 2001 the former Benedictine nuns of St Mary's Priory returned to remember the one-hundredth anniversary of the completion of the Pugin Chapel. Archbishop Vincent Nichols celebrated the Mass.

College Chapel, together with a supportive chaplaincy team, offers individuals space and time to grow in faith. 'Taking time out' is still highly valued and in the 1990s Sixth Formers went on retreats to Soli House in Stratford upon Avon, Hazelwood Castle Retreat Centre near York, and even farther afield to the MSC's retreat house at Waterford in Ireland. Indeed, the exploration of faith led to the ordination of OPs John Bennett, Tony Horgan and Carl Tranter.

Archbishop Dwyer, Princethorpe College opening Mass, 1967

Fr Charles Sweeney receives the gifts from parent Sheila Lewis

Christmas Carol Service, 1977

Stained glass detail from the Pugin chapel

With Psalm 150 in mind, music has always accompanied the worship of Almighty God. The Chapel can boast a splendid Binns' organ, meticulously restored by the late Hugh Page, who is still remembered in a series of memorial concerts performed annually by Tim Campain. The organ also accompanies singers and the College choir which emerged through hard-work and determination still flourishes and contributes to liturgy and other activities. In 1989 for instance, the choir sang Haydn and Elgar at the prize giving ceremony held in St Bede's Hall. The choir has also taken its music to a wider audience. In 1988 the choir travelled to Cork and sang the uplifting 'Magnificat' by Pergolesi at the Manor House at Bantry Bay, and the 'Mass of St Patrick' at Killarney Cathedral. Links were also forged through a visit to the MSC's sister school at Carraig na BhFear.

Music is still a large part of the school's life with orchestras, bands and choirs entertaining and enriching people's lives. On occasion, the sacred and secular come together. In the 1990s, a number of Christmases were celebrated by hosting traditional Wassails. The one held in 1996 started in the Chapel with a solo sung by Vikki Ball, followed by Bible readings and a rendition of '*Stille Nacht*'. There was then a procession to the Quad where the bell ringers demonstrated their musical abilities. Participants then made their way to the Theatre for a more 'secular' programme, when the orchestra played music and 'sleigh rides' by Wolfgang Amadeus Mozart and Frederick Delius, together with the 'Toy Symphony' by Wolfgang's father.

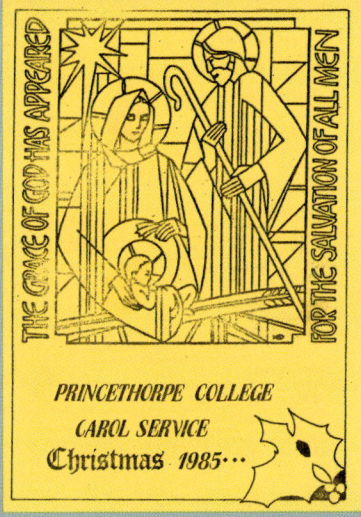

Christmas Carol Service, 1985

Official opening of St Bede's Hall by Wing Commander M M Kayne, summer 1979

The first fifty years of Princethorpe College

Visit by The Right Rev Philip Pargeter, Auxiliary Bishop of Birmingham, July 1991

Opening of Year Service, September 2007

The choir with Sue Francis, 1997

Vincent Nichols celebrates Mass for Princethorpe@40, January 2007

ORDINATION TO THE
DIACONATE
OF

TERENCE O'BRIEN M.S.C.
and
CARL TRANTER M.S.C.

by
THE RT. REV. PHILIP PARGETER
Auxiliary Bishop of Birmingham

Princethorpe College Chapel
Saturday 5th December 1992
5.00 p.m.

*Order of Service for the ordination of
Terence O'Brien and Carl Tranter, 1992*

*Terence O'Brien (l) and Carl Tranter following their
Ordination to the Diaconate, December 1992*

Inspirational teacher Stuart Labran delivers his Easter message. Shortly afterwards he began training for ordained ministry in the Church of England

Choir tour to the Rhineland

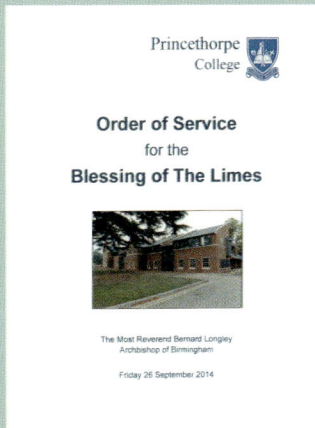

Blessing of The Limes, 2014

The choir, Christmas 2010

Christmas carol service, 1973

Hillfields Evangelical Church Harvest Collection, 2007

Year 7 retreat in the Chapel, summer 2011

We own all that you can see! An iconic picture of Head, Fr John Kevin Fleming with some of the first Princethorpe pupils. (Photo courtesy of BPM Media)

Fr Pat Courtney MSC who was initially at St Bede's and became Bursar at Princethorpe. He went on to be chair of governors of WCISF and was Provincial of the MSC congregation. He was succeeded as Bursar by Joan Elliot

Careers interview: Fr Nick Harnan and David Kerrigan

Br Finbarr O'Sullivan MSC watches a football match with boarders, 1970

The multi-talented Br Kevin McAteer MSC, before leaving to take over the Transvaal mission

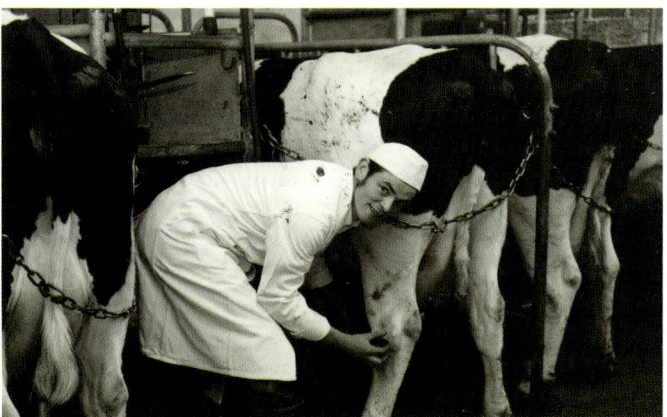

Br Pascal McKenna MSC hard at work on the College farm

MSCs by the front door. (l to r) Fr Chris Coleman, Fr T J Boyle, Br Donal Hallisey, Fr Teddy O'Brien and Br Seamus O'Rourke

Fr Michael Buckley MSC who was the College's first Head of History

Fr Mike Serrage MSC who for many years was the College Chaplain, having also taught Religious Studies and been responsible for boarding

(l to r) Fr Dan O'Connor MSC, Fr Sandy Murray MSC & Fr Charles Sweeney MSC

Fr Charles Sweeney shakes hands with Head Boy David Reti, 1991

Bertie, Fr McManus's beloved Labrador

Missionaries of the Sacred Heart

Princethorpe College

**James Francis McManus MSC
1935 - 1999**

Funeral service booklet for Fr James McManus, 1999

Alan Whelan's Silver Jubilee of ordination to the priesthood, 2006. (l to r) Fr Mark Van Beeumen MSC, Fr Teddy O'Brien MSC, Fr Alan Whelan MSC, Fr Carl Tranter MSC & Fr Ton Zwart MSC

MSC gathering at Princethorpe, January 2007

The late John Hales, Bursar, with Fr Joe McGee MSC

Superior General Fr Michael Curran MSC during a visit to Princethorpe

Harold Crossley plays the piano and Peter Jewel conducts. Orchestral practice, 1980

Music group: Melvin Glynn, Anthony Bennett, Louis Mora & Giles Hudson, 1971. (Photo courtesy of John Wright Photography)

Guy Rylatt plays the bagpipes,1980. (Photo courtesy of BPM Media)

Kieran Molloy plays at the South Africa tour fundraising Firework Concert, September 2008

The talented Kenny Choy in recital

Gaines residential music workshop, 2005. Sue Francis ran successful visits to Worcestershire for Year 7 pupils for many years. Music rehearsals were punctuated with fun outdoor activities such as karting, swimming, football and canoeing

GCSE Music Recital, 1995

Choir on tour in front of St Peter's, Rome, Easter 2006

Gospel music workshop, 2010

Music awards, summer 2009

Tim Campain (c) with Princethorpe organists before an annual Hugh Page memorial organ recital. The 22nd recital took place in July 2016 and Tim has played at every one

Gil Cowlishaw conducts the spring orchestral concert. Methodist Central Hall, Coventry, 2014

Christmas soirée, 2014

Buskers, Christmas Fair, 2009

Music leavers with Sue Francis

Prize Giving ceremony, Butterworth Hall, University of Warwick

Orchestral Day, November 2011

OP, teacher and talented trumpeter, Jodie Fisher

Orchestral Bonanza Day, February 2010

Heather Harris

1954 to 2011

Heather Harris, former headmistress of St Clothide's, Lechlade, joined the staff in 2001 when the College merged with St Joseph's School in Kenilworth, of which she was then headmistress. Together with trustees and Princethorpe's Head, John Shinkwin, Heather played a significant rôle in patient negotiations over many months, resulting in the creation of a new trust, then known as the Warwickshire Catholic Independent Schools Foundation: co-educational juniors at St Joseph's and co-educational seniors at Princethorpe; now simply known as The Princethorpe Foundation.

On the completion of the merger, Heather became Academic Deputy Head at Princethorpe, with responsibility for staffing, teaching cover, coordinating school trips and much else. Her warm-heartedness and gentle, caring, selfless personality had a great impact. She was instrumental in integrating the Kenilworth staff and pupils who came to Princethorpe and a constant source of support to all of the community. She ran Heads of Department meetings and was an exemplary member of the Foundation Executive Committee, often the meticulous minute-taker.

Heather was indefatigable, capable of working long hours whilst remaining cheerful and optimistic. She loved her Religious Studies teaching as her profound faith was the bedrock of her life. She could engage pupils in thought-provoking discussions but also encouraged a reflective, spiritual approach. She enjoyed contributing to many areas of school activities, for example, with the Japanese schoolgirls were welcomed to the College in 2005.

Heather was a loving mother of two and a devoted wife to Chris, with whom she collaborated, creating resources and delivering courses on religious education. She was ever-willing to indulge his passion for railway travel and enjoyed many continental train trips, as well as sorties to France to buy wine and cheese.

Having always helped with retreats, taking Year 10 to St Albans and others to Lindisfarne, in 2009 Heather relinquished her Deputy Headship to work as Chaplain, and found great fulfilment in the rôle. Ever patient, sensitive to individuals and infinitely supportive, her untimely death on 13 May 2011, aged only 57, robbed the College of a special person.

The orchestra plays for Prize Giving

Spring concert, 2015

The School of Rock was set up by teacher and OP Matthew Parsons to promote the playing of rock music amongst pupils. The School of Rock performed at the Princefest Golden Jubilee celebrations

Head of Music Gil Cowlishaw conducts the orchestra in the Round House, September 2012

The brilliant Drum Workshop delivered by teacher Alan "Sticky" Wickett and his son Lars, June 2016

08

Sport

Sport has always played a colossally important part at Princethorpe. After relatively little space at St Bede's, sporting life in the early days was helped enormously with about 60 acres of the Princethorpe estate devoted to games facilities. The MSCs were ambitious and established a well-drained 1st XV pitch, an outdoor swimming pool (decommissioned in 1978), gymnasium and tennis courts. St Bede's Hall followed in 1979 and was built entirely as a result of generous subscription by parents and friends. It provided a large sports hall and two squash courts (now the fitness centre and climbing wall). The Astroturf was completed in 2001. Over the years the facilities have been ably looked after variously by Fr Jim Mannix, Lewis Baines, Jim Keegan, Donal Murphy, Edward Robertson, Tom Probert, Nathan Reynolds and Clive Randle.

The journey began with basketball, volleyball and rugby as the predominant sports. This was driven by the strong boarding community which gave talented pupils the opportunity to develop and shine. The grounds gave ample scope for cross-country (and even the Leamington Road, Burnthurst Lane and the Coventry Road formed part of the weekly run!) Cross-country certainly meant that the College's name was out in the community and starting with the British Catholic Schools' event, Princethorpe has since hosted the full-range from inter-house, inter-school, Independent Schools' Association (ISA) Nationals, three English Schools' Finals, Schools' International and two European Championships (for visually impaired athletes and for the Police).

In the late sixties, Peter Wilks and Ian Jones were ably helped by many of the MSC clergy: Fr Dan O'Connor, Fr Bill Clarkson, Fr T J Boyle, Fr Chris Coleman, Fr Liam O'Callaghan and Br Finbarr O'Sullivan were all very keen sportsmen. There were enlightened alternatives, too, for those who were not traditionally sporty; canoeing on Switzerland was one such activity.

To have four schoolboys' international rugby players within five years, thanks to the dedication and talents of Mitchell Hoare, Angus Shillinglaw, Jonnie Fielding and Lee Rees was no mean feat, coupled with unbeaten 1st XV seasons from 1979 to 1981 and the same for the U12s to U16s between 1987 and 1992.

Kevin Marchant (top centre) reaches for the ball, Rugby, 1971

Athletes Stephen and Francis Massey

Gwilym Price with senior staff and athletes after the news of his MBE for services to education and sport, spring 2014

Junior rugby, 1971

Adam Shaw was called up for the England U16 team

Sports today are vastly different, with a much wider range of activities on offer which also take into consideration girls joining throughout the school from Year 7 after September 1994, when netball and indoor hockey formed the basis of their staple diet. In those early days of co-education many 11-year-olds were chosen for both teams! The core inclusive values for sport remain as they always were, but have been refined, developed and enhanced to meet the demands of a 21st-century-world.

Hockey has developed hugely since the artificial pitch was laid 2001 and this is now a major activity for both boys and girls, with numerous Warwickshire and *In2Hockey* titles. Home nation internationals in the form of Danielle Black (Scotland); Sean Whitehouse (England); James Simpson (England); Tom Czerniewski (Wales); Becky Redmile (England) and Lloyd Ellis (Wales) have all been talents which have been honed on Princethorpe turf.

Outstanding Cricket successes are notable for both Ian Bell (England) and Dominic Ostler (England A); two Warwickshire titles in the same season plus competing in the quarter finals in the National Knockout Cup - 2003 season - with Elliot Seal and Mark Lewis as the two team captains.

In athletics, Princethorpe's Simon Moore was a Great Britain race walker, Annabelle Pask an England Combined eventer and Paddy Mills and Patrick Price were both UK Games athletes.

The diverse nature of Princethorpe sport outside the traditional major games is one of which the Physical Education Department is incredibly proud. The activity list which boasts support from the grass roots to international level athletes includes Irish dancing, clay pigeon shooting, riding (schools' national two-day event in 2015 and 2016), skiing, golf, ballroom dancing, karting, motor racing, polocrosse, sailing, swimming, orienteering, tae kwon do, athletics, cycling, triathlon, ice skating and rock climbing.

Fr Jim Ryan and Geoff Clarke with hockey first XI, 1972. The late Geoff Clarke contributed a huge amount to the school, not only by his superb physics teaching but also through his involvement with sport and the extra-curricular life. (Photo courtesy of John Wright Photography)

Racing driver, Robbie Kerr, secured the British Formula 3 title in 2002 and was followed and supported hugely by Jane Middleton and the late Fr James Mc Manus. Jordan King, starting his racing career in karting, progressed through Formula Renault UK and on to Formula 2. He drove four races in Formula Palmer Audi at the Silverstone round in 2010, managing to get a podium and in February 2015, moved up to GP2.

Memorable trip and excursions include:

- Ski trips to Zermatt, San Moritz, Davos, Zell, Grindelwald, Kitzbuhel, Bardonecchia, Val Die Fiemme, Oberau and St Anton

- Rugby, boys' and girls' hockey and netball to South Africa in 2005, 2007, 2009, 2011, 2013 & 2015

- Outward Bound Trust personal development courses in Aberdovey and Duke of Edinburgh expeditions to Snowdonia, Lake District and Dark & White Peak areas

- Cricket tours to Somerset, Lancashire & Yorkshire

- Watching world class sport for super league netball; Warwickshire cricket, England ODI, Wimbledon; Twickenham; Franklin's Gardens; The Ricoh Arena; Leicester Ladies' hockey; National League indoor hockey finals

- Coast-to-coast cycling

- Day excursions to Draycote for sailing; Manchester and Derby Velodromes for cycling; Real Tennis in Leamington Spa

PE has formed part of the weekly curriculum for all pupils over the last 50 years and members of the Physical Education Department over the same period include:

Paul Adams, Danielle Black, Will Bower, Debs Brookes, Sarah Cockayne, Fr Chris Coleman MSC, Bob Cooper, Chris Cox, Jonathan Croall, Julie Douglas, Donna Edmondson, Marc Edwards, Charlie Ellison, Simon Ferris, Jon Fitt, Caroline Gilbert, Louise Harrison (née Champion), Sue Hoyle, Sophie Hughes, Emily Johnson (née Lark), Ian Jones, Sally Marshall, Neil McCollin (Head of Department), Chris McCullough (née Abery), Bernie Moroney, Brian Neil (Head of Department), Alan O'Grady, Sharon Patmore, Gwilym Price MBE (Head of Department), Leah Rowcliffe, Sean Schofield, Mike Turns and Peter Wilks (Head of Department).

Racing driver, Jordan King, moved up to GP2 in February 2015. He is pictured here at Princethorpe in 2011 showing off his 170mph F2 car

Cricket on Switzerland, 1970

South Africa Tour programme, 2005

Rugby U15, 1975

Chris Kerrigan at Sports Day, 2014

Cricket U12, 1980

Sports Day at Edmondscote. Andrew Walters and Eddie Craig compete over hurdles, 1992

Kevin Hardwick and Sean Kerrigan take part in a prospectus publicity shot, 1969

Dominic Batt completes the Great North Run, 2003

Long jump, Sports Day, 2009

Cricket U13, 1991

Rugby practice with Stephen Crisp going after the ball, 1972

Tennis with Alan O'Grady, c. 1970

U14 Rugby team, 1969

Hockey team, 1992

U14 Cricket team with Mike Taylor, 1992

U15 Rugby team, 1970. (Photo courtesy of John Wright Photography)

U15 Rugby team with Stan Silcock, 1980

Sports day scorers: (l to r) Fen Whittle, Eileen Sharpe & Kerri Boller

Dressage rider Maddie Dohery, 2015

Sports Day programme, 1975

Martial arts with Ted McArdle, who also taught art

U14 Rugby team, c. 1991

The first fifty years of Princethorpe College

Annabelle Pask, after her call-up for the England U17 athletics team

Cricket U13 team, 2003

Cricket practice, Switzerland, 1971

U12 Rugby team, 1974

Jason Evans receives the Victor Ludorum Trophy at the ISA Championships from Gwilym Price

U16 Rugby team, 1973

Simon Craig, Angus Shillinglaw (England Schools' cap) and Carl Elkerton

Martin and Jenny Sharp donated the Fr Mac Trophy to be awarded to the best boy dressage score in the inter-schools competition. It is seen here being received by Callum Henn

U15 Rugby, autumn 2006

Lewis Moody MBE, a former English rugby union player, with (l to r) Head of Rugby, Jon Fitt, Ed Hester, Oscar Thornton & Paddy Mills

Runners Tom Warne, Matthew Rush & Mollie Dibb at the Kenilworth Festival

Sarah Cockayne & Carmen Simpson played alongside each other at the Investec Women's Hockey League Finals, April 2013

1st XV Rugby, 1980-81

U14 Rugby, 1973

Alexandra Kennedy competes at the inter-schools' Offchurch Two Day Event, May 2012

First Teams' Dinner, spring 2006

Football team with Fr Teddy O'Brien, 1973

Sports Day, Edmondscote track, 1999

Josh O'Brien plays Hockey on the Astroturf, 2008

Nearly there! Runners at Sports Day, 2008

Rugby 7s vs Berkhamsted, 2006

U18 hockey indoor winners, 2013

Colin 'Dex' Dexter with Archery Club in the Orchard, May 2008

Sean Philpott and Rachel Taylor, Sports Day, 2010

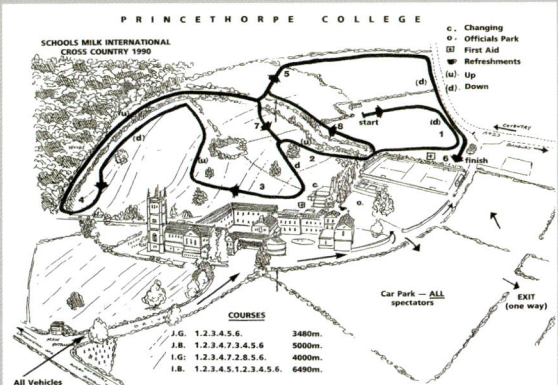

Cross-Country course, 1990

Wellingborough show jumping winners, September 2008. (l to r) Tom Fletcher, Lucy Tallis, Abi Morris & Hannah Logue

ESAA Cross-Country start on the Princethorpe estate, 2011

Crackley Hall team at the Junior Schools' Football Tournament, 2009

Rugby, autumn 2006

The first fifty years of Princethorpe College

House banners, Sports Day, 2010

U12 Football, summer 2004

Senior Cross-Country team, 2014

U14 Rugby team with Bernard Moroney, 1980

Make sure you wrap up well! Preparing to go outward bound: Biologists Simon Robertson, Catherine Warne and Bernard Moroney

Girls' Rugby: (l to r) Liz Buck, Judy Rose & Jo Mitchell

Tai Kwan Do champions, summer 2004

Gwilym Price MBE

Gwilym Price MBE, who started teaching in 1969, joined Princethorpe College in 1974 as Head of Sport and stayed for three decades, is one of those teachers whose career has been a described as something of a legend.

Gwilym dedicated thirty-one years to Princethorpe and was known for his wonderfully inclusive attitude to school sport, where he encouraged hundreds of pupils to find their sporting strengths, which were not always in the traditional pursuits of rugby, hockey, cricket, netball and athletics. Gwilym was just as interested in those who were a bit reluctant, as those who gained representative honours.

A workaholic, held in universally high regard by all of the Princethorpe community, Gwilym would do whatever was necessary to get the job done. He could be seen out on a shockingly wet January morning at 4 am finishing off country courses and later might well deliver home the last team member who could not easily get a lift. Every single person mattered and Gwilym would do whatever he could to offer support and encouragement.

When asked about the highlights of his long career, you would expect him to pinpoint elite athletes such as Old Princethorpian and England Cricketer, Ian Bell, but it's not. What brings a tear to the eye of this gently spoken Welshman is the nine-year-old who has forgotten her gym routine, yet soldiers on in the face of adversity, or the boy whose name is never mentioned in the rugby team yet whose tenacity has held the game together.

Awarded an MBE for his services to education and sport in the Queen's New Year's Honours in 2014, Gwilym Price helped generations of children to enjoy competitive sport. He has been involved with the Independent Schools' Association (ISA) sports programme since 1988, during which time he organised hundreds of sporting events for schools – both in the UK and abroad.

When he retired in 2005, Gwilym became National Director of Sport for the ISA and an ambassador for them, organising sport at Midlands and national level, such as preparing for national championships in rugby, hockey, swimming, cross-country, athletics and basketball, covering 330 independent schools from all over the country. National ISA cross-country and Rugby sevens meetings have been held at Princethorpe for many years.

At county level he has also been secretary of Warwickshire Schools' Athletics and Cross-Country for some years. He was also chairman of Warwickshire Schools' Rugby.

"My whole involvement in sport has been incredibly pleasurable. Seeing children active in sport and then watching their development as they rise up the ladder, knowing I've played a small part in it, is very rewarding," he said.

"It's all about creating opportunity", Gwilym added, "sport is about presenting the ordinary child with the opportunity to be extraordinary." Being extraordinary is what Gwilym Price is all about; an unassuming man with an indefatigable passion for making a difference.

National Catholic Schools' Boys' Cross-Country meeting at Princethorpe, 1985

Evie Bonsall and Lauren Whitfield support Fisher, Sports Day, 2015

Kenny Owen as Austin Powers, Sports Day, 2010

Loughborough Hockey Tournament triumphant winners, 2013

Opening of the Astroturf, 2001

Rugby U13, 1970

David Hare with Junior Ski winners, April 2008

International Honours Board since 1990

Name	Sport	Princethorpe	Country	Level
Ben Lewitt	Rugby Sevens	1990 – 1996	England	Full
Carl Pettersson	Golf	1992 – 1994	Sweden	Full
Ryan Turner	Rugby	1994 –1999	England	U18
Robbie Kerr	Motor racing	1992 – 1996	England	A1 racing
Ian Bell	Cricket	1994 – 2000	England	Full
Craig Lakey	Clay Pigeon Shooting	1994 – 2000	England & GB	Full
Tom Tombleson	Rugby	1994 – 2001	England	U18
Rory Kirwan	Golf	2001 – 2008	England	U18
Mark Lewis	Cricket	1999 – 2006	England	U17, U19
Tom Lewis	Cricket	2002 – 2007	England	U15, U16
Danielle Black	Hockey	2002 – 2009	Scotland	U16, U18
Callum Spencer	Irish Dancing	2003 – 2010	England	U16, U18
Katherine Brett	Ballroom Dancing	2003 – 2010	England	Junior
Sean Whitehouse	Hockey	2004 – 2009	England	U16, U18
Lucinda Cornforth	Polocrosse	2005 – 2012	Great Britain	
Ashleigh Burbidge	Polocrosse	2005 – 2012	Great Britain	
Alasdair Spencer	Irish Dancing	2005 – 2012	England	U16, U18
Tom Czerniewski	Hockey	2006 – 2011	Wales	U15
James Simpson	Hockey	2006 – 2013	England	U16, U18
Daniel Lane	Golf	2006 – 2013	England	U18
Isaac Marsden	Clay Pigeon Shooting	2007 – 2014	England	Junior
Libby Williams	Ballroom Dancing	2007 – 2014	Great Britain	
Ollie Eaton	Skiing	2007 – 2012	England	U16
Ailis Spencer	Irish Dancing	2007 – 2014	England	U16
Connor Flower	Irish Dancing	2008 – 2013	England	U16
Ellie Lewis	Tae Kwon Do	2009 – 2014	Great Britain	U14, U16
Annabelle Pask	Athletics	2009 – 2016	England	U17
Adam Shaw	Rugby	2009 – 2016	England	U16
Lloyd Ellis	Hockey	2010 – present	Wales	U15
Freya Eaton	Skiing	2010 – 2013	England	U14
Jane Furness	Sailing	2011 –	Great Britain	
Henry Lewis	Tae Kwon Do	2011 – 2013	Great Britain	U14
Theo Cornforth	Polocrosse	2012 –present	Great Britain	
Becky Redmile	Hockey	2009 – 2016	England	U18

Games Captains

Year	Games Captain	Second Games Captain	Year	Games Captain	Second Games Captain
1969-70	Adrian Mulleady		1993-94	Daljit Takhar	
1970-71	Sean Kerrigan		1994-95	Jason Evans	Michael Edwards
1971-72	Kevin Hardwick		1995-96	Edward Craig	
1972-73	Jonathan Aston		1996-97	Anthony Johnson	Kevin Elvin
1973-74	Michael Cox	Christopher Evans	1997-98	Alistair Seal	
1974-75	Christopher Evans	Philip Clements	1998-99	Kieran Harris	S Jacques
1975-76	Michael Evans	J Rogers	1999-00	Raymond Bethley	Fleur Oldring
1976-77	Anthony Burdett	Michael Naguar	2000-01	Thomas Tombleson	Vicky Cooper
1977-78	P Cairns	S Brookes	2001-02	James Ferris	A Borg
1978-79	Barry Cotter	N Thomas	2002-03	Peter Williams	Anna Southgate
1979-80	Mark Cotter	C Martin	2003-04		
1980-81	Michael Pennington	J Jenkins	2004-05	Francis Batt	Carol Hield
1981-82	P Smith	Vitus Leung	2005-06	Mark Lewis	Jenny Shortt
1982-83	Sean Mckeown	Neil Surman	2006-07	Jack Stockport	Amy Prendergast
1983-84	Richard Relton	Amit Patel	2007-08	Tom Warner	Josephine Brayshaw
1984-85	Nicholas Dando	Christopher Allan	2008-09	Kyle Murray	Danielle Black
1985-86	Vincent Lau		2009-10	Felix Heath	Amy Hale
1986-87	Karl Mace		2010-11	Kieran Molloy	Laura Newitt
1987-88	John McAuliffe		2011-12	Harry O'Brien	Lucy Fisher
1988-89	Christopher Lowe		2012-13	Clark McCallum	Carmen Simpson
1989-90	Nick Brown		2013-14	Alastair Jenkinson	Laura Brazier
1990-91	Sukhi Johal		2014-15	James Hobbs	Katie Brown
1991-92	Mitchell Hoare		2015-16	Thomas Pullen	Rebecca Redmile
1992-93	Daniel Price	D Mahida			

Zac Wiseman, high jump, Sports Day, 2015

U14 Rugby team, Paddy Mills runs with the ball

Hurdles, Sports Day, 2015

The annual De Hopbel Holland Hockey club tour at Princethorpe

Isaac Marsden was called up for the England junior team for clay pigeon shooting

During his time at Princethorpe, James Simpson was called up for the England U16 and U18 Hockey teams

13-12 win to Princethorpe, September 2009

09

Drama and entertainment

Early drama was in the hands of the wonderfully creative Jim Mannix, who as well as being Head of Art taught drama and singing. He was great at improvisation, so that was the form which the lessons took and he was also the inspiration behind a new portable stage which was still in service well into the new millennium.

Mike Nolan's arrival in 1969 extended the drama offering in the classroom and he also ran an extra-curricular activity as well, which led to the formation of the Princethorpe College Amateur Dramatic Society in September 1970, with Bernard Kennedy as one of the leading lights. Early plays were *Red Herrings* and *Billy Bunter*, but *Albert's Bridge*, the adaptation of a radio play written by Tom Stoppard, was the first seriously staged production, with lighting arranged by Richard Bunch and performed in the Study Hall.

Anthony Cowland took the top billing in *Herrings* as Harry Collas and in *Bunter*, Christopher Cowan played the part of Bunter himself, with Melvin Glynn and Charles Lawton looking after scenery and lighting, as well as having acting rôles.

One of the first major shows to be produced in the gymnasium in 1975 by Teddy O'Brien, was a three-night run of *Joseph and the Amazing Technicolor Dreamcoat*, with musical direction by Mary Woodward and back stage help from Howard Enstone, who worked on the home farm and was also involved with lighting at the Royal Spa Centre. This was followed shortly afterwards by *Half a Sixpence*, from the same production team. So popular was *Joseph*, that the production appeared again in 1979, with key parts played by Ian Higham, Paul Adams, David Barmes and Emilio Doorgasingh. Michael Pinchen starred as Joseph.

Paint Your Wagon followed in 1977 with Fr Teddy O'Brien as Musical Director and Fr Jim Mannix as Producer. Guy Marot was on guitar in the eighteen-strong orchestra and his brother Marc was on sound with Andrew Frain.

With the opening of the Sports Hall in 1979, the gymnasium was decommissioned and Fr Teddy O'Brien spent evenings and weekends building a permanent stage, which was extended several times, ultimately with an orchestra pit included, which gave a very professional facility. Curtains had come as throw-outs from St Paul's College at Newbold Revel.

Albert's Bridge, by Tom Stoppard, was one of the first plays to be staged by the Dramatic Society. (Photo courtesy John Wright Photography)

Tom Sawyer, 1981

It was about this time that Lou Skiffington, Pat and Moira Weir, John Hopwood, Frank McGreevy and Alex Darkes got together with *The Thwarting of Baron Bolligrew* as their first offering. Robert White took the part of the aristocratic Baron, the young, lively and capable Tim Atherton as the eccentric magician, Dr Moloch, Ian Lucas as Magpie, Tim Hunt as Sir Oblong Fitz Oblong and Matthew Lewis as Squire Blackheart, who also painted much of the scenery. Lou, Pat and Moira were responsible for the creative bits, with Frank, John and Alex doing the back-stage duties and Bessie deVries the costumes, ably helped by Rosemary Booth. There was very little in the way of permanent infrastructure, so John Hopwood designed and built much of the lighting and sound equipment, which did several decades of sterling service. This coincided with the opportunity to build a control balcony in the early eighties, which spanned the width of the theatre, to make a teaching space, as well as somewhere to operate the lighting and sound.

The late Vincent Hamilton, who taught Maths, had produced a number of Gilbert & Sullivan musicals in his previous school and decided that his debut at Princethorpe would be *Pirates of Penzance* which was staged in 1982 as the school's first Gilbert & Sullivan production and enjoyed a four-day run. Casting had to be done creatively, with the costume and make-up departments challenged to turn half of the performers into girls! Nigel Denton was the Pirate King, Richard Relton his lieutenant, with the perfectly cast Andrew Tilley as Sergeant of Police. Edith, Kate and Isobel were played by Paul Maoudis, Giuseppe Caputo and Simon Loasby.

Viva Mexico in 1979 was meticulously planned, right down to a list of pupils doing car parking and there was an impressive guest list of local heads and clergy who were invited to enjoy the show.

Cinderella in 1981 was one of the most lavish productions of the eighties, complete with a horse-drawn carriage which glowed brightly in the dark under ultraviolet light and a staircase worthy of any stately home, down which the principals made their impressive entrance! Nicholas Hanlon and Louise Gusterson both had parts as Cinderella, with Tim Atherton as the Fairy Godmother, Ian Lucas as Zips, John Beauchamp as Bathsheba, Carl Tranter as Esmerelda, Andrew Wadland as the Scout Leader and Sean Philpott as Hubert. Having done a magnificent job writing the script, Moira Weir cast a humorous part for herself as Felicity Wrigglesworth!

Ciaran Murtach (Kasim Baba) & Michelle Ovens (Olive Baba), Ali Baba, 1994

Year 8 Musical Extravaganza, 2004

The Thwarting of Baron Bolligrew, 1980

Revue 81 was staged to raise money for lighting equipment and the target of £190 was successfully reached. *Revue 86*, was another of many impromptu productions which had a stream of home-grown acts, ranging from dancing and singing through to poetry recitals and magic tricks, which without careful management by Lou Skiffington, could have easily gone on until the small hours. Peter Rex and Paul Norris appear to have picked the short straw on the programme, with both appearing as caricatures in nappies on its cover! Colin Morgan, as usual, managed to get his photograph on the back! Early Revues tended to be compèred by Caspar Davies and Tommy Hilditch whose natural repartee made for great entertainment. In recent years, *Princethorpe's Got Talent* has continued the theme of revue and added another house event where Austin, Benet, Fisher and More have competed against each other on the stage before an invited panel of judges.

The artistically talented Nick Essex had his design on the programme cover for a highly successful three-day-run of *The Three Musketeers* in December 1982, with familiar principals by way of Tim Hunt, John Beauchamp, Andrew Wadland and Carl Tranter, but they were joined by Jeremy Masding (D'Artagnan the elder) and Jeremy Taylor (Monsieur de Treville). Lianne Hardcastle was Milady de Winter, Carolyn Bolli was Madame Bonacieux and Sarah (Sybil) Grinnell played Marie. Peter Rex trained the actors in fencing and musical direction was by the inspirational Peter Jewel.

A Midsummer Night's Dream in June 1983 was an ambitious and successful outdoor production, which was Peter Jewel's brainchild and took place for three nights on the North Lawn and unusually the weather co-operated, too! Greg Deeley, Clare Leddy, Jeremy Masding and Lianne Hardcastle took the top rôles, backed up by Richard Relton, Carl Tranter, Sarah Grinnell and Richard Hill. Once again, Nick Essex was responsible for the spectacular design.

There was still energy left to do three nights of *Snow White and the Seven Dwarfs* for December in the same year, when again Moira Weir skilfully put pen to paper, with additional material contributed by Rosie Neal. Snow White was Joanne Doyle, Ian Lucas was the Mirror, Mark Cannon played Dracula and Paul Tickell appeared as Frankenstein. Essex's brilliant cover features caricatures of Paul Norris, Marguerite Jones, John Hopwood and Moira Weir.

The *Princethorpian Night* in February 1984 had two fashion shows, a make-up demonstration and hair dressing feature and in Part 2, Carl Tranter produced *The Wages of Sin* with a fairly familiar cast list. May of the same year saw Peter Jewel produce *She Stoops to Conquer*, with Sue Francis as composer and musical director. Parent, Angela Cowley, played first violin, with son Guy also in the orchestra, unusually on percussion rather than on clarinet. Classmate, Graeme Budd, was on trumpet. Ian Lucas's father kindly donated fabrics for the costumes. Both *Sir Gawain and the Green Knight* and *Gunslinger* were produced for 1985.

G&S was billed again for March 1987, still with a nautical theme, but this time it was *HMS Pinafore*, produced by Pat and Moira Weir with musical direction again by Sue Francis. Sr Julian played the part of Cousin Phoebe and Fr Dave Lee played Ralph Rackstraw, Rebecca Hilditch was Josephine and Marie Noble took the part of Little Buttercup.

Tim Atherton as Tom & Stuart Nordon as the Minister in Tom Sawyer, 1981

Chris Todd & Katie Rado, 1997

A Midsummer Night's Dream on the North Lawn, 1983

Roger and Hammerstein's *Oklahoma!* was chosen for 1990 and produced by the familiar team of Lou Skiffington and Moira & Pat Weir, with assistance from Rosie Neal. This was strong in all departments and particularly in music, with direction by Sue Francis, who was joined by all of the family in the orchestra: Ray, Trystan and Morwenna. Sophie Hughes took the part of Ado Annie, Danny Walker was Judd, Mitchell Hoare was Joe, Conrad Howard was Curley and Catherine Silcock played Kate, all to packed houses.

A Tale of Two Cities in 1993 was accompanied by a very lavish programme, full of illustrations and history penned by John Harwood and Moira Weir. Chris James, Warren Howard, Caroline Maggs and Stephen Hamilton all had the top billings for England with Matthew Williams, Annette Ovens, Will Grant and Mandy Graham on the French side.

Ali Baba in 1994 made for another memorable show with the talented Paul Madia taking the lead, Clive Jones appearing as Fatima Kebab and Michelle Ovens as Olive Baba. Madia enjoyed it so much that he debuted next time round taking a key rôle back stage looking after sound production and he subsequently went on to make his career in teaching.

Lost on the Yellow Brick Road came with comprehensive biographies of all the actors in the programme and *Peter Pan* in 1998 saw Jordan McCrindle, Leanne Meaney, Guy Oldring and Alex Sedgefield making their stage names, with music composed by OP Trystan Francis.

An atmospheric *Murder in the Cathedral*, produced by Margaret-Louise O'Keeffe for part of the millennium celebrations, was staged in the chapel and glorious costumes were hired from the Royal Shakespeare Company.

Susan Dadley (later Olden) joined the staff shortly afterwards and started the enduring Year 8 *Musical Extravaganzas*, which took place for over a decade, always performed at The Royal Spa Centre. These included *The Dream Club* (2003) and *Godspell* played a big part in the 2004 offering. *Big Sister* followed, as did *The Power of Music*, *The Film Star* and *Let Us Entertain You* (2006).

Tim Atherton (Fairy Godmother) & Louise Gusterson (Cinderella 2), Cinderella, 1981

Hotspurs, 1995

Nils Gruske, Chris Todd, Jamie Dury, Tim Donnelly, Allan Watts & Peter Stevens, Hotspurs, 1995

It fits! Cinderella, December 2008

Rosie Neal's *Alice Everywhere But Home* was performed by the Year 8 Drama Club in 2004, an activity which Chris Kerrigan has very successfully continued ever since; David Hare also made a guest appearance later in *Daisy Pulls it Off*. In recent years, drama has been in the capable hands of Vicky Roberts and Aileen Cefaliello who have taken the subject to exam level, with Mary MacDonald teaching LAMDA speech and drama.

Sixth Former Gareth Watkins wrote and produced a home-grown musical version of *Robin Hood* in 2005, which was directed by Chris Lee and co-produced by Kim Maxwell. Billed as "definitely not the stuff of legend" it was performed to packed and greatly amused audiences! The same year saw a production of *A Sixth Form Christmas Carol*, written and directed by Margaret Robinson, starring Elizabeth McCollum, Adam O'Brien, Roderick Spollon, Sam Brown, Ben Heath, Oliver Perkin, Charlotte Clarke, Sophie Porter and Jenny Shortt.

A highly memorable performance by Ollie Dewes as Seymour in the production of *Little Shop of Horrors* for three nights in 2012, was directed by Vicky Roberts, with music by Gil Cowlishaw.

Oliver! and *Grease* have followed in recent years, both starring Josh Popham and Ed Statham, both of whom made their recent debut at Leamington's Loft Theatre. Popham and Statham also featured in the 2015 production of *Guys and Dolls*, produced by Alison Wakeley, as did the very capable Charlie Blackwood (who has already made his TV debut), Miriam Isaacs, Lottie Morton, Matt MacLellan, Imogen Holmes, Lilli Draper and Erin O'Rourke.

The stunning February 2016 production of *Romeo and Juliet*, in the modern idiom, was superbly supported by Aileen Cefaliello, Vicky Roberts and Gil Cowlishaw, with Rob Southern heading up the technical crew. Blackwood (Romeo) and Isaacs (Nurse) featured prominently again, but were joined by Lizzie Carr (Juliet), Georgia Newborough (Benvalio), Lily Blunsom-Washbrook (Tybalt), James Walker (Mercutio), Alana Eckland (Lady Capulet) and Luke Dunkley (Lord Capulet).

As Moira Weir wrote perceptively in the programme of *Peter Pan* in 1998:

> Involvement in drama is one of the high points of schooldays, something our Old Princethorpians always remember with laughter and affection. They forget the late rehearsals, the rushed homework, the missed supper and the tiredness. They remember the moment when the orchestra struck up, the house lights went down and they stepped out onto the stage to give it their all…

Paul Madia (Ali Baba) & Clive Jones (Fatima Kebab), Ali Baba, 1994

Housekeepers, Kath Mercer (l) & Flo Bush, watch Pirates of Penzance, 1982

Dwarfs: James Varley (Sleepy) & John Heneghan (Happy), Snow White, 1983

Pirates of Penzance, 1982

The Cast, Robin Hood, 2003

Gerard Byrne (seated) as the Prosecuting Attorney and Schoolmaster, Tom Sawyer, 1981

1st XV dancers, Princethorpe's Got Talent, March 2014

(l to r) Tom Barrett (Mr Darling), Amy Wright (Mrs Darling), Leanne Meaney (Wendy) & Alex Hine (John), Peter Pan, 1998

Matthew Lewis as Squire Blackheart, The Thwarting of Baron Bolligrew, 1980

Talent Show, December 2015

Carlie Ayres (Sweet Charity) & James Oldring (Big Bucks), Hotspurs, 1995

Alex Healy (Flo) & Kate Morton (Lucinda), Snow White, 1983

(l to r) Piers Varley (Daughter of Dracula), Ian Lucas (the Mirror) & Mark Canon (Dracula), Snow White, 1983

Megan Godden & Tom Cross, Cinderella, November 2008

Snow White (design by Nick Essex), 1983

Zoe Leigh, Christine Müller, Morwenna Francis, Michelle Pratt, Estelle Holmes & Michelle Foist, Ali Baba, 1994

Edward Halliwell-Ewen as Mr Bumble in
Oliver! February 2011

Hairspray, Royal Spa Centre, May 2008

Ugly sisters, Pantomime, April 2011

The Francis family musicians: (l to r) Morwenna, Trystan, Francis Pettifer,
Sue & Ray

Lucy Coulson & Robert Mackenzie on the lighting desk
for the Fantastic Mr Fox, July 2007

Tom Thorogood juggles, Talent Show, 2008

Alex Sedgefield (Smee) & Guy Oldring (Captain
Hook), Peter Pan, 1998

The Fantastic Mr Fox, July 2007

Tom Sawyer from 1981

Oliver! February 2011

Dolly the compère (aka Emma Litterick),
Princethorpe's Got Talent, 2014

Little Shop of Horrors, 2012

Ollie Dewes (Seymour), Little Shop
of Horrors, February 2012

Talent show judges, Sue Millest, Pat Armitage, Mike Taylor
& Sue Francis, March 2008

Grease, November 2007

We Will Rock You, February 2013

LAMDA performers with Mary MacDonald

Talent Show, Jack Van Spall & Malachy O'Keeffe, spring 2006

Hamelin High, summer 2006

Grease, 2014

Katherine Brett, Pageant, December 2009

Princethorpe's Got Talent, Tom Pilling, March 2014

A-level Theatre Studies, spring 2006

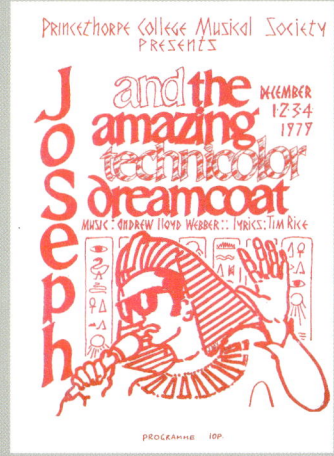

Joseph and the Amazing Technicolor Dreamcoat, 1979

Toby Harper-Lawrence in Disco Fever, May 2009

Adam O'Brien (Scrooge), A Sixth Form Christmas Carol, 2005

10

Celebrations

Celebrations take many forms at Princethorpe. One of the most important in the life the College took place in 1967, only a year after the school was born, when the Most Rev George Dwyer, the Archbishop of Birmingham, officially opened the school. Similar events provide a good excuse for a party, like the opening of the Sixth Form Centre in 2008 and blessing of The Limes in 2014.

Events are held for other significant moments in the school's life. On 6 June 1992 a grand ball was held at Princethorpe to mark the twenty-fifth anniversary of the foundation of the College, an occasion commemorated the previous year by way of a Mass, cricket tournament, barbeque and other entertainment. And the House of Commons hosted a splendid occasion to mark the Golden Jubilee in 2016. One hundred guests, who had to enter a ballot to obtain tickets, enjoyed pre-prandial drinks in the Terrace Pavilion and dined in the Churchill Room. *Princefest*, a weekend of music, good eating and fireworks marked the end of a significant year.

It is also proper that academic, sporting, artistic and many other achievements are recognised and given the attention they so rightly deserve. One of the most important events in the school's calendar is the annual prize giving, now held at the University of Warwick. Accompanied by musical performances, not to mention speeches summarising the school's life over the past year, it is a time for friends and family to join and celebrate the hard work and dedication of the pupils and staff. Guests of honour come from different walks of life and have included Anne Widdecombe, Theresa May, Mark Pawsey and Dr Lavinia Byrne.

Celebrations of all sorts bring people together in friendship, and this is something which characterises Princethorpe. Staff and pupils join for Christmas dinners, birthday and retirement parties, to say goodbye to our 'leavers', and even to rejoice in different cultures and traditions. A wonderful 'Africa Day' was held in 2000, complete with music, food and traditional costumes. We can add to this list other festivities, such as a champagne lunch organised by the Parents' Association in 1989, an occasion which raised over one thousand pounds for a new computer system.

Jan Matthew, recipient of The Princethorpe Shield, with Fr James McManus and other Sixth Form leavers, 1984. (Photo courtesy of the Rugby Advertiser)

Princethorpe @40 fireworks, summer 2006

Jan Matthew and Alex Darkes at the Cocktail Society's 20s evening, Eathorpe Park Hotel, 1982

Adrian Charlton receives the Princethorpe Shield from Dr Philip Pettit, 1973. (Photo courtesy of the Rugby Advertiser)

Leavers' Ball with Sr Julian (2nd from right), 1985

OP Marc Marot, MD of Island Records, distributes Sixth Form prizes in the chapel, 1996. Marc's brothers Guy, Christopher and André were all Princethorpians

(l to r) Margaret & Gwilym Price, Barbara Skiffington, Bernard & Kate Moroney at the Parents' Association Ball

The Archbishop of Birmingham, the Most Rev Maurice Couve de Murville, enjoys a beef curry during a pastoral visit, 1985

Emilio Doorgasingh and Colin Taylor receive the award for the best O-level results

Sixth Form Leavers' Ball, 1995

Tim Hunt collects his prize

Best public exam results, 1976: John Cowland, Peter Rollason & Joseph Emmanuel. (Photo courtesy of the Rugby Advertiser)

Alasdair Spencer and Patrick Durkin at the Irish Night in the Sixth Form Centre, March 2011

The Pinnacle, showcases exceptional work by Princethorpe pupils, June 2016

The Tower magazine, February 2007

Desmond Jack, Director of Boarders, addresses the pupils at their Christmas party, flanked by Pat Weir (l) and Ralph Moore

Summer Fête, 1970s

Pam Hamilton, widow of the late Mathematics teacher Vincent Hamilton, flanked by her prizewinning sons, Philip (l) and Stephen

The late Alex Wallis with the Head, John Shinkwin in 2009. The fitness suite is named in Alex's memory after he tragically died in a motor accident in 2010

Prize Giving visiting speaker Dr Gerard Hyland, with Heads of School and Headmaster, Fr Charles Sweeney MSC, October 1989. (Photo courtesy of the Rugby Advertiser)

Juniors say goodbye to Headmaster, John Shinkwin, after eleven years service, July 2009

Prize winners Stephen Matthew and John McKenna with Head Fr Bill Clarkson MSC, and visiting speaker Jim Pawsey MP, 1979

Angela Hales (l) and Mary Hodgkin were guests at the boarders' Christmas party

Boarders' Christmas party

Peter Griffin retires after thirty-seven years' service, during which time he had the rôles of Head of Economics, Exam Secretary and Deputy Head. Pictured with his wife, Liz (r) and Debbie Taylor

Prize Giving guest speaker Kathleen O'Gorman with Head Fr Alan Whelan MSC and prefects, 1993. (Photo courtesy of Leo Tomson)

Parent and Coventry City goalie Steve Ogrizovic receives a cheque for £960 on behalf of charity Shelter, October 1999

Christmas Wassail in The Quad

Sixth Form African evening, 2000

The parents of Christian Land with the bench to their late son's memory flanked by his school friends. Christian was tragically killed in a motor accident, 1998

Brenda & Brian Parry, and James & Gina Dick, present a Christus Rex crucifix in memory of the late James Dick

RAF Wessex helicopter arrives for a careers presentation; Fr James McManus greets the visiting officer

Fr James McManus MSC celebrates Christmas with Hong Kong Chinese students

Boarders' party. Head of MFL Ed MacFetridge with Rafael Fernandez Laina

David Terron

The Terron Brothers arrived in 1974 after a very unenjoyable term at the German boarding school at Hosert designed for the children of Forces' families. Sadly the two younger ones didn't settle at all and, after a series of escapades designed to ensure their return home to Mum, left after having been caught with seventy-two Penguin biscuits and a trail of wrappers all the way to their dorm.

Peter (nicknamed Peanut) was the wee footballing fanatic. He now runs his own building company and is currently converting an old barn for his latest project. Peter is the proud father of four sons, one of whom won the World Champion Bricklayer last year (and got a BEM aged 21!) Another is a quantity surveyor in London, the youngest is at LSE studying politics and economics whilst the eldest helps Peter in the building company.

Stephen, the middle and very quiet Terron, was a manager for one of the biggest building firms in North East Scotland. Married with two young sons, he died of cancer in 1997 aged 38.

David the eldest eventually went into the Army after leaving Princethorpe in June 1976, joining his local regiment the Queen's Own Highlanders. After a full career spanning 23 years and travelling to Hong Kong, HQ NATO in Brussels, Germany, Cyprus, Gibraltar and all over the UK, he went to Stirling University to take English, History and Professional Education. For the last ten years he has been teaching English at Elgin Academy in the North East of Scotland. Married for 36 years to Marlene, he has a son David who also did 12 years in the Army before becoming a plumber, Dorothy, who is a Customer Services Agent for the local Council and Lindsay who works with her Mum at the local hospital. The pride and joy of the family is now Lewis, aged 8, who will either be playing for West Ham in a few years or flying the Space Shuttle!

David writes: 'I have many memories of my time at Princethorpe. I still recall going to Stratford to watch *Macbeth* with Nicol Williamson. Our English tutor, Fr T J Boyle, knew Patricia Hayes, then a very famous actress who played one of the witches. She then came to our common room the following day and chatted about Shakespeare and *Macbeth*. I've always remembered this as one of the things that pushed me towards teaching English when I entered Civvie Street.

'As an English teacher I always correct my students as I was corrected by Fr Hanley, the Bursar who gave out pocket money. I would march in smartly and say 'can I have £5 from my funds please Father?' He'd always reply 'MAY I! MAY I!' 'May I have £5 please Father?' 'Of course you may!' Then I discovered as a teacher that it doesn't matter.

'I once went canoeing in the lake at Little Switzerland wearing a full NBC (Nuclear Biological and Chemical) warfare suit from the Air Cadets because I didn't have a wet suit.'

Paul Hubball receives the Liam Bennett Award for Art from Ann Widdecombe MP, 1991

Longest serving employee Judy Vick receives a gift from Estates Manager Mark Johnson (l), flanked by Lester Gibson & Cynthia Carpenter, on her fortieth year of service, September 2015

Brothers Christopher and James Tolcher at the Princethorpe@40 party, September 2006

German visiting Sixth Formers from Kardinal von Galen Gymnasium, Münster, Christmas 1997. In boarding days, Princethorpe had a strong relationship with this German MSC school

Twins Megan and James Godden (r) take up their Heads of School positions from Tim Smith and Hollie Adams, March 2009

Jazz Band Christmas Soirée, 2012

(l to r) Dermot O'Keeffe, Heather & Chris Harris and Margaret-Louise O'Keeffe at the Princethorpe@40 ball, June 2007

Opening of The Sixth Form Centre by former Deputy Head Margaret-Louise O'Keeffe, with students Rodothea Kefalas and Tom Cross, September 2008

Sixth Form British Night, November 2010

Prefects' Dinner, summer 2008

Chapel Restoration Appeal launch, May 2008

Prize Giving, University of Warwick, November 2010

Guest of honour, Gwilym Price MBE, at Prize Giving with Peter Rollason (Chair of Old Princethorpians), Mary O'Farrell (Chair of Trustees) and Ed Hester, University of Warwick, 2014

Prize Giving guest of honour Sr Frances Orchard, founder of Katharine House Hospice, pictured with John Shinkwin, Head Boy, Tim Smith and Head Girl, Hollie Adams, November 2008

Ed Smith; native American at the Indian evening, November 2008

Cake for all! Boarders' birthday party

50th birthday celebrations! A joint party was held by John Shinkwin, Heather Harris, Loretta Curtis, Carolyn Booth, Fr Alan Whelan and Sean Philpott, 2003

Cake and celebrations for Fr Bill Clarkson MSC to mark his retirement from the parish of Wappenbury

Member of the Bursary team Trish Simmons (centre) on her retirement with Ann Grant (l) & Maria Lawless, February 2008

Landmark birthday treat for cook, Julie Griffin, who had a day in a Jaguar, 2009

The first fifty years of Princethorpe College

Prospective Sixth Formers, the annual Suits Lunch, summer 2004

The Olanrewaju family with Head Boy Oliver Perkin, Prize Giving 2005. The family gives an annual prize to an outstanding pupil

Prefects' Dinner, May 2011

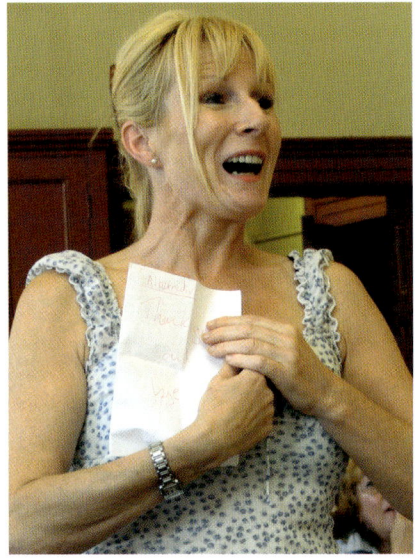

The lively and humorous Janet Holden-Ross says her farewells to the English Department, July 2006

Christopher Bond receives The Princethorpe Shield from Jeremy Wright MP, November 2013

Frank Gahan (r) presents Bernie Moroney with a bicycle on his retirement, summer 2010

Felicity Coulson (flute) and Sue Francis play at the retirement concert for Margaret-Louise O'Keeffe, summer 2007

Mexico comes to Princethorpe! Mike Taylor at the Salsa Evening, April 2004

Ken and Mary Baimbridge thanked by the Head and David Ratcliffe for their help with Parents' Association events over a period of more than thirty years

Musicians Richard Sibbick and his father Michael at the farewell concert for Head of Music Sue Francis, June 2011

Upper Sixth last day, 2006

Farewell concert for Deputy Head Margaret-Louise O'Keeffe, who retired after thirteen years of service, 2007

Catering Manager Lesley Topham says farewell to colleagues, August 2015

The Headmaster addresses guests at the opening of The Limes, September 2014

Prefect inauguration, Easter 2008

Cat Welch

My first memory of Princethorpe is the opening of the sports hall in 1979. I was five years old and my father (Stan Silcock) had been offered a position as a teacher at this beautiful school.

During the four years he spent there, it felt as though the sun always shone, despite distinctly remembering watching Dad refereeing rugby on muddy pitches, or running an Easter cricket camp in the aforementioned sports hall, during which I learnt how to skip with a rope. I remember even falling in love with the slightly damp but unique smell of the old place, which was particularly prevalent in the rooms and tunnels under the college which were used to store cricket equipment at the time. Sport, especially cricket, was particularly prominent during those years and, as Dad coached through all seasons, we spent many a wonderful summer afternoon up at 'Little Swiss' exploring the oasis with the Weir girls.

Maybe it was because it was a boarding school that its family feel was very real, made more so when Dad would bring home and mend *Scalextric* tracks for the boys during the weeks when he was the study master. There always seemed to be joy emanating from the place, especially during the school performances. I'll never forget Dad taking a custard pie in the face during one particular pantomime. Then there was the summer fete when I won a piglet, and of course the Christmas market. There was even something very special abounding during the summer language schools. So it will come as no surprise that I begged my parents to send me there for my Sixth Form years. (Joy of joys, they'd let girls into the Sixth Form during Dad's time!) It did not fail to live up to ALL the promise of my childhood!

Boarding came with all the usual shenanigans... ghost walks up the tower, breaking into the kitchens to top up on the food we'd been too busy to eat at the allotted times, parties that saw us barred from every venue we hired, being snowed in with no electricity for nearly a week, elicit sherry drinking which resulted in a collapsed cricket hut, moonlit trysts with... ah, now that WOULD be telling!

I was miraculously asked to take on the rôle of senior girl - one I cherished at the time, even if my husband has told me I must never mention it. The two years I spent there are two I look back on, through pink specs, as some of the best!

11

Beyond the classroom

Co-curricular activities, intended to broaden the learning experiences of pupils, are still a major part of Princethorpe life. These events take many forms and can include sports, field trips and tours, be it in this country or another. It also encompasses opportunities to help others, such as raising money for worthy causes, like 'Mary's Meals' or 'Whizz Kidz', or offering assistance and a welcome to others in the community. Sixth Formers often entertain local elderly residents in December by providing turkey with all the trimmings and seasonal entertainment. Clubs and societies of all sorts allow eyes to be opened. These embrace robotics, photography, electric cars, origami and climbing to name but a few.

Even from the very beginning of the College's life, teachers have always encouraged pupils to look outside the familiar brick walls. A school magazine from 1971 highlights the Princethorpe farm, something the MSCs inherited from the Benedictine community. Run by Lewis Baines, there were two-hundred acres for growing crops and to graze animals, together with forty-five Friesian cows which provided milk. Pupils used to assist Mr Baines, helping him to care for the cows and to milk them. Other activities instilled commitment and discipline. There was the Air Training Corps, which was a detached flight of the ATC at Southam. In 1972 the ATC cadets travelled to Shrewsbury to fly in a Chipmunk and fire .22 and .303 rifles, all for the cost of five pence. The pupils found the experience of flying at twelve thousand feet an exhilarating one.

Tower of strength. 820 pupils raise money for the Team Bryant cancer charity set up by Joanna Bryant, 2013

Will Bower locked up for charity

David Hare and owl. Shakespeare properties visit, June 2009

Former Deputy Head Fr Joe McGee MSC outward bound on a Duke of Edinburgh expedition, 1992

Olympic challenge, February 2012

Lettie Heath abseils down the tower, March 2013

The College is fortunate that it has attracted such enthusiastic and dedicated staff over the years to deliver learning 'beyond the classroom'. A great deal of planning and preparation goes into these outings, not to mention the supervision whilst in the field. Geography trips have always been popular and in 1971 five boys and three teachers travelled to Dinas Mawddwy (Montgomeryshire) with two tents and two caravans; the destination was a spot owned by Mr Pugh of Tyn-y-Pwll Farm. Visits included Pen-y-Pass, Bala, Dolgellau and Barmouth. Further south, forty-two students and four staff went to Swanage in 1993 to investigate coastal land forms and vegetation in relation to land development; the sand dunes at Studland provided a case study. More exotic places have been explored. In the late 1980s the History Department flew to Istanbul, Turkey, to study the Blue Mosque and other important landmarks. Margaret-Louise O'Keeffe led art historians to Florence in 2001 to examine the Bargello Museum and wonder at churches like San Lorenzo and San Marco.

The sporting world offers superb venues. On 1 July 1989 Alan O'Grady organised a trip to the Wimbledon Tennis Championships, where a can of pop cost sixty pence and a doughnut seventy. John McEnroe was on court but without the usual fireworks! Ski trips take in the delights of Alpine passes and cultural outings to France allow pupils not only to practice their linguistic skills but also to sample the superb cuisine. Margaret Robinson, Sarah Stewart, Colin Morgan, Ralph Moore and Fr John Tuohy escorted a five day visit to Brittany in October 1990. After having arrived at Cherbourg, they made their way to the town of Rotheneuf and explored St Malo, Cancale and Dinan. Culture includes literary excursions to the Hay Festival, and trips to performances by great Shakespearean actors and actresses at Stratford upon Avon. There was a memorable viewing of Rossini's *Le Comte Ory* by eighty-one boys and nine staff in 1973; it was performed in Birmingham as part of the 'Sadler's Wells on tour' programme.

A special mention must be given to the Duke of Edinburgh's International Award, which celebrates its sixtieth anniversary in 2016. It encourages children from the age of fourteen, and beyond, to engage in different activities that will help them to develop as individuals and to contribute to society in a meaningful way. It involves a wide-range of undertakings such as expeditions and practical work in the community.

Visiting French pupils, Bourton-on-the-Water, 1997

Ready for the zip-wire, Joe Guest-Bourne and Callum Carsley in Normandy, March 2011

PGL Normandy trip, (l to r) Kenny Owen, Suzy Ellis, Salima Belloundja & Sarah Stewart, March 2011

Michael Spelman enjoys an ice cream in France, PGL trip, 2011

House Activities Day, summer 2011

French Immersion in Milton Keynes, April 2013

Marc Edwards and Sarah McKeever, House Activities Day, 2014

The first fifty years of Princethorpe College

Charity Pink Day, 2014. (l to r) Mitchell Cook, Alex Fraser, Anna Fraser, Alexander Rooney & Ed Statham

Janet Griffin's farewell in 2004, after 27 years' service as cook

Ski trip to Val di Fiemme, February 2007

To be or not to be? Princethorpians in Stratford, summer 2007

Senior citizens' lunch hosted by Sixth Formers. John Kenward and Etienne Callaghan, 2016

Charity appeal, Valentine's Day

Snowdome trip, Form 7AD, April 2008

Climbing wall, Open Evening, October 2011

Sixth Form enrichment: car maintenance with Ian Sellars, 2011

Austin's model Olympic torch! Robert Rollason; House Fun Day, 2012

Birmingham Art Galleries A-level art & photography visit, July 2012

Suffolk Films talk to James Fletcher, 2012

The inspirational Phil Packer MBE with Matt Parsons, November 2012

Charity coffee morning, September 2014

St Omer town trail, July 2009

Myeloma UK cake sale, August 2012

Christmas Fair, 2014. (l to r) Lynne Dyke, Ruth Dyke & Suzy Ellis

Year 7 annual form walk, 2012

House Activities Day, 2013

On location: Graham Bullock, November 2009

Smiles all round for Poverty Lunch, spring 2004

Jack Bailey with his home-made buggy, Motoring Festival, 2010

Matthew MacLellan and Father Christmas, December 2013

School photograph, September 2011

D of E expedition group, summer 2010

Clowning around! House Activities Day, July 2011

Rhiannon Edwards and Edward MacFetridge on Interview Practice Day, 2013

Try the food: parents' lunch, November 2011

Mary's Meals Coventry Way Walk 2008. (l to r) Rod Isaacs, John Shinkwin, Catherine Warne & Simon Robertson

Berlin trip, 2009

Charity coin collection, October 2008

Tom Oliver: Photo Club, summer 2010

Careers Fair team, 2014

House Activities Day pro soapbox racing, 2015

Warwickshire Air Ambulance publicity shot, December 2008

William, Melanie & Jessica Butler, Christmas Fair, November 2008

Pancake race, Shrove Tuesday, 2014

Pupils with Jim & Jane Middleton, together with Stuart Labran & Irene Minehane, hand over a cheque to Helen Ley House, the Multiple Sclerosis respite home

Sixth Formers dress in blue for charity, 2014

Sixth Formers present a cheque for £492.75 in support of Breast Cancer Awareness, November 2003

Birmingham German Christmas Market visit, December 2005

Offchurch Photographic Competition winners Kate MacIntyre and James Trigger

Fun Day in aid of Kids 'n' Cancer, June 2014

Warhammer Club members with Dr Simon Peaple, 2006

Johnny Reay gets a helicopter ride home for his birthday in 2008

Pupils at Chateau Du Tertre, Normandy, on a PGL language course, March 2007

Sixth Formers present a cheque to HCPT, the charity which organises pilgrimage holidays to Lourdes for disabled and disadvantaged people

Crackley Hall pupils attend a Forensics Day

Jack Burr and Stephen Calcutt receive certificates from Sean Philpott in recognition of their fundraising for Lepra, the leprosy charity

Mary's Meals promotion, 2008

Parents' Association Quiz Night with question master Tony Pugh

Computers to Uganda. (l to r) Robert Mackenzie, Lester Gibson, Robert van Spelde & Paul Whitehead, 2009

The Headmaster with Charlotte Holmes, former Miss England, who visited the school with OP Dave Douglas, to talk to the Sixth Form about confidence skills

Year 11 Fun Day, May 2008

Crackleyograms, photographic workshop, November 2012

Foundation charity appeal for Mary's Meals, April 2013

The Hedderwick family: Grandparents' Tea, summer 2014

Movember warriors, 2014

House Activities Day cavalcade with Jon Fitt, 2014

da Vinci away day to the National Space Centre, Leicester, 2015

Rhineland German language trip, May 2014

Packing Christmas gifts for those in need by Jack Bromage-Eccles

Alexander Corkhill

I was a student at Princethorpe from 2000 until 2006, during which time I was appointed Deputy Head Boy, represented the College in many activities and sporting competitions, and was also awarded the Princethorpe Shield.

I will always remember my first day as a pupil at Princethorpe. The place (and people) seemed so big! I recall nervously getting out of the car, saying goodbye to my Mum and being greeted by both Margaret-Louise O'Keeffe and Loretta Curtis. Both members of staff were able to remember my name, house and form group, as well as those for hundreds of other students. I am pretty sure that they knew me better at that stage than I did myself. It was this meticulous, supportive and caring attitude that I experienced at Princethorpe, even during games and Bernie Moroney's rugby coaching sessions. It was fitting that Margaret-Louise was the one who handed me the envelope with my A-level results. From start to finish, I was looked after, and cared for, as a pupil and was taught by the very best. By the way, I am pretty sure that I still owe Alex Darkes some physics homework. I hope that he has forgotten by now . . .

After leaving Princethorpe, I studied for a bachelor's degree in Political Science at the University of Birmingham. I worked in the Estates Department at the College during the holidays between 2007 and 2010, and I remember working with Paul Shaw and Anne Davey, bless her soul. On graduating with a BA, I returned to the College as the Foundation Estates Assistant Manager, alongside Eddie Tolcher, Mark Johnson and Alex Darkes (2010 – 2013). We completed many projects at Princethorpe and at Crackley Hall. I also taught A-level Government and Politics. During this time, I was a resident at Princethorpe and lived at the College with a number of young teachers and gap year students; I held the position of Head Resident between 2011 and 2013.

Some of my favourite memories come from the time when I was a resident at the College. At one point there were sixteen of us living up in the old boarding wing. We had some fantastic fun and this was another wonderful example of just how special the wider Princethorpe community can be. We were a mixture of teachers, support staff, gap year and overseas students of varying ages. Regardless of our different experiences and backgrounds, nationalities and ages, we became a tight-knit family. For me, that is Princethorpe in a nutshell.

I have had the extremely privileged position of being able to see the College from so many different angles – as a pupil, a member of both support and teaching staff, as a resident and now as an Old Princethorpian. These experiences have given me an amazing perspective on life at Princethorpe and I have had the honour to meet so many lovely people. It is just one of those places that attracts kind, caring and loving characters . . . and is very reluctant to let them go! There really is no other place like it and I am extremely proud to be a part of its history.

I left the College in 2013 after the completion of my MA studies at the University of Warwick. I now live and work in Tallinn, Estonia, where I have moved to be with my wife whom I met at the University of Birmingham.

12

Old Princethorpians

Old Princethorpians encompasses past pupils, parents, teachers and friends of Princethorpe College, Crackley Hall, St Bede's College, St Mary's Priory, St Joseph's School, Abbotsford School and Crescent School.

The Old Princethorpians' Association gathered momentum in the 1970s, principally through the enthusiasm of Fr Bill Clarkson and a close group of friends who met regularly, centred on the late Christopher Hannon OP. Through Bill Clarkson, the group was given administrative assistance by Helen Jackson, who was Fr Clarkson's secretary.

Christopher was a true Princethorpian, and the school had meant a huge amount to him. He rose to the office of senior prefect in the late sixties and was a natural leader and acted as an excellent conduit between the staff and pupils. Early OP meetings had no regular cycle, but a number of successful reunions were held in Warwickshire and at the College.

The advent of the personal computer in the early eighties meant that at least address labels could be produced electronically and a lot of work was carried out to transfer paper records onto computer, with John Hopwood in the Physics Department helpfully writing a contacts database.

Periodic reunions continued, but were only held every year or so and the association did not really get fully established until around the millennium when the school agreed to devote some permanent resources to raising the profile of Old Princethorpians and Gill Price, as school database manager, was given the rôle of secretary. This meant more regular communication and the beginning of a cycle of frequent meetings. At around the same time, Peter Rollason was arranging regular meetings for the Year of 76 and later Martin Holland did much the same for the Year of 75.

Gill's responsibility for school databases grew and ultimately the secretary's job passed to Marketing Manager, Melanie Butler, whose three children attend the school and who has worked exceptionally hard at further friend-raising and establishing regular committee meetings and events, including OPs Festival Day, which grew out of the memorial gathering for Fr Bill Clarkson.

The current committee, which is led by Peter Rollason, has representatives from a broad range of age groups and as well as organising a comprehensive annual programme of events, acts as a communications channel between past pupils and the school, with the Headmaster and current staff representatives attending meetings, which take place termly on a Tuesday evening, over an informal supper in the Sixth Form Centre.

OPs' stand, Christmas Fair, 2010

St Joseph's 70 year birthday celebrations, March 2015. (l to r) Lesley Cox, Sr Philomena Bowers, Robert Duigan & Jane Le Poidevin

St Mary's Priory reunion, September 2014. (l to r) Biddy Allen, Annette Toner, Jackie Hardy, Mary Brown and Ann Chester

Old girls celebrate 70 years of St Joseph's School, March 2015

Gerard Grady with Ed Hester, September 2014

Maria Lawless's retirement in July 2014 after 40 years' service as Senior Matron.

Colin Morgan and Parminder Badial, OPs' summer supper, 2014

St Mary's Priory reunion, September 2014

OPs' year group visit, March 2015

OPs' Sports Day, 2014

Juan and Sylvia Contreras' wedding in Spain, May 2008

Former St Mary's Priory girls, Mary Wheildon (l) and Marianne Horne, with Archivist Nick Baker, May 2015

Alex Healy (later Johnson) with Peter Kafno

The Old Princethorpians' committee has been involved with the organisation of the wide variety of events planned for the Golden Jubilee in 2016-17, including the May 2016 dinner at the House of Commons and the enormous *Princefest* during the weekend of Saturday 3 and Sunday 4 September 2016.

Membership of the association starts as soon as pupils leave the College and provides opportunities for all of these groups to re-visit and to stay involved with their old school. In recent years there has been a substantial growth in active membership and there is a busy timetable of annual events.

The association has an important impact on the life of current pupils. Old Princethorpians are involved in the day-to-day life of the school in a variety of ways such as sharing their professional experience, providing business and personal network contacts and even becoming trustees of the Foundation. Past pupils also support careers events, including contributing to the successful biennial Careers Fair, giving advice through lectures and discussion groups, as well as providing mentoring and work-experience opportunities.

Past pupils have provided financial donations through our Development Office, including gifts to support the restoration of the Round House. A past pupil generously funds an annual scholarship of £1,000 awarded to a member of Lower Sixth. Our Development Office has key links with Old Princethorpians and we hope over time that we may benefit from further financial donations and legacies which will help with the on-going development of the school.

Annual events for leavers start with the OP Festival Day (early September), an informal event which includes an OPs' Sports Day with matches between OPs and current pupils, followed in early November by Prize Giving where the association holds a reception before the ceremony for immediate leavers and their parents. Each year there is a reunion in London, another held locally in the town and also a summer supper meeting at the College; there are even reunion meetings held regularly in Hong Kong.

Art Show, June 2011. OPs (l to r) Jean-Pierre Parsons, Paul Hubball and Anthony Cowland

Paul Yeung and OP friends, 2011

Visit of Marcos Gonzalez from Spain, November 2012

Fr Bill Clarkson's memorial service, April 2009

OPs' side: 1st XV vs OPs XV, September 2012

Tower visit, Old Princethorpians' reunion, May 2011

OPs' London reunion, The Porcupine, Charing Cross Road, November 2009. (l to r) Jethro Towers, Bernard Molokwu, Alex Darkes, Seamus O'Keeffe, Alice Boardman & Nick Cahill

OPs' Chair Peter Rollason, OPs' picnic, 2011

OPs' London reunion, The Porcupine, Charing Cross Road, November 2009

OPs' Sports Day, September 2012

St Mary's Priory reunion, September 2008. (l to r) Anne Yates, Pauline Wilby, Mary Robertson & Janet Haynes

Tom Cross, winner of The Princethorpe Shield in 2010, with OPs Paul Gallagher, Luke Hedderwick and Nick Cahill

Malcolm Stevens' visit from the USA, autumn 2007

St Mary's Priory reunion, September 2008. (l to r) Delphine Kingston, Margit Tumin & Christine Bell

The Shinkwin Cup 2012: John Shinkwin with Ben Warner & Richard Sidaway

Adrian Moore, former Feldon pupil, currently piano and organ teacher, looks at an old Feldon photograph with Archivist, Nick Baker

Beryle Peeke and Margit Tumin, St Mary's Priory reunion, September 2008

Alex Darkes with quiche, Form 7D cookery lesson, June 2009

OPs' London reunion, University Women's Club, May 2015

OPs' London pub meet at The Guinea, Bruton Place, Mayfair, May 2012

Old Princethorpians reminisce

Old Princethorpians' committee, 2009

Maria Cecilia Cordoba Good (l) came to Princethorpe from Colombia in 1956 as a nine-year-old with no English; she stayed until 1962 and made life-long friends. She travelled all the way from Miami to attend the Golden Jubilee dinner. Her time at Princethorpe was clearly very happy, formative and important

Unveiling of the Princethorpe shield, East India Club, May 2014

Former Spanish pupils' reunion, September 2011. The late Ann Grant (centre), who for many years was the key link with Spain

Golden Jubilee Dinner, The Churchill Room, House of Commons, May 2016

Old Princethorpians is Princethorpe College's thriving and popular past pupils' association. We are interested in hearing from all past pupils and how life is treating them post Princethorpe.

We aim to keep past pupils, staff and parents in touch and to foster links with the College, particularly in terms of networking and careers guidance and in the build up to our Golden Jubilee celebrations in 2016-17.

Register on the Old Princethorpians section at www.princethorpe.co.uk for the latest news, events and access to our database of OP profiles. You can also subscribe to The Old Princethorpian termly e-newsletter www.oldprincethorpian.co.uk or check us out on Facebook.

The Wheildon family at the House of Commons dinner, May 2016. All are Old Princethorpians. (l to r) Emily, Peter, Mary, John & Michael.

Subscribers

This book has been made possible through the generosity of the following subscribers:

James Ackrill

Don, Helen, Rory & Miles Aitkenhead

Steven Arnold

Peter & Gill Ashley-Smith

Toby Austin

Milo & Rowan Baker

Saffron Baker

Mary & David Benham

John Berry

Edward Bickerton

Laura Bickerton

The Bond Family

Alison & John Boothroyd

Sarah Breen

Deborah Brindley

Nigel Bromley

James Broughton

Tom Bull

Jack Burr

Richard Butler

Callum & Dominic Channing

Chan Pang Chi

Daisy, Millie & Devon Christie

Jonathan Cocks

Grace Cockerill

John & Caitlin Conmy

Mark Conmy

Mitchell, Saxon & Archie Cook

Michael Cooke

M M Cooke

Alexander Corkhill

Quintin Cornforth

Peter Coulls

Felicity Coulson

Lucy Coulson

Rosie Coulson

Tony Cowland

Michael & Terence Cox

Kate & Peter Critchley

Loretta Curtis

Judith Cussen

Giles Darkes

Zainah, Hasan & Adam Darr

Catherine Davenport

Emily Wheildon Dawber

Steve Doherty

Basil Drobyk

The Dyke Family

Mike Edwards

Kevin Elvin

Jason Evans

Samuel G. Evetts

Tobias Feilding-Crawley

Damian Fitzgerald

Charlotte Fitzpatrick

Richard Fitzpatrick

Mike Fletcher

Ray & Sue Francis

Peter Friswell

Frank Gahan

Martin Glynn

Maria Cecilia Cordoba Good

Ellen Goodwin

James Goodwin

Miles Goodwin

Jack Green

Paula Greig

Cameron Griffin

Peter, Liz, James & Christopher Griffin

Mark Edward Grundy

David Hall

Lauren Hall

Edward Halliwell-Ewen

Archie & Amelie Hancock

Ciara Hancox

Anne Healy

Martin Heffron

Ana Paula Rodriguez Hernandez

James, Lizzie, Katherine, Tracey & Ed Hester

The Hill Family (Clare, Terry, Declan, Richard, Lauren & Angela)

Adrian Hollier

Carter Hollier

Deborah & Steve Horsley

Paul Hubball

Angus Hudson

Maura Hudson

James Hulbert

Carl Ives

Ryan Ives

Aaron Jaffer

Jennifer Jayasundera

Elizabeth Jeffs

Alexandra Johnson & the Healy Family

Will & Tori Jones

Amy Kaye

Margaret Laidlaw

Cecilia Lane

Stephen Langford

Charles Lawton

Matthew Lee

Simon Leung

Anthony Jacob Lock

Gerard Lovely

Philip Lovely

Edward MacFetridge

Annette Mansie

Michael Masding

David Mason

Antoine Matarasso

Sarah McGinlay

Alison, Shirley & Heather McLean

Michael C. Meredith

Sue Millest

Irene & Liam Minehane

Roger Moore

Bernie Moroney

Harry, Jack & Lily Murley

Anne Naylor

Laurence Neal

Mark Neal

Donna Nixon

Emma & Mathew Nobes

Harry O'Brien

Josh O'Brien

The O'Gorman Family

Alex Osborne

Helen Pascoe-Williams

Annabelle Pask

Jean-Pierre Parsons

Mark Patterson

Paul Patterson

Gary Peacock

Greg Peacock

Jeremy Peacock

Barbara & David Plumtree

John Pope

Olivia Pope

Karl Radzikowski

George & Rob Redwood

Margaret Robinson

Kelly Maree Rogers

Peter & Moira Rollason

Alexander Rooney

Charlie Rooney

Rory Rooney

Tom & Ben Rothwell

Diane Rowicki

Joe & Noel Ruddy

Patrick Rutter

Eqbal Samra

Suki Samra

John Sarl

Mary Sears

Richard Sibbick

Jane Smith

Randall Smith

The Spelman Family

Liam Stanier

Gerard Starling

Pauline Stearman

Sarah Stewart

Dominic Strange

Katie Strange

The Sweeney Family

Jeremy Taylor

Rachel Taylor

David Terron

Diane Thomas

Mark & Jane Thompson

Amy Elizabeth Thorne

Becky & Josh Tidd

Philip Tillman

Chris Tolcher

Eddie & Ann Tolcher

James Tolcher

Phillip Tomson

Fr Carl Tranter MSC

James Trigger

Sam Turner

Dominic Turner-Burr

William Uglow

Maria & Anil Vohrah

Alison Wakeley

Bernard Warner

Otterly & Chumley Warner

Louise Warr

Cat Welch

Prudence Welton

John Wheildon

Mary E. Wheildon

Michael Wheildon

Peter Wheildon

Fr Alan Whelan MSC

Arthur Whitehurst

Lauren Whitfield

Ben Wilcox

Janet & John Willock

Richard J.D. Willock

Mark Woods

Peter Yang

Alan Young

Further Reading

N.G. Baker, 'Princethorpe Priory and College', *Journal of the Midlands Catholic History Society*, 22 (2016): 21-29

L.A. Bowers, *Montargis to Fernham, 1630-1901*, 1(pts. 1-5) (Priv. ptd., 2004)

P. Harris, *The Architectural Achievement of Joseph Aloysius Hansom (1803-1882), designer of the Hansom Cab, Birmingham Town Hall, and the churches of the Catholic Revival* (Edwin Mellen Press: Lewiston, Queenston and Lampeter, 2010)

D. Mac Cárthaigh, *Fifty Years of MSC Mission, 1952 – 2002* (Missionaries of the Sacred Heart: Cork, 2002)

D. Mac Cárthaigh, *A Hundred Years of MSC Mission, 1909-2009*, 2 (Missionaries of the Sacred Heart: Cork, 2005)

M. Page, *A History of Crescent School: the first 60 years* (Crescent School: Rugby, 2008)

N. Pevsner and A. Wedgwood, *Warwickshire*, Buildings of England, 31 (Penguin: Harmondsworth, 1966)

P.C. Rex, 'The Origins of Princethorpe', *Princethorpe* (1983): 2-4

F. Stapleton, *The History of the Benedictines of St Mary's Priory, Princethorpe* (Samuel Walker: Hinckley, 1930)

[Stoneleigh Abbey] 'Country Homes in Wartime: No 14, Stoneleigh Abbey, Kenilworth', *The Tatler* No 2044 (28 August 1940): 293-295

Princethorpe College houses archival material on St Mary's Priory, St Joseph's Convent, St Bede's College and Abbotsford School. Other major collections on these establishments can be found at Douai Abbey (St Mary's Priory), the Birmingham Archdiocesan Archives (St Mary's Priory), the Archive of the Union of the Sisters of Mercy GB (St Joseph's Convent) and the Warwickshire Record Office.

Heads of School

Year	Head Boy	Year	Head Boy
1966-67	Charles Crowley	1981-82	Stephen Reed
1967-68	Richard Lawlor	1982-83	Richard Attrill
1968-69	Philip Newbold	1983-84	Jeremy Masding
1969-70	Philip Newbold	1984-85	Mark Cannon
1970-71	Richard Walsh	1985-86	Simon Hall
1970-71	Thomas Aldridge	1986-87	Michael Masding
1971-72	Sean Kerrigan	1987-88	James Pope
1972-73	Nicholas Warwick	1988-89	Alan Beesley
1973-74	John Berry	1989-90	Adam Sturt
1974-75	Andrew Kirwan	1990-91	John Welbourn
1975-76	Kevin Kerrigan	1991-92	David Reti
1976-77	Marc Kirby	1992-93	Sukhvir Samra
1977-78	David Yirrell	1993-94	Eqbal Samra
1978-79	Stephen Matthew	1994-95	Dominic Convey
1979-80	Eamonn O'Brien	1995-96	Jonnie Fielding
1980-81	Noel Ruddy		

Year	Head Boy	Head Girl
1996-97	John Palmi	Eugenie Hales
1997-98	Joseph Gaffney	Helen Rich
1998-99	Edward Hope	Ruth Foist
1999-00	Michael Kerrigan	Polly Poulter
2000-01	Yemi Olanrewaju	Amy Bleasdale
2001-02	Nicholas Cahill	Alice Boardman
2002-03	Dominic Batt	Philippa Mills
2003-04	Timothy Douglas	Kim Maxwell
2004-05	Oliver Warner	Catherine Burns
2005-06	Oliver Perkin	Sharne Drewitt
2006-07	Hugh Bissett	Abigail McGaw
2007-08	Malachy O'Keeffe	Kathryn Price
2008-09	Timothy Smith	Hollie Adams
2009-10	James Godden	Megan Godden
2010-11	Jacob Mitchell	Alice Holden-Brown
2011-12	William Harper-Lawrence	Ellie Eaton
2012-13	Christopher Bond	Millie Bray
2013-14	Patrick Mills	Hannah Brindley
2014-15	Simon Fisher	Maddie Wigmore-Sykes
2015-16	Joshua Popham	Sophie Nicholls

The Princethorpe Shield

Year	Recipient	Year	Recipient	Year	Recipient
1966-67	Charles Crowley	1984-85	Christopher Allan	2000-01	Tom Tombleson
1967-68	John Baines	1985-86	Michael Cleary	2001-02	Alice Boardman
1969-70	Michael Mulleady	1986-87	Joseph Clune	2002-03	Joanne Lee
1970-71	David Ryan	1987-88	Anthony Mogboh	2003-04	Daniel Farrell
1971-72	Christopher Hannon	1988-89	Rafael Fernandez Laina	2003-04	Sion Williams
1972-73	Adrian Charlton	1989-90	Colin Byrne	2004-05	Elizabeth Sharpe
1973-74	John Berry	1990-91	Damian Ward	2005-06	Alexander Corkhill
1974-75	Alexander Darkes	1991-92	Adam Budworth	2006-07	Josephine Mitchell
1975-76	Robert Cox	1992-93	Mark Wood	2007-08	Malachy O'Keeffe
1976-77	Robin Abeyesinhe	1993-94	Richard Sibbick	2008-09	Lucy Coulson
1977-78	Seamus Edney	1994-95	Jason Evans	2009-10	Tom Cross
1978-79	Stephen Matthew	1995-96	Jonnie Fielding	2010-11	James Street
1979-80	Malcolm Stevens	1996-97	Mike Edwards	2011-12	Daniel Leung
1980-81	Duncan Hynes	1997-98	Jide Olanrewaju	2012-13	Christopher Bond
1981-82	Jeremy Claridge	1997-98	Tunde Olanrewaju	2013-14	Thomas Pilling
1982-83	Joseph Ruddy	1998-99	Mark Bates	2014-15	Maddie Wigmore-Sykes
1983-84	Janine Matthew	1999-2000	Paul Yeung	2014-15	Simon Fisher

Christus Regnet

Christus Regnet, tell the story,
To him be the power and the glory.
Praise the Lord, lift up your hearts,
Sing a song of joy.
What 'though the way be weary,
Times hard, and life seems dreary,
Lift your hearts, lift up your voice.
In Christ rejoice.

Through death's dark vale he will guide us,
Through storms, whate'er betide us,
We will walk steadfast in faith.
We are not alone.
We strive, we strive ever onward;
We look, we look ever upward.
Christus Regnet, Christ the Lord
Reigns in our hearts.

Christus Regnet goes before us,
Christus Regnet swells our chorus.
Hear our voices, give our thanks
Unto Christ our King.
May we in our endeavour
Give service true for ever.
As he lives, so shall ye live
For evermore.
Amen.

Rosie Neal